Control and Urban Planning

by the same author

URBAN AND REGIONAL PLANNING
A Systems Approach

Control and Urban Planning

J. BRIAN McLOUGHLIN

FABER AND FABER LIMITED
3 Queen Square, London

First published in 1973
by Faber and Faber Limited
3 Queen Square, London WC1
Printed in Great Britain by
Western Printing Services Ltd, Bristol

ISBN 0 571 10143 7

Contents

List of Figures

7

Preface

My motivation to write this book has a number of specific roots. In general, however, it reflects a continuing interest in the development of ideas about the nature of planning itself, its place in public life and the development of the people who do planning. In particular, my job helping to prepare a sub-regional study left me wondering about the purpose and relevance of these and similar 'strategic' planning exercises both in Britain and elsewhere. I was concerned about their translation into actions by public authorities and their relationships to action in and by the communities ostensively on whose behalf they were undertaken. The report of the Planning Advisory Group had concentrated, as its terms of reference required, on the future of development plans. But in suggesting considerable changes in the scope and content of plans, the directive instruments, they advocated little or no change in the scope and operation of development control which is a vital implementative tool in British planning.

The widening range of public issues embraced by the new planning procedures seemed to me to raise many difficult questions about the intellectual development of planning, the education and training of planners and the inter-related matters of departmentalism in local government and professionalism in their staff deployment. The expanding concerns of the debate about the nature planning called for a view which transcended technical and operational concerns and which came face to face with social and political issues.

All of this seemed to require a recognition of complexity in another order of magnitude from land use or physical planning. Such complexity might be studied within the framework of cybernetic and general-system approaches to urban systems and planning systems. I wondered if it would be possible to relate the detail of what British planners did in their interventions to the generality of cybernetic ideas about control in highly complex systems.

I was fortunate in being awarded a generous grant in order to pursue this line of enquiry by the Social Science Research Council. This enabled me to spend two and a half years at the University of Manchester where Professor John Parry Lewis offered me a place in the Centre for Urban and Regional Research. There, helped for over two years by Judith Webster, for one year by Tony Hall (both full-time) and for eight months by Barbara Solomon (part-time) I reviewed the application of cybernetics and related ideas to fields of interest to planners and carried out field studies of development control in Britain.

We were greatly assisted by the willingness of several planning authorities to co-operate. Manchester City Planning Department was especially kind in allowing us to conduct a pilot study to help in the design of the subsequent full investigation. This included visits to planning offices in Aberdeen, Bromley, Camden, Crawley, Durham, Greater London, Herefordshire, Leicester, Lincoln, Luton, Manchester, Newport, Oxfordshire, Peak Park, Ross and Cromarty, Skelmersdale and Southend. In addition we had advice and help from officers in Brent, Lancashire and West Sussex. It is clearly impossible to name all those who gave so generously of their time but I know my ex-colleagues would want to be associated here with my gratitude for the courtesy and kindness with which we were received everywhere. Some of the officers we interviewed later agreed to serve on a small working group which evaluated our findings and sharpened our ideas about the present and future of development control. To them and to the research workers who were also included, I owe another debt of gratitude.

The working group meetings were a direct outcome of the interest shown in the research project by David Donnison, Director of the Centre for Environmental Studies. The Centre provided the facilities for the meetings and a great deal of informal criticism and encouragement. My membership of two other C.E.S. working groups – those chaired by Peter Cowan on 'The Future of Planning' and by Jim Amos on 'Educational Objectives for Urban and Regional Planning' – has been of considerable help in developing my understanding of professional, educational and other problems in planning and I acknowledge the debt I owe to the members of those working groups.

Since I joined the staff of the C.E.S. in August 1971 I have benefited from working relationships and friendships with many people there. This book has been influenced by many discussions at the C.E.S. including my current work on the development of structure planning in Britain. Some of the most searching criticisms of the ideas in the following pages have been made at lectures and seminars to students in several universities, but especially during my weekly sessions at the School of Environmental Studies, University College, London.

Needless to say, none of these friends, acquaintances and colleagues is in any way responsible for the faults of this book. Barbara Solomon, apart from her contribution to the research project, researched and wrote the whole of Chapter 2 which appears substantially as she wrote it; Judith Webster spent innumerable hours in discussion as part of her invaluable work and several parts of the book have been written with the help of drafts which she wrote at Manchester. But apart from Chapter 2 the whole of the text is my own writing and I must bear the responsibility for its errors and infelicities.

It has proved a difficult book to write and I hope it is not, therefore, too difficult to read. I was sometimes tempted to consider two quite distinct texts: one on the generality of cybernetics and general systems analysis of urban and regional planning; the other on the administrative and procedural details of development control in Britain. But to have taken this undoubtedly easier way out would have been to deny the very importance of connection between the two, of avoiding the attempt to demonstrate or at least to suggest the relationships between overt, deliberate, statutory intervention and the general ideas of complex-system regulation.

I am sure that I have failed to make completely clear and explicit just what those connections are. One will search in vain here for a specification of how it really is or how it ought to be. There remains much ambiguity but I hope that the book as a whole will in part inform but for the most part suggest what might be possible in thought, research and action, in planning administration, institutional design and management practice at a time of considerable change in local government, education, research and professionalism. Many people are already involved in these debates and actions and many more contributions will be needed; the Law of Requisite Variety suggests that this should be so.

I hope the book will be useful to a number of people, perhaps especially to students, research workers, local government officers

11

and all those who are directly interested and active in the demanding world of urban and regional management.

Several typists have helped to prepare the manuscript from my appalling handwriting but the vast bulk of this effort has been borne with great good humour, diligence and unfailing efficiency by my private secretary Audrey Halsted and I am ever grateful to her.

All of the original illustrations were prepared by Jacquie Porter.

My long-suffering family – Marie, Fiona, Rory, Niall and Angus – have again endured my moods, absences and idiosyncrasies during many months of writing. To them I owe my greatest debt of gratitude.

Bramhall, Cheshire
Summer, 1972.

1 · Controlling Urban Change

This chapter will try to establish what is meant by controlling towns and regions. It will do so first of all not by reference to theoretical arguments but rather by a review of examples of actual intervention by governments. We will confine ourselves largely to Britain and North America and primarily to the present century. Also our review will be illustrative only; any attempt at comprehensiveness would probably be self-defeating or founder, at this stage, in problems of definition. Our aim will be to provide a 'taste' of governmental intervention in what are called 'town-and-country' or urban and regional matters. We shall cast the net wide in order that the selection of examples shall be reasonably representative and then an attempt will be made to pose some general questions about such interventions and to reach some tentative conclusions. For example we shall ask how far such interventions have been directed to short-term urgent problems or to longer-term issues; what frames of reference have been used for defining these problems and issues? What political, professional and philosophical ideologies have such interventions embodied or implied?

In the beginning was . . . the scheme

In the early years of this century, most of the aims which inspired Victorian reformers were still clearly apparent. Before the landmark of the 1909 Housing and Town Planning Act (the first statutory use of the words 'town planning') physical controls had been largely those exercised by local public health authorities through the bye-laws. Otherwise, physical control was in private hands – those of philanthropists like Cadbury, Salt and Lever with their model villages and garden cities. Landowners of all kinds could exercise control over physical development by means of covenants restricting the use of

13

land and buildings, the manner of development, the appearance of buildings, their physical relationships to each other and to open space. Bye-law control was exercised by the legal requirement that the developer (say of a street of houses or a workshop) should ask permission from the local authority who could then scrutinize his (drawn) plans to assure themselves that legally and administratively specified standards were observed. In similar fashion, private landowners exercised control because the restrictive covenant (transmitted with the title deeds on conveyance) usually demanded express consent for proposed action relating to matters dealt with by the covenant clauses. This form of control was very often used in private 'building estates', i.e. tracts of land, often formerly in agricultural use on the edge of towns which were divided into plots for the erection of private houses. Covenants typically were designed to protect the associated characteristics of low densities (e.g. by restricting the subdivision of plots), boskiness (e.g. by requiring the planting and care of trees) and middle-class social ambience (e.g. by prohibiting industrial and commercial activity but nevertheless allowing private professional practice in houses by surgeons, lawyers, writers and fine artists).

In either case – control through the bye-laws or covenants on private building estates – the enabling power or sanction is that of the law. In the former case it is largely a question of administrative law and in the latter it is predominantly the civil law. But in both cases a variety of purposes are involved. The welter of bye-laws introduced by the great Public Health Act of 1875 are concerned mostly with the health of the individual, the family and the community, but also to some extent they were concerned with orderly physical development in its own right and with traffic circulation, access, safety from fire hazards and so on. Covenants as we have seen were concerned with the quality of the physical environment and with ensuring that only people with certain incomes and styles of life could occupy the area and that 'undesirable' activity such as manufacturing and trading was excluded. This variety of ends was achieved, however, by a much narrower set of means; for the most part these purposes were served by controls over physical forms – i.e. position, size, shape, distance, spacing, ground cover and planting – together with some degree of control over activity or 'land use'.

But twentieth-century British control over towns and regions begins with the Housing and Town Planning Act of 1909. Prominent among its major aims were a drive for healthier living conditions and better urban amenities in general. The President of the Local Government Board, John Burns, introducing a debate on the Bill in the House of Commons referred to the advantages of *planned* as opposed to *haphazard* development of towns and cited a number of estates developed by public corporations and enlightened private owners as examples. This view forms an important part of the planning ethos and echoes the vision of HOWARD (1898) who wrote of his proposed garden city that

> 'there should be a unity of design and purpose – that the town should be planned as a whole and not left to grow up in a chaotic manner as had been the case of all English towns. . . .' (p. 46 of 1946 edn.)

The planning system centred on the *planning scheme* – a set of written clauses and accompanying maps – which was clearly modelled on the legal structure of the private estate development schemes. It was essentially a local extension of the 1909 Act and gave the local authority enforceable powers. The matters which could be dealt with in a scheme included the width and alignment of streets, the number and spacing of buildings, their design and external appearance and the uses to which they could be put. This could be done by defining 'Use Zones' and by specifying the class of proposals which would need permission from the authority. The scheme could also specify that where development permission was refused, the planning authority might be liable to pay compensation to the owner of the land (typically for the prevention of industrial development in residential areas).

Between the wars

For about thirty years – up until the outbreak of war in 1939 – the concept of the planning scheme, both in general and in detail, dominated successive Acts of Parliament concerned with town and country planning. That is, they were essentially concerned with control over *physical development* including the specification of the use to which land could be put, the appearance of buildings and the landscape, the alignment of streets, densities of development and so forth. The control was exercised by the full force of *the law* and was

15

very largely negative in effect, i.e. the schemes and their implementation were concerned with what should not occur rather than what should come about. Finally, therefore, they were *indicative* rather than prescriptive and tended to be unrealistic in terms of how much and what kind of developments were envisaged; usually far more land was zoned for development than was ever likely to be used.

These characteristics are to be found in the Housing and Town Planning Act of 1919 and the Housing Act of 1923, the Town Planning Act of 1925 and the major Town and Country Planning Act of 1932. In this latter Act the original notion of the 'scheme' was broadened considerably from its application to 'land which is the course of development or appears likely to be used for building purposes' to include undeveloped land and land of considerable natural or aesthetic interest. In effect, 'planning schemes' under the 1932 Act often covered the whole of a local authority's area. But the procedures involved were cumbersome and slow; also the making of 1932 Act schemes (despite new powers to exclude the possibility in certain cases and areas) was still hampered by the problems of claims for compensation both for refusal of permission and for failure to zone land for development.

Perhaps these were the main reasons why the 'restriction of ribbon development' i.e. building along the frontage of trunk and arterial roads was attempted under the 1935 Act of that name and administered by the Ministry of Transport. By developing in this fashion, speculative builders and their customers could take advantage of the accessibility provided by the road and often of pre-existing utility services as well. The uncontrolled spread of this sort of development had become a serious problem by the early 1930s and the Act required developers to seek the permission of the Ministry of Transport and the local authority for all proposals falling within 220 feet of a trunk or classified road.

The planning of roads, and the provision for traffic taking account of the relationships between physical development, population and movement was nevertheless very badly served. And such measures for the prevention of ribbon development were administered quite separately from the town and country planning schemes. Equally the underlying problems of population and economic activity were being studied and tackled in separate ways via the Special Areas legislation and the creation of 'trading estates' (ASHWORTH, 1954, pp. 218 et seq.).

Moreover, the growing problems of the countryside resulting largely from the depression of world trade, lack of investment in agricultural technique, indifferent farm management and rural depopulation, although resulting in considerable changes in the physical environment (e.g. derelict agricultural land, encouragement of suburban sprawl and shack developments) were also being dealt with in contexts quite distinct from town and country planning.

The post-war period

The great trilogy of reports – popularly referred to as 'Barlow', 'Scott' and 'Uthwatt' after their respective chairmen – were the foundations of planning in Britain from the wartime period until the changes of the late 1960s. They have been described, discussed and analysed so much by other authors that it would be tedious and unnecessary to do so here (e.g. ASHWORTH, 1954; COMMITTEE ON THE QUALIFICATIONS OF PLANNERS, 1950; CULLINGWORTH, 1972). The point which interests us is what sort of central objectives for planning did their conclusions embody? What did the legal and administrative powers and procedures seek to influence and control?

In essence, the reports taken together made these recommendations: that planning control should cover the whole country; that there should be a national policy for industrial location and population distribution; also that there should be a central planning authority concerned with: urban redevelopment, reduction of congestion; achieving industrial 'balance' within and between regions; examining the potential of garden suburbs, satellite towns and trading estates; research and information about industry, resources and amenities; correlation of local planning schemes in the national interest.

The resulting legislation was formidable: Town and Country Planning Acts in 1943 and 1944 extending and confirming the 1932 Act and giving powers of 'comprehensive' reconstruction and redevelopment of war-damaged areas; the Distribution of Industry Act in 1945 (administered by the Board of Trade) empowering government to license new industrial development with the intention of effecting growth in the Development Areas (previously called the 'Special Areas'); the New Towns Act of 1946 enabling government to set up development corporations for building new towns to aid in

17

providing housing and employment away from the conurbations, especially London, and thus to aid in decentralization and reduce urban congestion; finally the benchmark Town and Country Planning Act of 1947 which repealed most preceding planning legislation.

In 1950 the 'Schuster' Committee in reviewing 'the scope of town and country planning' examined possible definitions of the field and the range of objectives which then comprised the activity. First, they noted that the 1943 Act charged the Minister of Town and Country Planning (an office created by the Act itself) with the duty of 'securing consistency and continuity in the framing and execution of a national policy with respect to the use and development of land throughout England and Wales'. This however begged the question of the range of objectives which should be taken into account and how the functions of the planning authorities were to serve such objectives. The committee found that there had been a change in the conception of planning which now recognized the reciprocal relationship i.e. that all human activities depend on land and that the actual spatial patterns of development have profound effects on 'social, economic and strategic issues' (p. 13).

A brief analysis of the functions of planning authorities led to their recognizing a two-fold planning function: first the determination of policies, social, economic and strategic; and second, the making of land use and development plans in conformity with those policies. The plans for London and Greater London prepared by the late Sir Patrick Abercrombie, the other regional plans, e.g. for West Middlesex, South Wales, North Staffordshire and the Clyde Valley, made very wide-ranging proposals for urban redevelopment, industrial dispersal, a network of arterial roads and the location of large new residential developments including complete new towns. Plans for the reconstruction of blitzed cities such as Coventry, Liverpool, Plymouth and Manchester also proposed changes which would have considerable effects on the lives of their citizens and the business and commercial communities.

As far as control was *physically* practicable over such matters it was 'very nearly absolute'. That is, with respect to 'any building, engineering, mining or other operations, in, on, over or under land, and to any material change in the use of land or buildings' planning authorities had considerable powers under the law. But at the same time their positive powers of implementation had greatly increased. This was especially so because the legislation has in most cases removed liability for compensation to owners for refusal of permission to develop land or to change its use. Moreover, the 'comprehensive development' powers under the planning Act of 1947, and the power to build new towns are only the most striking examples of the ability to take public *developmental* initiatives set alongside the power to regulate those of others.

A good idea of the official view of the scope and objectives of town and country planning in the mid 1950s can be gained from the Report of the MINISTRY OF HOUSING AND LOCAL GOVERNMENT (1956). In this the long-term objectives of development plans were identified as 'remedying the defects of environment created during the nineteenth century . . . reducing congestion and rebuilding . . . [and preventing] . . . sprawl into the countryside around and between the old towns, disruption of compact communities and a wasteful daily movement to work'. But plans had to prepare for the future also, to respond to higher standards of living and the changing patterns of demand these would create. This would require 'intelligent anticipation, experiment and continual revision of assumptions'. In particular, a heavy demand for more land for development was implied. These problems and the context for their solution were then discussed by reference to specific examples of plans for Greater London, the County of London, the St. Paul's Cathedral area, and other city and county development plans which the Minister had considered. This revealed a multitude of objectives ranging from tackling the problems of slums, traffic congestion and lack of open space in Leeds, via mineral extraction, port development, coastal recreation and rural depopulation in Lincolnshire to a relief road to remove extraneous traffic from the University area in Oxford.

Mention was made of the statutory need for regular reviews of development plans and particular attention drawn to the problem of 'overspill' of population from one planning authority area to another; usually this occurred when a county borough redeveloped outworn housing at a lower density and could not find new land within its own boundaries to accommodate those families displaced by the operation. Very complex problems arose: some were administrative in which a county borough, a county and one or more of its districts were involved; some were 'technical' and involved the provision of all

19

the necessary infrastructure and services for the incoming population; some were socio-economic and involved efforts to ensure the availability of local employment in or near the 'overspill' development.

No reference to an official report of 1955 would be complete without mention of the Green Belt policy introduced in that year by the then Minister, Mr. Duncan Sandys. In his own words the aim of green belts was in general 'to prevent the further unrestricted sprawl of the great cities' and in the subsequent Ministerial circular (42/55) three specific aims were identified: to check the further growth of a large built-up area; to prevent neighbouring towns from merging one with another; and to preserve the special character of a town. Fairly severe restrictions on most forms of building development were intended with the exception of 'appropriate' uses such as golf courses, sewage works, recreational activities, agricultural developments and a certain amount of 'infilling and rounding-off' of existing towns and villages inside the green belt.

It is not necessary to enter into an analysis of green belt policy here since our purpose is merely to note it as one of the express objectives of British statutory planning at this time. In any case there are some useful critical analyses available (e.g. MANDELKER, 1962 and THOMAS, 1970).

Other sections of the 1955 official report deal with the problems of land acquisition (so as 'to secure the proper use of land'), with the reclamation of derelict land, the external appearance of buildings, the design of street lighting, caravan developments, the control of advertisements, and the creation of long-distance footpaths (such as the Pennine Way), the preservation of trees, woodlands and historic buildings. Other major sections of the report deal separately with mineral workings and with New Towns.

Still, for the moment, keeping within a British context and still emphasizing statutory planning, we can bring the time forward to when KEEBLE (1961) saw 'planning at the crossroads'. Keeble was in no doubt that 'land use planning, town and country planning, physical planning, or whatever other name may be preferred . . . is of profound importance to human welfare.' Listing a very wide variety of human activities he points out that physical arrangements including design of buildings, their arrangement with respect to others and indeed the whole gamut of spatial relationships of activity and communication can either increase or decrease 'a relatively harmonious' way of life and that, in addition, the deliberate inculcation of visual beauty can make a major contribution to life's enjoyment (p. 1).

But Keeble's main burden of argument concerns the 'piecemeal' nature of planning as he saw it at that time – the number of different people both lay and professional with a finger in the planning pie, the multitude of different and often conflicting opinions as to what planning in general was *for* and how in particular it ought to be done. He was afraid that 'there is a considerable danger of the ultimate objectives of comprehensive town and country planning being lost sight of altogether.' (p. 5.) So far he was arguing in general for a renewed sense of the *gestalt* or of Geddes's 'synoptic vision', for the notion that the whole is greater than the sum of its parts. But he quickly goes on to become very much more specific in what he admits is a personal 'vision': an unviolated countryside, largely devoted to agriculture and having well-designed and sited buildings; wild country should remain wild; an adequate, well-designed system of rural roads; settlements with 'clear, clean edges . . . and interesting silhouettes'; uncongested urban roads; a balance of population and employment to avoid mass journeys to work; a clear urban structure i.e. a pattern of land uses and communications which maximized accessibility and minimized congestion and danger; pedestrian shopping precincts; playing fields and other open spaces accessible to all who want them; well-designed industrial areas; the widest possible choice of house-types in residential areas with private outdoor space if possible; 'proper design and integration' of a multitude of natural features and artifacts in the urban scene.

Keeble admits the largeness of his vision and that, so far, it has not been attained but is adamant as to its desirability. He nevertheless puts it forward seriously as being a central requirement of civilized social policies. Although 'the stubborn individuality of human beings is as strong as bindweed . . . it surely seems preferable for it to manifest itself as incidental disorder superimposed upon basic orderliness, rather than as fundamental anarchy.' (pp. 6–10)

In Britain, the statutory planning scene in the 1960s was dominated by the report of the PLANNING ADVISORY GROUP (1965). In their opening review of the British system as they found it 'P.A.G.' (as it has come to be known) reaffirmed that planning was concerned not simply with land-use allocation but also with the quality of the

21

physical environment. At central government level, objectives of broad distributions of population and employment were of interest, as too was the whole 'urban structure' including traffic patterns 'development standards, recreational opportunities and community services'. But at the local level, physical planning and development control were regarded as the essence. And although the planning system had to serve 'an immense range of purposes', P.A.G. saw their complex inter-relationships as being studied and resolved by spatial and physical means to a very large extent. Throughout their report the Group refer to the objectives of planning. In talking of future *urban* (as opposed to rural or regional) planning they list the major tasks for the next twenty years as including: the physical reshaping of large towns and cities; the redevelopment of town centres; 'radical reappraisal' of the town's functions and land-use structure; 'balancing' accessibility and environmental standards.

This last point is but one example of the enormous influence of the report *Traffic in Towns*, by Sir Colin BUCHANAN (1963). British planning ideology and practice responded to this report perhaps more widely and deeply even than it had after 1955 following Duncan Sandys' green belt policy statement. Quite quickly everyone it seemed had become sharply aware that in having cars we were 'nurturing a monster of great potential destructiveness'. Not only were existing plans re-examined to see how well or not they could cope with motor traffic, and individual development applications scrutinized for their traffic effects, but in addition a whole new series of special 'land use and transport' studies was inaugurated. We can note in passing that in several ways (as had ribbon development control in the 1930s) both the broad policy formulation and the implementation and control passed into hands other than those of town planners.

We will not follow this line any further at present since enough has been said about the P.A.G. report to illustrate its views on major planning objectives and also because the whole realm of statutory planning in the late 1960s and early 1970s is taken up in a later chapter.

North American planning objectives

Instead we shall try and widen the perspective a little by looking at stated planning objectives in North America in roughly the same period, bearing in mind before we start the considerable differences in administration, the virtual absence of anything like the British statutory planning system and the different attitudes of Americans to relationships between the individual and the various organs of the State.

At a very broad level there are, of course, many points of contact concerning the ideology of planning and its more concrete objectives. Geddes and Howard were inspirational forces in America in their own lifetime and their messages have been amplified and developed over two generations by Lewis MUMFORD (1961). He shares one intellectual position with northern European planners and that might be called the ideal of organic order – order given in nature not imposed by man, an order which is subtle, complex and adaptive rather than simple, direct and firm. Obviously such a position owes much to Le Play and Geddes. For Mumford, haunted by the pre-monitions and early harbingers of a final holocaust, of Megalopolis and Necropolis,

> 'Significant improvements will come only through applying art and thought to the city's central human concerns, with a fresh dedica-tion to the cosmic and ecological processes that enfold all being. We must restore to the city the maternal, life-nurturing functions, the autonomous activities, the symbolic associations that have long been neglected or suppressed. For the city should be an organ of love; and the best economy of cities is the care and culture of man.' (p. 575)

Americans, inheritors of revolutionary liberalism set in the rural and small-town economy of the eighteenth century have long been anti-urban, whether they were born or brought up in Manhattan or the Kentucky hills. Rural romanticism, fear of the urban mobs, fear of rapid and radical change for some, fear of drab uniformity and conformity for others – these are some of the elements of anti-urbanism in American thought (see WHITE and WHITE, 1960). And whilst it is true that American planning, like that in Britain, has claimed to be 'the preparation of long-range comprehensive plans for communities' it has tended to focus on 'the efficacy of means to the exclusion of ends' and has thus failed to make effective use of the utopian tradition (MEYERSON, 1960). Rather more specific objectives in American planning can be deduced from a reading of some im-portant collections of essays produced by academics, researchers and

23

practitioners during the 1960s. For example in the collection edited by WINGO (1964) contributors discussed aims and objectives concerning: open space; urban form and structure; localized space and design. EWALD (1968) edited a volume of papers presented to the 50th Anniversary conference of the American Institute of Planners in 1967. There the substantive concerns were with the plight of disadvantaged minority groups; health, urban form; transportation choices and the threat of the car; housing conditions including alleviating overcrowding and clearing slums; the management of natural resources.

This latter question – what has come to be called the 'ecological' problem – characterizes the present and immediate past. The 1972 United Nations Conference at Stockholm emphasizes a world-wide movement of concern about the effects of rapid population growth, the depletion of natural resources, the pollution of the environment and the dangerous effects of (e.g.) artificial fertilizers on ecosystem balance and supersonic aircraft on the physical-energy systems of the atmosphere. It is much too early to evaluate these movements, less still to judge their complex arguments and controversies. But already some decisions are being influenced by pressures brought on 'ecological' grounds.

A very good idea of what American planning seeks to do at the 'sharp end' i.e. at the point of effective implementation, is provided by BAIR (1970) who begins by stating that 'any planner worth his salt in the years ahead is going to have to be aware that in large measure he won't know what he is planning for.' This turns out to be the prelude to a critique of the ideals of long-range planning and a plea for a heightened sense of the immediacy of problems and the need for planning to become more integrated with politics. He then goes on to give a confident statement of what city planning should be and do. Physical form and function are emphasized but not forgetting that they are but one manifestation of social and economic processes. Planning should often concern itself, of necessity, with seeking improved governmental forms. Once again entering a caveat at overconcern with unrealistic long-range forecasting, he nevertheless feels that 'some planning objectives seem valid for as long as cities will be with us.' Thus planning must control air and water pollution; conserve land resources; seek efficiency and economy in services provision; promote the general welfare (though 'here some soul-

24

searching is indicated' as to which publics and what kind of welfare is meant). More specifically, Bair lists ('of course') such matters as reducing traffic congestion; securing safety from fire and 'other dangers'; adequate light and air: adequate transportation; water, sewerage, schools, parks; prevention of overcrowding, promotion of orderly development and the prevention of sprawl (pp. 18–21).

We have spoken only of Great Britain and North America so far in this attempt to illustrate (rather than define) the range and character of objectives which are officially adopted in town and country planning. We lack adequate and accessible accounts of other countries' principles and practices. Yet we do know that the kinds of *problems* which have been discussed are experienced in widely differing nations – for example those comprising the membership of the Organisation for Economic Co-operation and Development (O.E.C.D.) as evidenced in a number of publications (e.g. THORNLEY, 1973). Included prominently are differential rates of growth between regions, rapid urbanization, congestion, housing, traffic congestion, decentralization of large cities, environmental pollution and so on. And if we in Britain have suffered from an outworn pattern of local government areas and functions, many O.E.C.D. member countries find urban planning difficult because their highly centralized 'Napoleonic' governmental systems imply the lack of any effective *local* government comparable with the British system.

What is planning for?

What sense can we make of this rapid scanning of town planning objectives? Is there some simple underlying rationale? For it is clear that the first impression is one of astonishing diversity and the sheer extent of the variety of these stated aims. Can one give a useful and clear answer to the question 'What is planning for?' whilst mentioning the general welfare, the design of sewer systems, reducing air pollution, controlling the design of outdoor advertisements, ensuring an adequate choice of housing types, reduction of traffic congestion . . . and so on, *all in the same breath*?

One possible way of organizing all this is to look at it dynamically, that is, with respect to the way the scope and emphasis of the whole set of so-called planning objectives has evolved *through* time and also how they are related *to* time. For example, some issues and objectives seem to be in Bair's words 'valid for as long as cities will be with us', e.g. those related to basic human physical functions such as breathing unpolluted air, drinking unpolluted water and so on, whilst others seem to arise quite suddenly and after a time cease to be in the forefront of concern because they have given way to new matters of urgency. In recent years, the threat of the car has yielded its prime place to housing and other factors contributing to 'multiple deprivation' in the inner, decaying areas of big cities. This problem in turn may be ousted from the limelight by the 'ecological' issue and environmental pollution. But having passed out of the realm of prime urgency these objectives do not thereby go away or become unimportant. To the extent that political action in bringing them to the notice of government has been effective in changing or instituting policy and action, these objectives thereby become part of the set of ongoing concerns.

Thus we can conceive of *a process of growth in the set of objectives* which have been listed in this chapter. At any point in time a set comprising a large number of objectives (reduce overcrowding and traffic congestion, control caravan development, encourage new industries in an area, etc.) is related to a set of policies and actions to serve them. As time passes new issues arise which may or may not be added to that set. This will depend upon a number of factors: who perceives and defines something as a problem, the force with which the issue is presented, the distribution of power between groups in society (including government) who would either oppose or promote policy and action on the problem.

Such 'candidate' problems are seldom new in any absolute sense. People were badly housed in cities, towns and countryside long before the Victorian reformers pressed for and achieved governmental action. Traffic congestion and conflicts between accessibility and environment were common in ancient Rome, eighteenth-century London and nineteenth-century Paris, i.e. long before Professor Buchanan drew our attention to the problem with such persuasive force. At least three important overlapping factors seem to be at work in this process. First of all, *technological change* may exacerbate and magnify a problem which at its previous levels was not perceived as critical; secondly, *information*, especially the mass media, and education, makes more people aware of conditions and of differentials between various groups or geographical areas; thirdly the dynamic process itself, in altering and enlarging the set of objectives for planning *thereby alters standards or norms* as to what is or is not tolerable.

Thus in the last hundred years town planning in Britain began with an emphasis on sanitary conditions in urban housing areas, became enlarged to incorporate a 'civic design' concern for the aesthetics of estate development; later still it incorporated the conservation of agricultural land, controlling sprawl and ribbon development, containing the growth of large cities and decentralizing their activities to new towns, the provision of open space in urban areas . . . and so on. All of these concerns have been 'taken on' by government in response to initiatives of its own or of groups in society at large in response to a *constantly shifting set of values and norms*.

Two other points are worth making. First, that not all of this growing set of objectives has been dealt with by so-called town and country planning departments whether of central or local government; industrial location policy was for long controlled by the Board of Trade; highway and transport-systems planning was until recently separated from other aspects of physical planning in central government and still is in the majority of local authorities; agricultural land-use policy and control is divided between the Ministry of Agriculture and other central departments. The list could clearly be extended.

The second point is that as more issues are admitted into the set of objectives loosely defined as planning objectives and become translated into policy and action, so the whole business becomes not only bigger in the sense of having more 'bits' to it but also *much more complex* – or at least our conception of the problems does.

So, to some extent, those things which come to be regarded as 'town planning' matters can be defined in relation to the administrative structure and function of government central, regional and local. This is a necessary condition for understanding but not a sufficient one. What is lacking is the *motivation* which raises the issues and governs their perception in the first place. For that we must turn to look at the *ideology* underlying British town planning.

One of the most thoughtful analyses of this is due to an American architect, FOLEY (1960), addressing British social scientists. Foley found that British planning comprised not one ideology but three

– which were often in mutual conflict. First of all, he found that planning in Britain was concerned

> '*to reconcile competing claims* for the use of limited land so as to provide a consistent, balanced and orderly arrangement of land uses';

the second element of ideology was

> 'to provide a good (or better) physical environment . . . for the promotion of a healthy and civilized life';

whilst the third he identified was

> 'providing the physical basis for better urban community life'.

The great appeal about a physical-environment goal is that it is simple and easy to understand. The visual sense is that which conveys by far the majority of the important information to the brain and with which most aesthetic experiences are connected. Physical benefits can be seen and appreciated by electors and demonstrated by politicians. Intentions, i.e. policies which are conceived in physical terms can be represented with force and economy on plans, charts and diagrammatic maps, which as Foley rightly discerns, 'have their own aesthetic'. (Perhaps Foley recalled his days in architecture school, where, as any student knows, pretty presentation was often half the battle.) Physical-environment policies, expressed on such plans are powerful in reinforcing physical symbolism such as the linked ideas of order and control. What appears orderly on the plan in the office will surely result in an orderly town or neighbourhood. The plan itself is a clear and simple policy instrument *and* a device for implementation via construction projects and development control (see Chapter 5). Finally, there is the element of 'environmental determinism', which holds that since social and economic disorders are often associated with poor physical environments, improvement in the latter will result in improvements to the social and economic aspects of life. Foley notes the essentially middle-class, educated basis of much of this ideology e.g. the prevention of urban sprawl and the preservation of pretty landscapes and townscapes by means of such instruments as green belts and conservation areas.

Planning seen as providing the physical basis for a better community life merges with the 'pure' physical goals to some extent. This occurs for example when planners discuss the clear distinction

28

between town and country in social terms. However, the classic example of this aspect of planning is the *neighbourhood unit* which reached its highest expression in some of the 'Mark I' new towns such as Harlow and Crawley. In neighbourhood planning, the aim was to provide for certain functional relations in daily life such as between homes and shops, open spaces, school and certain 'facilities' like doctors, dentists and other services to be ordered by spatial relationships. In this way, the evils of inter-war suburban developments would be avoided where houses were built for sale without any regard to such needs. But neighbourhood ideology extended to the notion of the 'balanced' community in which the proportions of socio-economic groups in the development would approximate to some norm such as a national or regional average. Significantly, this was to be achieved by constructing certain proportions of different types of houses – usually a small proportion of larger, higher-rented ones in which it was hoped the middle class would settle and larger proportions of various types of smaller houses and flats for lower-middle- and working-class people.

Outside of the new towns (which, it can be argued are special cases) a similar ideology can be discerned in the way county planning authorities treated small towns and villages. Usually major expansions were resisted and the nucleated, contained physical forms of many English villages and small towns have been nurtured through detailed planning and control not only for aesthetic reasons but also because of the assumption that the 'balanced, integrated' community life of such places would thereby be perpetuated (see BROADY, 1968).

Foley seems to detect an overriding concern with spatial order however and he advances one or two possible reasons for its pre-eminence. As noted earlier, it is not only a very powerful symbolic medium but also space standards 'can be treated in a technical manner in convincingly professional style'. This inheritance from the architect, the engineer (and to some extent, the lawyer and surveyor) may also account for the apolitical, neutral pose assumed by most British planners. But such 'technical' treatment of location and space, whilst handled with great confidence about villages, housing neighbourhoods, medium-sized towns and green belts seemed to break down at large geographical scales such as the conurbation or region. Perhaps this is because planners recognized unconsciously or consciously that environmental determinism would then be much more difficult to sustain as a concept. Foley remarked that issues like the total population, employment or kinds of people and jobs in these larger areas tended to be regarded as 'given' by British planners who

'in thinking of themselves as technicians, may sometimes be disinclined . . . to venture too far into the social and/or regional'.

Foley sums up his impressions by recognizing a central ambivalence between 'neutralism . . . and social advocacy'. As others have noted, planning had its earliest roots in liberal middle-class social reform but the movement quickly became *professionalized* in the form of the Town Planning Institute, dominated for its first fifty years by architects, engineers, surveyors and lawyers. As the professionals came to dominate the practice in the local and central government institutions so has technical, functional neutrality in a bureaucratic setting tended to oust the original social advocacy. So, the profession's image was technical, despite the fact that its activity touched on the deepest social and political issues (e.g. housing, recreation, employment opportunities). But even in 1960, Foley could detect that

'a flexible, administrative view of planning has rather taken over in the past decade or so from an earlier architectural, schematic, advisory-plan view.'

Whether or not that is a fair interpretation of events in the 1950s (or whether Foley was simply seeing the effects of the then Conservative government's steady withdrawal of interest in town and country planning) is beside the point here. Elsewhere in the book we shall have occasion to look at the 1960s and illustrate the shift from a narrow interest in land use as such towards a wider concern for social, economic and political processes on the British planning scene. But there can be little doubting the primacy of concern for the physical environment as such within the planning profession and in the legal and administrative machinery in which planners have operated with increasing effectiveness through the last half-century. We want to close this chapter by asking, as did Foley and many others, whether physical environmental quality and orderly land use patterns can be *ends in themselves* or is there some *other* kind of ideology or set of beliefs behind the apparent ends of designing and controlling the physical environment?

The ideology of control

Our hypothesis is that the key to the question lies *in the notion of control itself*. Most of the foregoing discussion has been in terms of what, substantively, is controlled by urban planners – land uses, visual aesthetics, ribbon development, agricultural land, employment locations. One of the puzzling aspects about planning is the apparent random diversity of its applications, the feeling that 'anything goes'. Indeed, LICHFIELD (1956) remarked that:

> 'certain objectives . . . have been absorbed by planning merely because they cannot be pursued by any public authority under its current powers. In such circumstances planning, in cricket terms, acts as a long-stop for balls which cannot be fielded by other public authorities.' (p. 31)

But it may be that town and country planning is an ideology related to the common element of control irrespective of what is controlled. *Physical* entities and systems are, as we have observed already, more amenable to discussions of the *objectives* of control, the *means* of control and to demonstrations of the *efficacy* of control. But control is control.

We can discuss this from a number of viewpoints. First of all, a desire for explicit order, for clear-cut stable relationships and maintenance of steady states may define a certain psychological type and a philosophical ideal. In classical Greece the figure of Apollo represented this element in human nature and its expression is manifested in ideas of proportion and constancy in architecture, music, mathematics and the socio-political thoughts of Plato. In recent times Freud's concept of super-ego is that element of mind which is order-maintaining and stability-seeking. By contrast, the classical Greek figure of Dionysus and the Freudian id represent the forces of disorder, chaos, instability, latent forces for change. Much philosophical, political, artistic and psychological analysis has been concerned with the interactions, tensions and interplay of forces set up between these two poles of disruption and stability.

If we translate this into political and sociological terms we can identify the ideal types of the conservative and the radical, the former seeking adjustments of a moderate and incremental kind in order to

31

adjust the output characteristics of the existing social system, the latter seeking more fundamental changes including restructuring of the social system itself. Several commentators on contemporary planning in its social context have begun to interpret planning as a set of activities which seek to maintain the existing order rather than to initiate and even sustain radical changes. For example SIMMIE (1971) recalls how the original radical concerns of e.g. Patrick Geddes at the close of the nineteenth century were quickly narrowed into a physical and legal framework. He argues that this has drastically reduced the effectiveness of planning as an instrument of change for overcoming social evils.

> 'Very often plans purport to be normative in so far as they start with goals and then define the means for achieving these goals. On closer examination, however, it is usually found that these goals are not seriously referred to throughout the plan and that there is a continued tendency to revert to trend planning.'

And he goes on to argue the need for 'a radical political view of physical planning'. Because of lack of understanding of social and urban processes by planners and because of their predominantly upper- and middle-class values 'planning costs have fallen more heavily on the poor and its benefits more directly on those who can already compete in a market economy.'

There is a growing number of people – including a considerable number of American writers disturbed by the urban crises of the 1960s there – who would argue as does Simmie, that one of the prime functions of planning would be to seek *redistributive* goals (notably of incomes but also of housing, employment and educational opportunities) and that to do so requires restructuring of government and its relations with the public (e.g. GANS, 1968; DAVIDOFF, 1965). These views seem to be on the increase – certainly if the learned journals are any guide. More than that, one has the impression that a large proportion of the younger generation of planners is asking searching questions about the rôle of planning in government and society.

A good case can be made for looking at contemporary practice, the profession, the statutory framework, the planning agencies in central and local government as maintainers of existing patterns of order. Good cases are also being made for the use of planning as a

direct instrument for social change as its nineteenth-century origina-
tors may have intended. Jane JACOBS (1961) launched a powerful
attack on the neat-and-tidy mindedness of city planners who she
claimed might eventually destroy the rich and random diversity of
urban life. Richard SENNETT (1970) has perhaps gone a little further
and suggested that

> 'When conflict is permitted in the public sphere, when the bureau-
> cratic routines become socialized, the product of the disorder will
> be a greater sensitivity in public life to the problems of connecting
> public services to the urban clientele. . . . The fruit of this conflict
> . . . is that in extricating the city from preplanned control, men will
> become more in control of themselves and of each other. That is
> the promise, and the justification, of disorder.' (p. 198)

To many people, certainly to the great majority of less sophisticated
people – that is most of the various publics whose interests planning
and government may claim to serve – the idea of deliberately-induced
disorder must sound a little perplexing, even wilful self-indulgence
on the part of intellectual social scientists. For planning's original
claim to legitimacy, its *raison d'être*, was intervention to right manifest evils and to root out the disorders of housing, health, crime,
education and urban congestion. According to this view social evils
were (and are) associated with disorders, with the operations of the
laissez-faire market mechanisms having gone *out of control*. On this
view *intervention* by public authority is justified in order to counteract
various evils. This attitude has never quite been lost. A sample of
writing about planning since the Second World War would reveal a
crop of examples of the need to intervene *lest chaos ensue*. How often
have we been told that unless stringent measures were taken 'traffic
will grind to a halt' or that our cities are 'choking themselves to
death' or that we will shortly have 'formless suburban sprawl all the
way from Southampton to Carlisle'?

These things have not come about – or certainly not in the
apocalyptic fashion their authors feared. In part this must be the result
of certain self-equilibrating process in the situations themselves. For
example, as traffic congestion mounts, its material and psychological
costs increasingly act as deterrents which prevent further increases in
movements into and within city centres. Activities which generate
high volumes of traffic move out of congested areas. Central London

has not ground to a halt for many reasons. Some would agree that governmental policies have had significant effects via severe parking regulations and traffic management systems.

But at the same time there are clearly processes which are *dis*equilibrating. One fundamental form of deprivation is poverty. The 'poor and the poorest' by and large get the poorest housing, less effective teachers and schools, doctors and social services, or make much less effective *use* of the social services than the middle classes. The children of poor families end up being less healthy, wealthy and wise and thus have the worst possible chances of advancement in the employment market. It is argued that this 'multiple deprivation' is both cause and effect of a situation in which bad things get progressively worse.

The ideological basis for control is a difficult and complex one. Are those who intervene in order to control a situation really producing change and righting wrongs or emphasizing the status quo? Are certain kinds of intervention wholly superfluous and irrelevant anyway in that they simply reinforce or duplicate the market mechanisms of a society like ours? These are serious questions. Planning as a socially concerned *movement* as well as a profession and an arm of government must clearly be seen to do better than market forces which may of themselves prolong or perpetuate certain kinds of injustice and suffering.

Very obviously we have slowly come to realize the sheer *complexity* of our perception of urban and social phenomena. We are now 'prisoners of the realization that everything in the city affects everything else'. Modern system theory suggests that the very existence of complex systems logically requires a vast amount of *intrinsic* control or ordering, organizing processes (BEER, 1966). If that is correct, intervention, i.e. control applied from outside to a potentially 'chaotic' system is mistaken. At the same time, there are many like BUCKLEY (1967) who claim that the most complex systems we can conceive – the 'sociocultural' systems – depend on intrinsic control which *necessarily comprise both equilibrating (negative feedback) and deviating, disequilibrating (positive feedback) phenomena* (see Chapter 8).

This suggests that a simple dichotomy between equilibrating, structure-perpetuating 'baddies' and disequilibrating, structure-changing 'goodies' is at best suspect, at worst downright useless as a

34

basis for discussion. At the same time, complex-system or cybernetic insights suggest first, that on the basis for deeper understanding of the webs of relationships which constitute our societies, those who seek to 'intervene' will be doing so from within (see CHADWICK, 1971, Chapter 15) and second, that such care and concern must be for a large number of different kinds of phenomena, some of which are equilibrating (for these are necessary) and some of which are dis-equilibrating (for so too are these). To understand and operate *only* one *or* the other kind of process is to miss at least half the point of being alive.

A slightly more extended and penetrating analysis of cybernetic insights into urban, social, planning and governmental phenomena occupies the closing chapters of this book. We close this chapter with the view that in the sixty or seventy years of its existence, official planning in Britain has been ideologically and psychologically based on the general view that intervention was necessary, even urgently necessary to restore order to situations which threatened to become chaotic and on the specific application of that view first of all to detailed physical situations (like housing layouts and garden cities) and latterly to broader physical patterns at the scale of the whole settlement and region. At the detailed level action many have missed the point because of 'environmental determinism' i.e. social evils might have far better practical remedies. At the broad scale, much of the evidence (reviewed in later chapters) suggests that planning as it is currently practised may simply be reinforcing or paralleling intrinsic homeostatic (i.e. 'steady-state') processes.

In order to clarify and illustrate these later difficult propositions we will turn in the next chapters to an account of the workings of deliberate intervention: land use and development control in Britain today.

2 · The Legal Basis of Development Control*

The legal basis of control over the physical environment is of great importance and is essential to an understanding of its practice and procedures. An understanding of the anomolies, the gaps and the superfluities in the British system of deliberate controls over the physical environment and the place of 'town planning' or 'development' controls within this depends to a very great extent on understanding its basis in the statute law and in administrative regulation and action. Without an understanding of this it is difficult to appreciate just how or why British town and country planning is so concerned with procedural matters, sometimes to the detriment of matters of substance and policy. Also, some knowledge of this statutory and administrative basis helps in understanding various *relationships* notably between local and central government (and especially between local authority planning departments and the Department of the Environment), between departments within local authorities, and between these and the public.

The definition of 'development'

The foundations of the modern British system of development control can be traced in Part III of the Town and Country Planning Act of 1947 which established the need to seek permission for all development carried out after the 'appointed day' which turned out to be July 1948. 'Development' was straightaway defined for this purpose as:

'the carrying out of building, engineering, mining or other operations in, on, over or under land, or the making of any material

* Most of the research and writing for this chapter were carried out by Barbara Solomon, M.A. (Illinois).

change in the use of buildings or other land.' (Town and Country Planning Act 1947, section 12(2))

This comprehensive definition was then qualified so as to exclude normal building maintenance and internal alterations, highway maintenance and minor improvements, the maintenance of public utilities, activities within the curtilage of dwelling-houses 'incidental to the enjoyment of the dwellinghouse as such', agricultural and forestry activities, and changes of use in buildings or land *within the same class of use* to be defined by the Minister later. Furthermore, subsection (3) of section 12 states that the subdivision of a single dwelling into two or more involves a 'material change of use' as does the tipping of refuse or waste materials (even on an existing tip if the area or height of the tip is thereby increased). Subsection (4) declares that the display of advertisements on a building will be regarded as a material change of use.

It is obvious that the definition of 'development' in the 1947 Act was crucial since it governed the whole scope of planning control. We should notice that this scope comprises physical development operations, changes of use (and changes in the intensity of use) of land and buildings. Subsequent sections of Part III of this Act dealt with the way in which local planning authorities should deal with applications. Of special significance is section 14 which states that the authority may grant permission, temporary or permanent (subsection (2)), with or without conditions, or refuse permission. In dealing with applications the authority:

'shall have regard to the provisions of the development plan, so far as material thereto, and to any other material considerations'. (section 14 (1))

Permission could be granted for development *not in accordance* with the development plan and the circumstances in which this could be done would be prescribed later by Ministerial Order. (Like so much else, this was to be included in the General Development Order.) Section 15 empowered the Minister to 'call in' any application for his own direct consideration and section 16 established the Minister's importance and significant role in receiving and deciding with finality the *appeals* of those applicants who were aggrieved by the local planning authority's conditions (attaching to a permission) or because of refusal of permission. The logic of the Minister's position

37

with respect to 'calling in' applications and determining appeals has always been contentious being open to the charge of 'judge and jury in his own cause'. But so long as applications for permission to develop are judged in relation to a development plan which the Minister has already considered and approved (with or without modifications) then he has an inescapable relationship with applications.

The remaining sections of Part III dealt with the legal and financial matters of compensation for refusal or revocation of permission in certain curcumstances, the enforcement of planning control and other special *subjects* of control (trees and woodlands, buildings of special architectural and historic interest, advertisements, certain public-authority development) all of which we shall be discussing later in the chapter.

It is important to look at the 1947 Act in this way because although subsequent legislation (e.g. 1960 Caravan Sites and Control of Development Act and the Town and Country Planning Acts of 1968 and 1971) have done much to revise the *details* of development control, its incidence, rights of appeal, etc., there has been no fundamental change made to its statutory purpose. Indeed the P.A.G. found that the scope of developed control needed no change and that 'The General Development Order and the Use Classes Order have stood the test of time remarkably well' (para. 1:10). They further believed that the procedures were 'basically sound and can work efficiently'. Despite the obvious close inter-relationships between plans and controls they felt that the trouble with the planning system was not with methods of control but with 'the development plans on which they are based and which they are intended to implement' (para. 1:15). At the end of their report, having advanced their proposals for substantial changes to the development plan system, the Group looked at the implications – including development control.

They were sure that the new-style plans would 'provide in many ways a sounder basis for development control' than the current detailed plans which showed land-use allocations or 'zonings' as the Americans would say. They felt that the new policy-and-objective based plans would be a sounder guide to the way in which each individual decision should go. But the new plans, like their predecessors would never be binding in their effect. 'All planning applications must be considered on their merits, having regard to the

development plan and any other material considerations . . . '
(para. 7:11). *Plus ça change . . .*

Exceptions and extensions

The 1947 definition of development was repeated verbatim in section
12 of the 1962 Planning Act, i.e.:

> 'The carrying out of building operations, engineering operations,
> mining operations and other operations, in, on, over or under land,
> or the making of any material change in the use of any buildings or
> other land'.

This definition is followed by a list of operations or uses of land
not to be considered as involving development of land (section 12
(2) a-f) and several operations which *are* to be considered as development (section 12 (3) a & b), a clause dealing with external advertisements as material changes of use (section 12 (4)), and a definition of
new development (section 12 (5)).

Those operations and uses of land not involving development
include:

(a) internal or external improvements, alterations, or maintenance
works which do not materially affect the external appearance of
the building (expansion of a building below ground level con-
stitutes development from 1 Jan. 1969);

(b) maintenance or improvements works carried on by a local
highway authority to or within the boundaries of a road;

(c) inspection, repair, or renewal of sewers, mains, pipes, cables,
etc. by a local authority or a statutory undertaker;

(d) use of any building or land within the curtilage of a dwelling
house for any purposes incidental to the enjoyment of the
dwelling house as a dwelling house;

(e) use of land for agriculture or forestry and the use for such purposes of any such building occupied with land so used;

(f) the use of buildings or land for any uses within any single class
in the Use Classes Order.

The use of a single dwelling house for the purpose of two or more
separate dwellings is to be considered development as is the deposit
of waste materials on an existing dump if either the superficial area
of the dump is extended or the height of the dump is extended and

exceeds the level of the land adjoining it and the display of advertisements on the external part of a building not normally used for such display. A lengthy specification of what is to be considered new development is also included.

The General Development Order (MINISTRY OF HOUSING AND LOCAL GOVERNMENT, 1963b and 1969a) and the Use Classes Order (MINISTRY OF HOUSING AND LOCAL GOVERNMENT, 1963a) are designed further to amplify the definition of development. The G.D.O. states what categories of development are deemed to be permitted and, therefore, need no express permission from the local planning authority. The twenty-three classes of permitted development include many of those areas specifically mentioned in the 1962 Act and much of the development by statutory undertakers.

The Use Classes Order is designed to clarify the question of material changes of use by declaring certain changes within each defined 'class' of use as not material and, therefore, not development as defined in the Act.

The provisions of the Act and these two important Orders taken together with a number of legal decisions constitute a full definition of development. They spell out for the planning authority what applications it will receive and in what categories of application it will have to decide whether or not to allow development to proceed. We have said above that such legal definitions and their amplification are necessary to the functioning of the planning Acts. That this is so does not mean that these definitions are without policy implication.

Certainly the preservation of agricultural and forestry lands are written into both the definitions and the procedures for handling development applications. In addition the development rights of government departments and statutory undertakers are also safeguarded by the preliminary definitions and Orders. These mean that *certain developments are undertaken without the local planning authority being in a position to evaluate their merits in terms of development plan policies* and local concerns (except in so far as they can influence the Ministry to hold a public inquiry on a proposed development). These developments may involve changes in the nature of once prominent industrial uses, in the intensity of the use of industrial premises and in the type of agricultural uses from market gardening to factory chickens, as well as a vast range of governmental and nationalized industry developments.

There are two important implications to the narrowing of the definition of development. One, that the local authority is not in a position to evaluate all of the real pressures which arise for development in its area since many of them do not need its permission to proceed. Two, that a number of changes in the use of land and existing buildings with important local consequences, can take place outside of the control of the planning authority.

An example of the type of restraint on a local authority through the Use Classes Order is provided by changes of use from shops to launderettes. The authority may believe that the traffic generation potential and the hours of business of the two were materially different and hence affected the local environment in different ways. But under the provisions of the Use Classes Order most shops and launderettes are in the same use class and, therefore, change from one to the other is not considered a material change of use, therefore no application for planning permission needs to be made.

The Minister can make special orders suspending a specific class of permitted development in a given locality so that the planning authority can look at development it might not otherwise be able to consider. For example permission might need to be obtained for agricultural buildings in a green belt in order to examine the labour and traffic-generation potential of the type of buildings proposed.

At present the planning authority is only notified of changes of use in industry if the proposal is to change the industrial use from one industrial use class to another, e.g. light to heavy industry. The implications for labour intensity, the density of traffic on nearby roads, etc. in a change within a single industrial category and in some cases from general to light industry can never be formally considered by the planning authority.

The lack of general principles

It is our contention here that within the confines of the local development plan based on what are considered to be local problems, the planning authority should be in a freer position to look at the kinds of development it believes are relevant to local problems. This does not mean that the use classes and the areas of permitted development need to be abolished but perhaps that the terms in which the uses are designated be more relevant to current planning problems so that industrial classifications would be based on relevant criteria like noise levels, worker intensity, traffic, etc. rather than on the nature of the product produced and noxious odours which seem to have been the traditional criteria.

It is a reflection of the antiquated nature of the use classes that special industrial uses are stated in terms like catgut manufacture, fish curing, animal charcoal manufacture, bone boiling, blood boiling, etc. (Use Classes Order 1963, class IX). The other special industrial categories tend to state specific processes like manufacture of acetylene from calcium carbide for sale or for use in a further chemical process (class VIII), manufacture of glass, where sodium sulphate used exceeds 1·5% of the melt (class VII), production of calcium carbide or zinc oxide (class VI). Whilst most of the industrial classes have a unifying element linking the individual processes, like distilling, refining or blending of oils, treatment of metals in furnaces, treatment of ores and stone in kilns, there is no explanation of the criteria for the groupings in the Order or any statement of the criteria on which new processes might be added to a class. All of the distilling, refining and blending operations in class VIII produce offensive or noxious fumes yet there is no mention of this in the listing of the processes and hence new processes which might have the same effects cannot automatically be added to this class. A general statement of the nature and effects of the processes to be included in each industrial class would avoid the problem of new processes, not specifically listed in any class, having to make constant application for planning permission until the process is added to a revised use classes order.

The General Development Order authorizes development without permission of the local planning authority or the Minister for twenty-three classes of what would otherwise be classified as development under the preliminary definition in the Acts. These include development within the curtilage of a dwelling house, temporary buildings, certain agricultural buildings, works and uses, certain forestry buildings and works, certain ancillary developments for industrial purposes, development under local or private acts or orders, development within limitations by local authorities, development by statutory undertakers within certain limits (including river authorities and the National Coal Board), development previously sanctioned by a government department, and use of land as a caravan site within limits. These are subject to two standard conditions: (1) that no obstruction of view on a highway and (2) that no changes in trunk or classified roads are involved in the development.

The classes of permitted development are again stated in terms of *the nature of the use rather than of its impact on the environment.* Unlike the Use Classes Order certain of these categories relate to the developer apparently on the assumption that certain developments by public and quasi-public agencies require less scrutiny by planning authorities than the undertakings of private developers. It does seem a bit niggling to have a class of permitted development for fences up to a certain *height* rather than permitting all those fences which do not obstruct view on the highway. Changes in use class from general industrial to light industrial, from restaurants to most types of shop, and from excepted shops (fish and chips, etc.) to general shops are permitted under class III. These permitted changes meet with the same criticism as the use classes, that *they disregard some of the potential planning problems attendant upon these changes.*

The present categories of permitted development and the use classes do perform their intended simplifying function in that they reduce the number of applications received by and the administrative burden on the local planning authority. However, they are not altogether appropriate in that they do not match the planning problems facing the authority. They do not necessarily facilitate dealing with the environmental problems raised by industrial development and by solid waste disposal, or with problems of traffic generating in older town centres.

When a development control caseworker goes to make a recommendation on an application, to what extent do procedural or substantive controls prevent him from making that decision on the basis of any factors which seem relevant to the case?

The caseworker receiving the applications has to find decision rules for his determinations if all applicants are to receive equal treatment and intending developers are to understand their position to any extent prior to making an application. Its own local development plan policies are a major source of such rules, Ministry Circulars and Bulletins are another source whilst precedent in the form of decisions on applications and appeals decisions are a third major source (see Chapter 4 below).

The development control policy notes discussed earlier begin with a

43

discussion of the general principles governing the operations of planning control. The discussion emphasizes the primary requirement to have regard to the development plan so far as material to the application and to have regard to what are termed other material considerations. The development plan is referred to in terms of use zones, green belts, proposals for public uses and existing uses proposed to 'remain for the most part undisturbed'. Other material considerations are described as including such matters as: the effect of a proposal on road safety or the beauty of the surroundings; the effect on public services, drainage, water supply, etc.; conflict with public proposals for the same land; and the need to ensure that valuable minerals are not sterilized by erection of buildings over them.

These other material considerations must be, as the notes point out, 'genuine planning considerations', related to the purpose of the planning legislation to regulate the development and use of land and not to achieve some extraneous purpose. For example, authorities are urged not to refuse the establishment of betting shops on the grounds that there are too many in the area already. A recent appeal was sustained where councillors in a local planning authority had refused permission for amusement arcades on moral grounds. The obvious problem raised by such cases is that councillors will want to make decisions on these grounds and will end up disguising them in acceptable but vague 'planning' terms. The looseness of the standard reasons for refusal of many authorities means that a number of extraneous reasons can be subsumed under phrases like 'damaging to amenity and convenience', 'to protect amenities', 'to enable the Council to exercise proper control over development', 'to ensure satisfactory development', 'to avoid the creation of traffic congestion and dangers on the highway', and 'to ensure that future redevelopment is not prejudiced'.

Another major factor in reaching control decisions are 'bottom-drawer' maps and policies not a part of the development plan (see Chapter 5). The use of these maps, etc. as well as the tendency of the development plan to get out of date leads to local planning authorities desiring to approve proposals not in accord with the development plan. In the Development Plans Directions 1965 provisions are made for approval of applications not involving significant departures in the opinion of the local authority and of notification of the Ministry of intent to grant permission where a substantial departure from the development plan is involved.

Assistance from the Ministry in making decision rules could be framed in more helpful ways than the ones discussed here presently are. In deciding appeals the Ministry is frequently making policy through the handling of individual cases without providing guidelines that would lead the local planning authority to the same decision. The Ministry draws back from specific advice in many cases on the grounds that the ultimate decision in each case must be based on the unique policy issues which separate the case from all similar cases (SHARP, 1969). It seems easy to overemphasize this point of the differences between all individual applications. Certainly if the administrative burden on the local planning authority is not to become excessive, applications dealing with fairly simple matters could be handled by setting out in advance general rules governing certain cases of application.

There is, of course, the problem of defining the level of specificity appropriate to the local authority and the Ministry and avoiding the situation of historic buildings and advertisement control where the level of specificity at the central level is too great, leaving the local authority little opportunity to integrate local concerns into its decisions. Also there is the need to avoid the situation where the central guidance is so loosely framed that local authorities are unsure of how to apply it and the Ministry ends up making *ad hoc* policy through its individual decisions on planning appeals.

There is a general argument to be made that more of the burden in planning control should be shifted towards the developer. Doing this involves stating the authority's policy in a way which allows the developer to make certain preliminary judgements of his own about his proposals. Certain preliminary conditions may be formulated so that the developer has a relatively clear idea of what amount of space and type of design he needs before approaching the planning authority and some idea of what types of sites will be automatically rejected, and secondly that the authority has relatively clear decision rules to use in studying the applications.

This may not be a perfect solution and loosely drawn special permit ordinances have led to the exercise of arbitrary administrative discretion for narrow purposes like economic and racial segregation in the United States. But it does shift a certain amount of the burden of

45

examining a proposal forward from the local planning authority to the developer. The developer is in a position to examine his own proposal in light of the stated policies of the authority rather than making a certain prior investment of time and money and then having the planning authority give him the details of its policy and finding out that his proposal is likely to be unsuitable.

Obviously it is not easy to do this for major industrial proposals or shopping centre proposals, the nature of which would be difficult to anticipate. However, it is estimated that 90% of development control work is with the less complicated type of application involving minor floorspace additions, residential garages, individual dwellings, etc. It is in these areas that codifying decision rules would leave the development control staff with greater amounts of time to deal with major redevelopment, town centre, residential estates, and major industrial proposals. Not that decision rules are impossible to define for the more complex cases but they are more difficult to evolve. The case for each having obvious unique policy elements is stronger. It is worth saying again that such specific decision rules can only be formulated with any degree of confidence against a background of broad general policy from the Ministry and in the local development plan. If made without these the uncertainty is too great and the authority is in a less disquieting position if it falls back on its own previous decisions which have been upheld by the Minister on appeal.

Non-development controls

The exercise of special types of control has extended the sphere of planning control to include advertisements, caravan sites, tree preservation and buildings of architectural and historic interest. The specificity of these policies has been discussed above but bears repeating here. They are in general procedures which exist over and above the normal control process, involving licencing and controls, where development, as defined in the planning Acts, is not taking place.

These controls carry different types of enforcement provisions from the regular planning controls. In the particular case of historic buildings the controls are such that contravention of the various regulations ordinarily involves fines levied by courts. This initial involvement of the courts makes this a different form of legal enforcement procedure from the enforcement notices used in the normal procedures for the control of development.

In the case of caravan sites, planning control is closely involved with a local licencing procedure. Nationally issued Industrial and Office Development Certificates are a necessary but not sufficient precondition to granting permission for certain proposals.

The controls are built on different planning bases from the normal procedures; sometimes these are broader than the normal criteria and sometimes they are narrower. The vast edifice of advertising control is based on the interests of amenity and public safety. The caravan sites regulations cover public health considerations as well as aesthetic ones. With regard to tree preservation orders matters of amenity are the only relevant factors for consideration (1962 Act, section 29). The nature of the procedures for protection of historic and listed buildings developed under the 1968 Planning Act are considered by some lawyers to be a serious restraint on the owners of such properties in spite of the provisions made for compensation. The need to preserve the national heritage in both historic and architectural terms is held to be an adequate justification for these restraints.

While not all these controls are based on amenity considerations the elaborate controls over advertisements, tree preservation and caravan sites are partially or solely based on amenity. Amenity, of course, is a genuine planning concern but it is hard to see why it assumes more importance in the establishment of special control procedures than noise, air or water pollution, none of which are so clearly written into the planning code. Advertisements, to cite only one example, are obviously less durable than those factories which turn out to be major air or water polluters. Also it would seem that if the definition of amenity is taken as meaning pleasant circumstances, features and advantages (HEAP, 1969, p. 139), then tree preservation procedures are not designed to protect watersheds, prevent soil erosion, or preserve windbreaks. Certainly such environmental concerns are as important as screening mineral workings and preserving tree-lined streets.

The question of whether there should be such special controls over and above the normal planning control process must also be asked. These controls tend to enshrine a series of issues which may or may not be the most important planning issues, and by the existence of special procedures emphasize their importance in the planning process. The nature of the procedures places a heavy administrative burden on the planning authority to the possible detriment of the regular procedures. If planning control should be extended to things not covered in the definition of development like preservation of trees and woodlands, then it would seem to call for *modification of the definition of development* rather than establishment of special controls outside of that definition. Leaving aside the problem of irreplaceable buildings, it is not immediately clear why different enforcement procedures are necessary for the areas of special control. Why are the normal enforcement procedures not strong enough to cover these areas? Should they not be since the regular control procedure comprehends areas as important as those covered by the special control procedures?

Gaps in control of the environment

Our general discussion of the nature of planning controls has already indicated a number of gaps in the control over the physical environment available through development control procedures. Of course, it is possible to argue that some kind of general control over the physical environment is not the purpose of development control; that development control exists to regulate land uses, to conserve 'amenity' and to implement development plan policies. Even if this were ever true, the advent of the structure plans under the 1968 Planning Act, replacing the old land-use-oriented development plans, has changed things. The new structure plans appear designed to produce a more comprehensive type of planning, dealing with the physical aspects of the quality of life within the local planning authority's territory. If development control is to remain a major tool for the implementation of plans it must be adequate to its task of implementing this broader type plan. Unfortunately its present legal structure does not comprise a number of areas of current concern to local authority planning and to the public at large.

What follows is an exploration of a few of these areas, currently defined as problem areas in the physical environment, which the development control procedures do not cover adequately. This list makes no pretence at comprehensiveness; it is merely illustrative. And it is in the nature of things that even if comprehensiveness were attempted the list would soon become obsolete as *the definition o, environmental problems is constantly shifting* and technology seems regularly to produce new environmental threats. We shall be looking at: public development; agricultural land; air, water and noise pollution; traffic and traffic control; and the economic implications of development proposals.

Public development

Public development, i.e. by government departments, statutory undertakers and local authorities, is not entirely outside of the ambit of planning control. However, the gaps in the control are much broader than the areas of coverage.

Where a local authority or a statutory undertaker must have approval from a government department to undertake proposed development, formal planning permission is not necessary. The approval of the department is treated as 'deemed planning permission' (1962 Act, Part III, section 41). A local authority, within its own territory, has deemed planning permission when the proposed development is in accord with the development plan (1962 Act, Part III, section 42), or where the departure from the plan is not considered a major one. For development outside of its own territory the local authority must make formal planning permission to the relevant local planning authority. Development under local acts is also exempt from the need for planning permission.

Maintenance and repair work of local authorities and statutory undertakers is not considered development so it does not require planning permission (1962 Act, section 12 (2)).

Part X of the 1962 Planning Act deals with the methods of controlling development by statutory undertakers. The elaborate provisions include the rights to compensation if they feel they have been put at a disadvantage by such control. However, HEAP (1968 p. 107) points out that under the General Development Order 'statutory undertakers are given a good slice of permitted development' for which a blanket planning permission is accorded by the terms of the Order itself. In this area of permitted development it is the undertakers' 'operational land – land essential for carrying out the functions for which the undertaker exists' which is given what Heap terms 'favoured treatment' when it is being developed for the purposes for which the undertaker exists. Under the 1968 Act (section 69) non-operational land at the time the Act comes into effect does not enjoy this permitted-development status and specific planning permission is required for the development of such land for the purposes of the statutory undertaking (section 69 (2) (a)). However, the 1968 Act has extended the cases involving non-operational land where the undertaker can make a joint appeal to the Minister and the sponsoring Minister rather than accept the determination of the local planning authority.

The developments of statutory undertakers are considered vital to the continued functioning of the nation and this has led to the traditional exemption of their operations (as opposed to offices, etc.) from the need for local planning permission.

In essence, the planning consideration given to 'operational land' development proposals is at the Ministry level, frequently in conjunction with the sponsoring department. The Planning Ministry (D. of E.) is, of course, compelled to hear local authority representations regarding a proposal as well as the representations of the statutory undertaker. The sponsoring department in giving authorization for development to proceed no doubt must examine the environmental impact of the proposals. However, this is only one of the many factors to be taken into consideration by *the sponsoring department whose primary responsibility is not safeguarding the local physical environment*. The local planning authority whose primary responsibility *is* the quality of the local physical environment has very little to say about the location, scale and impact effects of proposed operational developments by statutory undertakers.

The nature of the developments necessary to carry out the duties of statutory undertakers are frequently out of scale with their surroundings, potentially damaging to the environment, and disturbing to the local community like the giant power plant stacks which dot the countryside and the high-tension power lines crossing national parks.

Problems such as those regarding the development of the Dee Estuary in West Cheshire and Flintshire highlight the need to scrutinize these developments with regard to local planning proposals regardless of the essential nature of the proposed development. The Central Electricity Generating Board was proposing a major atomic power installation at Connah's Quay on the edge of the estuary in Flintshire. It was incumbent on the Board merely to notify the

County Council of the intended development. However plans for development of the Dee Estuary as a recreation facility were being made jointly by Cheshire, Flintshire and the Welsh Office and a proposal for a major steel mill at the southern end of the estuary was expected to be forthcoming. Among other problems a determination needed to be made about whether the use of cooling towers or cooling pools at the Connah's Quay installation would best fit in with the other proposals for the area. A planning inquiry has been held to examine all of the various proposals for the area since they each have important implications for the others and finalizing any one of them would greatly lessen the alternatives left open to the others. Proper development of the area to cater for all of these developments requires a great deal of co-ordination not available through normal procedures. Under the normal procedures the statutory undertaker could have proceeded without formal involvement of the local planning authorities.

The extent to which major industrial projects can go forward without any type of local planning permission is a serious gap in the control of major planning problems by the local planning authorities. It seems imperative that the operational undertakings of statutory undertakers, given their potential for damaging the environment, must be treated in similar ways as other industrial proposals at the local level, subjected to the same kinds of questions and to the far-reaching *public health and pollution questions which should be a part of the planning code.*

Agricultural and forestry development

Agricultural and forestry lands presently have what amounts to immunity from development control. Under the 1962 Act (section 12 (2) (e)) the use of land for agricultural or forestry and the use for any of those purposes of any building, structure or erection occupied with the land so used is not development. Moreover, new agricultural and forestry buildings while considered development are 'permitted development' under the General Development Order. The only things *not* exempted from development control scrutiny are homes for agricultural and forestry workers.

The fact that the general presumption is in favour of any productive farmland remaining in active farming regardless of the nature

51

of the development proposed creates a gap in the local planning authority's ability to respond to development pressure and to take into consideration all relevant factors in planning for the physical environment.

The Environmental Handbook (BARR, 1971) comes to the conclusion that there is a need for 'a study of the costs and benefits of alternative uses of "agricultural" land, such as amenity, conservation, or recreation, and the need to look again at the assumptions that land outside towns must be farmed' (p. 287).

Under the present arrangements, which have existed as long as statutory planning in Britain, whole regions may undergo massive shifts in husbandry, in cropping patterns, in the balance between pasture and arable land, in the pattern of labour demanded by different farming methods, in the use of fertilizers and other aspects of advanced technology. As a result the appearance, the social structure and the economy of whole tracts of countryside may quite drastically alter. Despite the fact that the Planning Acts (and planning ideology) pay such regard to population, traffic, visual amenity, local services, public transport and so on and despite the fact that agriculture is the *largest single user of all land*, it is virtually unaffected by our elaborate system of planning and control.

Pollution control

Various forms of environmental pollution are covered by statutes other than the Planning Acts and enforced by other departments or special authorities. The planning code does not write these concerns into development control as material considerations in considering applications for development. (It is of course possible for local planning authorities to write such considerations into their development plans but it seems unlikely that a great many have done so given the preoccupations of old-style development plans.) Some local planning authorities co-operate with the local health department about the implications for clean air of alternative stack heights for proposed industrial developments, but such consultations are entirely voluntary.

The cost of the lack of such considerations in examining proposals for development can sometimes be counted in dead animals at Fort William, Scotland, but the issues are not always so obvious. More often the additional smoke or noise or polluted water just adds to what finally become an unpleasant place to live or work. The present concern with the noise level around airports has led counties like Cheshire to adopt planning policies which prohibit future development at certain distances from Manchester's Ringway Airport and require sound-proofing at further distances. However, *it is not clear that a decision to prohibit a development on the grounds of the noise or smoke or waste products it would generate is within the current powers available to development control.* On the other hand there seem to be no reasons why conditions could not be imposed on permissions with regard to these matters.

If development control decisions are indeed to represent meaningful control over the physical environment, *pollution control considerations should be written into the planning code* and not left entirely to the intelligent foresight of individual local planning authorities.

Traffic control

Much time seems to be devoted to questions of traffic generation potential and parking needs of proposed developments. Certainly the Ministry considers one of the 'material considerations' in judging an application to be its effect on road safety. A considerable amount of consultation on access requirements and other traffic-related matters takes place with the authority's traffic engineer in making control decisions. Parking policies for residential and commercial properties are usually established by local planning authorities.

Yet a number of matters with very direct impact on the amount of traffic and its impact on a given area do not come to the development control apparatus at all. Proposals for re-routing buses or for storage of vehicles with potentially dangerous cargo go directly to the local authority department concerned with traffic. Parking regulations may have a profound effect on land-use changes, etc. but can lie completely outside the ambit of planning and development control. The decisions are made without recourse to planning considerations as developed through a consultation procedure. Traffic-flow improvements and road locations are usually made through central department-local authority consultations which often involve solely traffic engineering personnel at both ends.

The impact of major road locations on planning for a locality really needs no additional discussion; it is vital to the location of various facilities and generates a rather predictable set of land-use pressures. The planning authority has to deal with these resulting pressures without having had much influence on the road location. In the case of matters like determination of bus routes, it is easy to underestimate their impact on minor planning and redevelopment schemes in cities where shop space may be planned along existing bus routes or children's playgrounds on a quiet road which is proposed to become a bus route.

What is good traffic planning may not always be good planning from a broader perspective. Adequate planning for the physical environment would seem to require this broader perspective especially if integrated land-use and transportation planning is to become a reality rather than the subject of lip service only.

Economic implications of proposed development

It is not so much that the economic or financial implications of proposed development are outside of the legal structure of development control but rather that the Ministry has generally refused to accept this as a valid consideration in making decisions on applications for permission to develop.

The classic example given in the discussion of planning appeals is that betting shops cannot be refused planning permission on the grounds that there are too many such shops in the area to make an additional one potentially profitable. The argument says that this determination is up to the licensing authorities in the case of betting shops. It continues by noting that *it is not the business of the planning authorities to put themselves in the place of market forces.*

This argument is certainly reasonable as far as it goes. However, there are more problems involved than whether or not Honest Joe will go bankrupt leaving a vacant shop. When a private developer is proposing new premises or a private renewal scheme it is senseless not to consider the economic feasibility of the project in terms of its location and the nature of the proposed uses. Most authorities no doubt do this. The Ministry recognizes this to some extent in its guidance on redevelopment in town centres. However, it has generally been reluctant to extend this to other areas of development.

The Ministry has generally rejected local authority attempts to make policies for given stretches of major roadways where it had received applications for petrol-filling stations and expected to receive additional applications. Such policies would typically have limited the number of stations based on the potential traffic on the roadway. The Ministry rejected this on the grounds that it was *up to the oil companies to make the determinations of economic feasibility* and not the local authority. The local authority must consider each of the separate applications 'on its merits'. One particularly unfortunate result has been several derelict petrol filling stations on a stretch of road in the South Midlands – filling stations which all passed the tests of good design, adequate access and traffic safety.

Development control acts as a brake on unlimited development and it confers substantial powers on local authorities to affect the pattern of development. In the matter of out-of-town shopping centres and so-called hypermarkets, these powers have often been used to confer advantage on one set of businessmen, those in the existing town centres. The fear of declining trade in town centres and the planning problems that would involve have clearly been motivating factors in the decisions. Local planning authorities have neither a tradition of considering the economic aspects of development nor adequate analytical tools and skills and this has left them without any adequate basis on which to judge the full range of factors involved in out-of-town versus in-town shopping areas. Guidance from the Ministry is still in draft form and only recently have some authorities begun to ask the serious questions about such development.

Most authorities faced with a proposed hypermarket have preferred to avoid any possibility of damage to town centres by rejecting the proposals.

The major issue raised in all such cases is *what is planning control for*? What are its criteria as embodied in the development plans and the 'other material considerations' which would provide a rationale for individual decisions to be made? What precisely is meant by treating each case 'on its merits'? On the specific question of financial or economic viability the official view for some considerable time has been that it is not the function of statutory town planning to interfere with the operations of market forces in e.g. deciding how many filling stations or how many square metres of shopping floorspace a town or region needs. These matters, it is argued, are the concern of the entrepreneur, not of the bureaucrat. To argue this is to limit the operation of development control and statutory planning to such matters as external appearance and land-use zoning. But at the same time, government has introduced, after lengthy discussion, legislation which calls for an explicit concern for physical and *economic* facts in urban and regional plans. Surely we cannot have it both ways.

An even bigger issue is at stake here and that concerns one's view of the purpose of planning in a society like ours. Is it conceived of as a regulatory process for gradual adoption of aspects of the status quo or as an agent for advocating and implementing structural changes? We shall take this question up in later chapters.

Conclusions

The burden of the arguments about the legal structure of development control has been that: (1) the present scope of development control is not as broad as the current concerns for the physical environment in British planning, and (2) that the nature of the current planning controls are at once too narrowly drawn in some areas and too loosely drawn in others.

The first point might suggest a broadening of the range of topics so that the scope of planning control is adequate to the concerns of the plans it is to implement. One area which has been mentioned at length and bears repeating here is the need to include much more public development, particularly that of statutory undertakers, within the scope of local planning controls, either under the regular permission procedure or under some modification which gives adequate consideration to the local concerns inevitably involved in such development.

The theme of the need to involve planning agencies more directly in decision making where they have a legitimate interest (but are not presently represented) is one which unites the seemingly disparate areas of concern which we have been discussing: traffic control, air, water and noise pollution, and road locations.

The actual *nature* of the present planning controls is as fundamental a question as their scope. The legal framework of planning control is not only tied to traditional land-use questions but it is a dual system with one set of controls dependent on the definition of development and another set of ad hoc controls *which have no clear rationale at all.*

This dual system not only has distinct bases in law but uses different types of enforcement procedures and involves different types of restraint on the individual's use of private property.

That part of the planning control system which is based on the definition of development tends to be loosely drawn, leaving a great deal of discretion to local authorities in giving planning permission based on local planning policies. It has imposed on it the rudiments of a national land-use policy through a variety of somewhat fragmentary methods, the main one being the adjudication of appeals from local planning authority decisions by the Ministry. The lack of either general principles or sufficient detail as well as the omissions in the range of subjects covered seems to be the serious problem with this part of the planning control system. Local planning authorities feel a lack of adequate guidance in formulating decision rules and an inability to discern government policy in certain areas. The Ministry appears to have defaulted in this respect on what GRIFFITH (1966) considers its vital role of providing a context of policy within which local authorities can operate.

The ad hoc part of the planning control system appears to have the opposite problem of being too tightly drawn. It comprises a set of separate issues about which there has been a great deal of public and governmental concern. The governmental concern has generally been with economic issues like the location of industry and the extent of office development. The public concern has largely been with amenity issues like advertisement control, caravan sites, preservation of trees and woodlands, and preservation of historic buildings. The controls are entire codes which operate over and above the normal planning control procedures for permission to develop. The local authority acts generally as the agent for the central government in administering these controls. The scope for the integration of local concerns or preferences into these control systems seems narrow indeed.

These codes are really very narrow in the number of issues they cover compared to the possible range of amenity and economic issues which might be covered in this way if the political demand were there. The question is whether this is a valid procedure for dealing with areas of concern like advertisements and office development. It is not possible to handle the amenity issues in particular through the normal mechanisms of planning control? Amenity is considered a legitimate planning consideration. The aims of both the amenity and economic

57

controls are within the scope of planning concerns, even if advertisements and tree preservation are not within the scope of the present definition of development. The question is whether the special handling of these issues does not accord them undue importance and whether the nature of the procedures established does not place an unnecessary administrative burden on local planning authorities. Are these not techniques which have been elevated to the level of dogma and which need to be examined in terms of alternative methods of achieving the same ends?

In dealing with the problem of making a context of policy for development control, the issue seems to resolve itself into one of what level of detail is appropriate to statements of policy made by central government and what level to those made by the local planning authority.

The mention of detail in the same breath as policy may tend to suggest a disregard for the policy element in each case being considered. This policy element makes each case unique and thereby renders general policy statements difficult to make and perhaps meaningless. However, it has been said before that this type of statement over-emphasizes the uniqueness of each case. It also seems that policy guidelines run the risk of being too specific, like the special control procedures. *It is, however, the very general statements of the objectives of town and country planning which are lacking in even such basic documents as the principal planning Acts.* The local planning authority is, therefore, left to weigh criteria in specific cases with regard to the goals of the local plan and local conditions. What are the general criteria for well-planned towns? Do they have carefully segregated land uses or do they use performance criteria rather than use zones to create a clean, healthy place to live and work? What are the important criteria to consider in industrial location and in studying industrial applications? How and when must the authority consider regional and other interests in its decision making?

Despite the differences in legal context between American and British land-use controls, BABCOCK (1966) in his review of American zoning practice comes to much the same conclusions we have here. One of the major changes for which he calls is 'a statutory restatement of the major substantive criteria by which the reasonableness of local decision-making criteria is measured' (p. 154). In suggesting changes in the legislation which establishes the legal context within which local legislatures draft their land-use control ordinances (local laws) Babcock is attempting to interject broader regional criteria into land-use control decisions and to have clearly established just what criteria will be used in judging the reasonableness of local decisions when appeals are made. Among the examples which he presents are (not all applicable to the British situation):

> 'The state should set forth in the statute whether the reasonableness (validity) of local decisions affecting land adjacent to state highways and navigable waters will be determined in part by the impact of the proposed uses on those regional resources. The state should articulate, whether the reasonableness of local decisions over density of development will be determined, in part at least, by the impact of a chosen density upon metropolitan transportation. The state should articulate in the enabling act what significance, if any, the impact of development on public schools shall have in a land-use dispute. . . . The state should indicate whether a decision to mix or not mix commercial and residential uses is solely a matter for the local community : are metropolitan considerations relevant to a determination of the validity of municipal regulation in such cases?' (p. 160).

No one would suggest that the writing of general goals for local planning is easy. The experience of the regional planning exercises in the United States clearly indicates this. However, even the rather vague structure of a governmental economic policy is lacking in the area of national land-use policy. It would be difficult to argue convincingly that local authorities would not be in a better position to judge the reasonableness of their own decisions if they had the background of a general policy context for planning control of the physical environment.

59

3 · Planning Authorities, Departments and Development Control

The aim of Chapters 3 and 4 is to present a fairly detailed picture of development control casework in Britain at about the time of writing. The evidence for this comes to a very large extent from studies carried out in seventeen widely contrasted types of planning authority during 1970 as part of a wider research programme financed by the Social Science Research Council (see Preface). In this fieldwork, structured interviews (based upon a questionnaire form) were conducted with seventy local government officers directly concerned with development control casework and some thirty informal conversations in the same offices.

The selection of authorities for empirical study was governed by a number of factors. In the first place we wished to have a reasonably good representation of different types of authority, that is, counties, county boroughs, new towns and so on. The 1947 and 1962 Planning Acts, operative at the time of our investigation, gave planning powers to the counties and county boroughs in England and Wales and the Scottish counties and large burghs were given similar powers by the equivalent legislation for Scotland. In addition, however, certain powers to make development plans, and most powers of development control, could be delegated by agreement from English and Welsh counties to their constituent (second-tier) districts. These arrangements vary widely from one county to another (see for example, MINISTRY OF HOUSING AND LOCAL GOVERNMENT (1967a)). Moreover, there were a number of special cases which merited study, such as the G.L.C. area, the subject of a new system of metropolitan government including planning and development control following the 1963 London Government Act, two of the national parks (Peak District and Lake District) which are independent planning authorities. It might be expected also that variations would be found between authorities with plentiful staff resources and those short of manpower, between areas with different major problems: congestion, poor housing and so on in major conurbations; rural development and the expansion of tourist development in Scotland and parts of northern England. Finally, we had to tailor our fieldwork effort to our own resources of time and money in the research project.

In the event we selected seventeen authorities for full study from the large number who had said they were willing to co-operate. They are:

Aberdeen Large Burgh
Bromley London Borough
Camden London Borough
Crawley Urban District in West Sussex
Durham County Council
Greater London Council
Herefordshire County Council
Leicester County Borough
Lincoln County Borough
Luton County Borough
Manchester County Borough
Newport County Borough
Oxfordshire County Council
Peak Park Planning Board
Ross and Cromarty County Council
Skelmersdale Development Corporation (in Lancashire)
Southend County Borough
In addition we visited the Horsham area office of the West Sussex planning department and the Wigan divisional office of the Lancashire planning department in order to understand better the context of development control in Crawley and Skelmersdale respectively.

During the course of this chapter we shall depend in turn for our understanding and explanation partly on the evidence provided by study visits to these authorities and partly on general knowledge and experience of local government and its 'town and country planning' function.

At the time of our studies and at present (until the reforms expected in 1973/4), local government in Britain consists of two parallel systems of authority. Most large cities are governed by all-purpose single-tier authorities – the County Boroughs – which discharge all of the statutory functions of local government within their administrative areas. The counties on the other hand are two-tier authorities in which there is a County Council for the whole county whose area is subdivided into three kinds of districts – the Municipal Boroughs, the Urban Districts and the Rural Districts. The powers and duties of local government are shared between these two tiers, but the three kinds of districts discharge slightly different mixes of functions. In general, however, the more 'strategic' functions (such as education, major roads, town and country planning) are the responsibility of the county councils, whilst the 'tactical' services (e.g. secondary roads, street lighting, building regulations) are discharged by the district councils. Additionally, certain minor powers (street lighting, children's playgrounds) are possessed by the rural parish councils in counties.

Full accounts of these matters are available in many standard works of reference (e.g. GRIFFITH (1966); ROYAL COMMISSION ON LOCAL GOVERNMENT IN ENGLAND (1969); MINISTRY OF HOUSING AND LOCAL GOVERNMENT (1967b)). The very brief sketch given here is sufficient for putting the development control operation into its context and we shall be concerned in other parts of this book to discuss the future of planning and development control in the context of the future patterns and functions of local government in this country.

Local authority management structures

Local authorities in Britain are characterized by a very strongly developed departmental structure. That is to say, both their bodies of elected members and their employees are fairly strictly divided into committees and departments respectively. These committees and departments are closely related to a specific function of local government, usually defined by a particular Act (or series of Acts) of Parliament. Furthermore, there are very strong and direct links between most of the committees and a particular department.

For example, the Education Acts placed the responsibility for local education (primary, secondary and 'further') on the county boroughs and the counties who have each created an education committee drawn from members of the council (with or without co-opted members) advised almost exclusively by a chief education

LOCAL AUTHORITY MANAGEMENT STRUCTURES

officer. In similar fashion, the Housing Acts have led to housing committees, housing officers and housing departments.

There are, of course, any number of variations in this apparently simple model. In response to widespread pressures based on the view that many problems of health, housing, children and welfare could not and should not be compartmented since their incidence on the individual and family were usually interlinked, we are now witnessing the creation of social services departments comprising all these functions within the same administration and reporting to a social services committee. But this kind of development is in a way a confirmation of the departmental model rather than a radical departure from it. And we should note that once again it was central government action in the form of the Social Services Act, 1968, which gave real impetus to these changes and not any particular desire for it on the part of local government members or their staffs.

Not all committees and departments are defined or required by statute either – libraries, parks, recreation, leisure, industrial development and many other functions of local government are a matter of individual choice for each local authority depending on its problems and predelictions. The departments-to-committees relationship is not always one-to-one. It is often the case that one department will report to several committees (e.g. engineer's department to the highways, finance and public works committees) and conversely several departments may report to one committee (e.g. to the finance and general purposes committee).

A special case is that of the Clerk's department and the Clerk's official function. The 1933 Local Government Act defined the Clerk, the chief legal officer and head of the council's staff as '*primus inter pares*' with respect to his fellow chief officers – the heads of the other functional departments. He and his department, in providing legal, administrative and (latterly) management services to all the staffs and committees of the authority, are therefore in a uniquely integrative position.

In general terms the reporting and supervisory relationships between committees and departments in British local government can be represented diagrammatically as shown overleaf, where the thicker lines represent a greater volume of reporting and directive control. Of course, to some extent the council itself, the assembly of *all* the members of the authority, served by *all* its chief officers, does provide a measure of 'horizontality' whereby the relationships between, say, housing and highways, education and public transport can be considered. But explicit and deliberate debate of inter-service and community-wide problems which cross committee and departmental boundaries are rare as many writers have pointed out (e.g. STEWART, 1971) and council meetings are typified by their 'rubber-stamping' of executive *and policy* decisions taken by their committees.

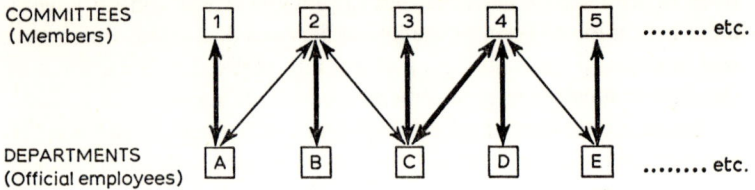

COMMITTEES (Members) 1 2 3 4 5 .... etc.

DEPARTMENTS (Official employees) A B C D E .... etc.

A major factor which tends to reinforce the compartmented, 'vertical' structure and behaviour of British local authorities is *professionalism* in their staffs (see McLoughlin *in* COWAN, 1973). By this we mean that many, if not most, of the major departments of local government, tend to have the greater part of their (non-clerical) staffs drawn from one major profession (or aspirants to professional membership). Indeed, the shaping of local government, its internal structure and functions, cannot be dissociated from the activities, aspirations and ideologies of certain key professional groups. Municipal engineers not only grew up as a body in response to the existence of more powerful and effective Victorian urban administrations but they in turn helped to shape the evolution of techniques, methods, attitudes and even legislation in dealing with evolving problems of urban life. If the clerk could be symbolized as the nerves of the nineteenth-century town hall, and the treasurer as its heart and blood supply then the intellectual and muscular power are virtually concentrated in the engineer and the medical officer.

Lawyers have tended to dominate the clerk's department, accountants the treasurer's, (ex)teachers the education department, doctors the medical officer's, and so on. In a strongly hierarchical departmental system, the predominance of one kind of professional in the staff has several obvious advantages: ease of communication on technical, functional issues; clearly established criteria for recruitment of junior professionals and subsequent promotion; ease of transfer for the staff themselves between local authorities; and so on. The disadvantages are also plain enough: difficulty of communication across departmental boundaries, the fragmentation of problems by different intellectual and professional points of view, the consequent lack of ability on occasion to perceive certain problems in the round, just because professional training makes one see things from a *particular* point of view, and susceptible to analysis and treatment only in particular ways.

The connections between the planning acts, planning departments and the planning profession exemplify most of what we have sketched out above by way of background. The (now Royal) Town Planning Institute was established in 1914 but its small membership had virtually no influence at all on local authority management structures for about thirty-five years. The explanation is that the 1947 Town and Country Planning Act made planning obligatory on all the counties and county boroughs for the first time. After that, attention had to be paid to staffing the authorities in order to discharge the new statutory function and in turn, the membership of the Town Planning Institute received an unprecedented stimulus to lobby for the creation of *separate planning departments with their own chief planning officer* in each administration. In this they were supported by the report of the COMMITTEE on the QUALIFICATIONS of PLANNERS (1950).

Progress was slow, and varied markedly between the counties where powerful 'technical' professionals were not so dominant as were the engineers (especially) in the county boroughs. Counties had their surveyors it is true, but a great deal of functions in geographical counties were performed by the engineers and surveyors of the district councils, whereas in the county boroughs the engineer/surveyor and his department performed all of those functions appropriate to his profession. So, immediately the 1947 Act was on the statute book most counties created a planning department and appointed a chief planning officer (who was, however, seldom accredited with full 'chief officer' status at that time).

In the county boroughs, several things happened. By far the most popular solution was to add the new mandatory planning function to all the others discharged by the city or borough engineer (or surveyor as he is often called). The planning staff was then a section of his department, headed by a person entitled 'chief planning assistant' or a similar label, working alongside other sections dealing with sewers, highways, building inspection and so on. In a smaller proportion of authorities the city (or borough) architect was given the planning function. In the absence of very detailed circumstantial knowledge we can only speculate about the basis of these decisions. Most probably the decision to give the planning function to an *existing* officer was based on the belief that planning was indeed something to do with physical development and *plans*. And the consequent choice between the architect and the engineer could be a function of personalities, the bargaining strengths of departments in the authority's private 'power game' and the authority's perception of its area's problems.

It was some considerable time before planning professionals registered their first success in persuading county boroughs to create separate planning departments. The first was Newport, in South Wales and was followed by Newcastle-upon-Tyne. The campaign for separate departments in major cities was led by the Royal Town Planning Institute (TOWN PLANNING INSTITUTE, 1963) and the Chief Planning Officer's Society. It is a good example of the relationship between departmentalism and professionalism in local government. For although the Institute made reference in its arguments to the distinctions between architecture, engineering and planning, there can be little doubt that they were conscious of the better prospects of promotion of their members to positions of senior responsibility – ultimately to chief officer status – which would follow from the establishment of planning departments in their own right. This issue is one which we shall refer to on other occasions later in the book. At the time of writing most local planning authorities in Britain have a separate department with its own chief officer reporting to a planning committee (and various sub-committees in some cases). Of the seventeen authorities listed earlier, eleven had separate departments. Three others had combined architecture-and-planning departments: Skelmersdale is a New Town Development Corporation and this is the usual arrangement in such situations; so too had Crawley Urban District in Sussex, reflecting its earlier new town organization. Lincoln invited its planning officer (who was also a qualified architect) to become head of a joint department when the former city architect retired some years ago.

Southend had a joint planning-and-engineering department as had Luton which achieved county borough status as recently as 1966. The Greater London Council merged its planning and transportation functions in a joint department in 1967, doubtless as a response to the 'Buchanan' report on traffic in towns – a movement to integrate land use and transport issues in government which was further emphasized by Lady SHARP's (1970) report on management, education, training and research for these linked fields.

The structure of planning departments

The structure of planning departments – that is to say the way in which their staffs are deployed into *sections* – is strongly and clearly related to the statutory functions demanded by the Town and Country Planning Acts. The 1947 and 1962 legislation demanded three principal classes of work:

The preparation and review of the development plan for the whole of the authority's area (the 'County Map' and the 'Town Map' for counties and county boroughs respectively) and for certain towns in counties 'Town Maps' also;

the preparation and review of detailed development plans for parts of the authority's area (Comprehensive Development Area Maps, Supplementary Town Maps, Town Centre Maps, etc.);

development control, i.e. the receipt of applications and the framing and issuing of decisions upon each application.

In addition there is a miscellaneous class of jobs to be done according to the statutes (see Chapter 2) e.g. tree preservation, buildings of architectural and historic interest and conservation areas. Finally, some tasks depend upon the nature of the authority's area and its problems. Thus we find special 'industrial' sections in areas where there is persistent unemployment and 'landscape' sections in areas with fine scenery or a considerable amount of derelict land (or both).

In general as we would expect, the largest authorities tend to have the largest and most specialized staffs. Not only do they employ more people and people with special skills and qualifications, but also their staffs are subdivided and grouped in more complex ways. Whilst all professional or 'technical' planning staff have access to administrative and clerical assistance its provision varies widely in quantity and quality. The most fortunate planners are those in the largest authorities where each section may have a small clerical staff – say a junior clerk and typist – attached to them; in the smaller authorities, or those with a tendency to greater administrative centralization, a busy professional officer will be fortunate if he can find someone in a central typing pool to prepare his routine letters and reports.

For the purpose of simplified exposition we recognize the three main types of non-clerical work in planning offices as those we set out above and which we shall label for brevity 'plan', 'design' and 'control' respectively. 'Plan' means the strategic or broad-brush work including studies going beyond the authority's administrative area (e.g. sub-regional studies); area-wide studies; plans for the area as a whole; 'aspect' studies such as retailing or transportation; information, data and intelligence work.

'Design' means more detailed (and usually physical) studies and planning work for parts of the authority's area; studies of the application of area-wide systems to particular localities; detailed feasibility studies; the work of specialized groups with a distinctive 'environmental' relevance (e.g. historic buildings, land reclamation, coastal recreation, urban redevelopment).

'Control' means the professional and technical operations leading up to development control decisions and all associated work.

The present chapter and especially Chapter 4 which follows, are concerned with the development control job and those who do it. Chapter 5 will have much to say about 'design' work and the staffing of sections doing detailed planning work whilst Chapter 6 includes a description and discussion of the work and the personnel of 'plan' sections and their associated research and intelligence functions.

Working on the reasonable assumption that the seventeen authorities visited in the research project are not untypical, there seem to be four main types of deployment of staff to serve these major planning-authority functions:

(1) | Control-with-design | | Plan is absent |

In this arrangement, the control and design staffs and functions are very closely related and, in a small number of cases are performed by the same individuals. The plan function is not found within the same office because it exists in another agency. This is commonly the case where a county district (like Crawley) possesses delegated planning powers from a county (in that case West Sussex) which retains the strategic planning and intelligence functions. It is also found in Development Corporations (e.g. Skelmersdale, where Lancashire exercises most of the planning powers and Skelmersdale enjoys certain special powers under section 6 of the New Towns Act) and in other special cases such as Ross and Cromarty County where the specially constituted Highlands and Islands Development Board provide the staff functions of strategic planning.

(2) | Control-with-design | | Plan |

This arrangement closely resembles (1) above but here there is a 'plan' function and section within the same authority. The technical work of the department is divided into two broad groups: strategic, policy oriented studies and proposals in the plan section and detailed design and control in another. The latter can be looked on as an *implementation* section for the wider proposals developed in the plan section. As we shall see, such a polarization is becoming a characteristic of the way in which physical planning (and local government as a whole) may be evolving. Among the authorities studied directly, G.L.C., Luton and Manchester exhibited such an arrangement. We noted some degree of association between this and the extent to which authorities had adopted the newer models of corporate management such as those proposed by the Maud Committee.

(3) | Control | | Plan-with-design |

In this arrangement of technical work, both broad strategic and detailed 'design' are regarded as aspects of an integrated

69

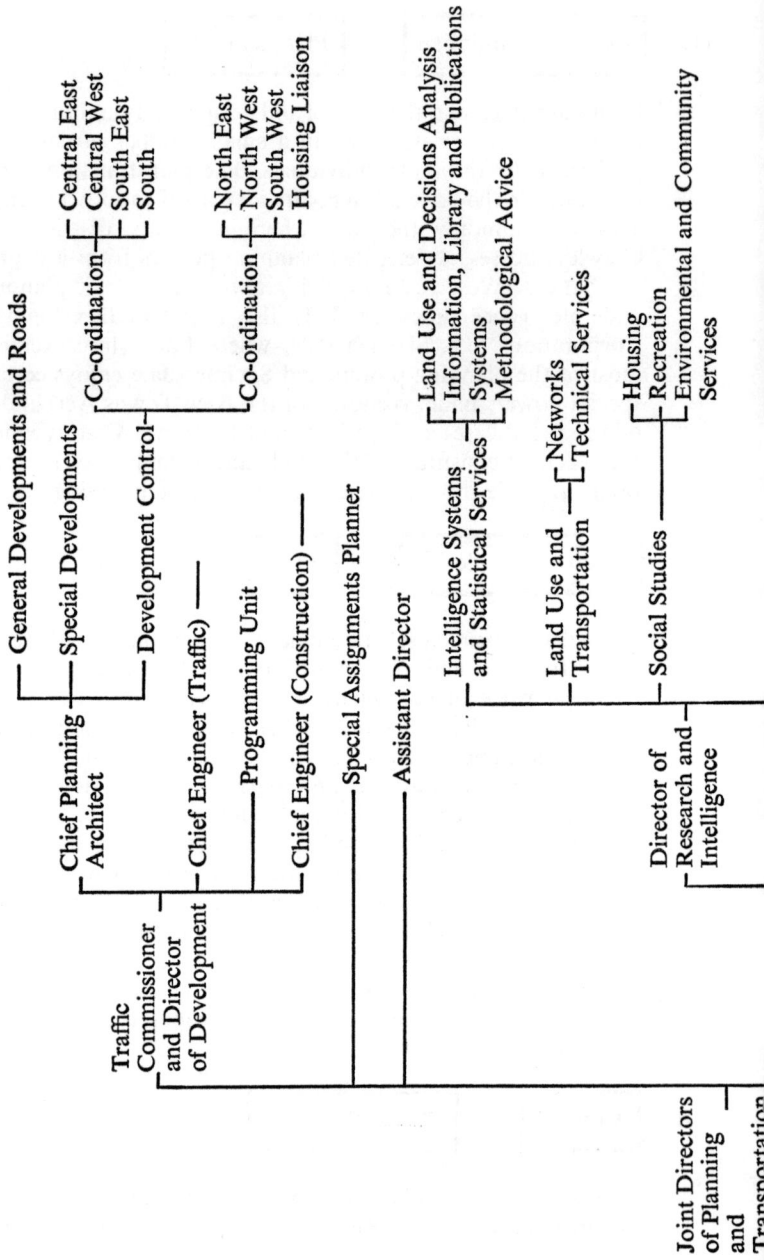

Joint Directors of Planning and Transportation

- Traffic Commissioner and Director of Development
  - Chief Planning Architect
    - General Developments and Roads
    - Special Developments
  - Development Control
    - Co-ordination
      - Central East
      - Central West
      - South East
      - South
    - Co-ordination
      - North East
      - North West
      - South West
      - Housing Liaison
  - Chief Engineer (Traffic)
  - Programming Unit
  - Chief Engineer (Construction)
- Special Assignments Planner
- Assistant Director
- Director of Research and Intelligence
  - Intelligence Systems and Statistical Services
    - Land Use and Decisions Analysis
    - Information, Library and Publications
    - Systems
    - Methodological Advice
  - Land Use and Transportation
    - Networks
    - Technical Services
  - Social Studies
    - Housing
    - Recreation
    - Environmental and Community Services

Chief Administrative Officer

Chief Planner (plans)
— Co-ordination
— Transport Liaison

Chief Planner (strategy)

Development Economics

Social and Economic Policy
— Residential
— Employment
— Regional Planning
— Services and Amenities
— Economic and Population Studies

Transport Policy

London Boroughs
— Planning Studies
— Finance, Housing
— Health, Welfare
— Education, Children

Population and Economic Studies
— Economic Intelligence
— Evaluation, Cost-benefit
— Employment

Greater London Development Plan

Initial Development Plan

Borough Structure Plans
— South West
— North West
— North East
— South East
— Central

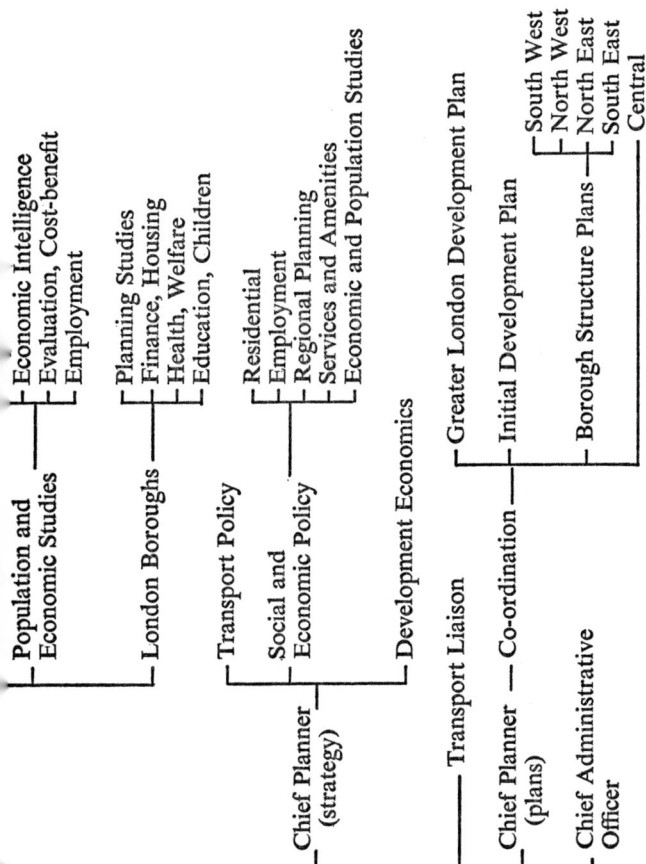

Figure 3.1: Part of the structure of the G.L.C. Department of Planning and Transportation in 1970

(See McLoughlin and Webster, 1971)

function of plan making. Control is looked on as a distinct operation which must relate to all scales and levels of detail in policy. But as we shall see in Chapter 4, the development control officers had significantly more interaction with those officers in the plan-with-design section who work on *detailed* aspects of planning. We found such arrangements in medium-sized authorities without much development of the new management structures and methods – Herefordshire, Newport and Southend.

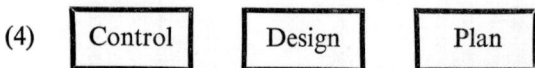

(4)
| Control | Design | Plan |

This complete separation into three distinct sections (or groupings of more specialized sections) was found to be the most popular form of arrangement of technical staffs in the local planning authorities studied. It was again noticeable that the greatest amount of interaction was between design and control. Generally speaking, it was the larger authorities which exhibited this pattern – Aberdeen, Bromley, Camden, Durham, Leicester, Lincoln, Oxfordshire and the Peak District National Park.

The development control section

Whilst planning authorities vary widely in their administrative and management structures as a whole, in the ways they deploy their planning department staffs and in their creation of specialist groups to study particular problems, all of them possess development control staff with posts permanently assigned to that function. The ubiquity of development control caseworkers is explained by the constant pressure to give decisions under strong sanctions of legal obligation. For whilst the Planning Acts require the submission and review of development plans and whilst the Minister possesses considerable powers to make a plan in default of a submission or review by the authority, it is almost inconceivable that they would be invoked if only because of the openly strained relationships which would then persist between the central department and the planning authority. Planning authorities can, therefore, be somewhat lax in discharging their obligations to prepare plans and reviews for submission.*

* We might add that the Minister has not always displayed a sense of urgency in considering and approving submitted development plans.

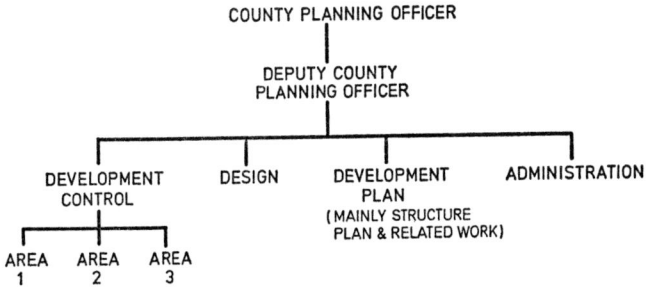

Figure 3.2: Staff structure of a medium-sized county

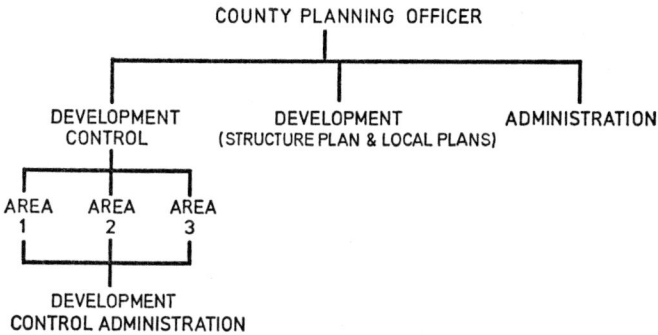

Figure 3.3: Staff structure of a small rural county

The pressure to sustain development control activity is relentless. Day in, day out, applications are submitted and must be dealt with (unless the applicant agrees to a delay) inside two months; if not, the applicant can appeal to the Minister against the failure of the authority to issue a decision. Now appeals cost everyone a great deal of time, effort and worry and the authority's staff are no exception. It is, therefore, in their interest to issue decisions within the statutory time limit. In 1968 an average of 8·8 applications per 1,000 persons were made in England and Wales, but this varied between 5·9 in county boroughs and 11·5 in counties. The average-sized county borough, therefore, had to deal with over 1,000 applications annually on average – say four per working day. Their colleagues in an average county have a much heavier load for they could expect to receive some 2,500 applications or about ten each working day.

Development plan and design officers have only their own consciences and the Minister to push their workpace – a Minister who is very reluctant to invoke his sanctions. The time-scale is the review period of the 1962 Act which calls for fresh surveys and appraisals 'at least once in every five years'. Development control people have *thousands* of applicants (and their professional advisers in many cases) to prod them and a time-scale of two months at maximum.

It is small wonder that one development control officer remarked that young planners are reluctant to come into control 'because it's too much like hard work'. Occasionally when control sections are particularly overloaded, junior plan and design staff may be called on to lend a hand; this hardly ever happens in reverse.

Development control sections are usually headed by a senior or 'middle-management' officer who may rank about third or fourth in the hierarchy. Thus above the plan, design and control section of the department there will be one or two deputy planning officers and the chief officer. In some authorities the deputy includes a special concern for development control among his functions; he it is who will attend a committee dealing with control and usually act as the authority's expert witness in appeal hearings. The section head may be called 'Assistant County Planning Officer (Development Control)' or 'Chief Planning Assistant (Development Control)' or a similar title.

The development control section will be staffed in the main by caseworkers who will be supported by a number of ancillary workers

– filing clerks, typists, draughtsmen and so on. In some authorities (especially those with large departments) the section may have its administrative and 'technician' staff directly attached and exclusively for their assistance; in others this clerical and technical help will be centralized and at the disposal of the department as a whole. Again, the daily pressure of routine development control work tends to affect the disposition of these non-professional people as much as the professionals so that in some cases we find ancillary workers attached specifically to the control section *in addition* to the centralized administrative, clerical and technical group.

The development control section itself may be subdivided in two different ways. First of all it may be divided into groups dealing with geographical sub-areas of the authority's area as a whole; thus for example, Manchester's staff (which as we have noted is a 'design-implementation-and-control' section) is divided into three groups of officers dealing respectively with the north, the centre and the south of the city and the G.L.C. had at the time of our visit eight 'sector groups' each dealing with a subdivision of Greater London. Secondly, the development control staff may be posted into 'out-stations' away from the headquarters office and have their own ancillary staff outstationed with them. This arrangement is almost always associated with counties and has the claimed advantages of officers being close to the sites of applications, ease of access to district council officers and the convenience of applicants. (MINISTRY OF HOUSING AND LOCAL GOVERNMENT, 1967a.)

The relationship with district councils in counties

Parallel to these deployments of a county planning authority's staff, there are three main ways in which the *district* councils are involved in the process of decision making. The Management Study called the three systems 'centralization', 'decentralization' and 'delegation'. *Centralized* systems are not common and mean that the county council reserves all rights to receive and determine applications. However, a considerable amount of consultation is carried out whereby the district councils and/or their officers are called to express their views on each application, sometimes involving two complete cycles of consultation in the event of disagreement. *Decentralized* systems have as their essence a geographical subdivision of the county into groups of contiguous district council areas and to form for each division a joint committee of county and district councillors. Most cases are determined by such area or divisional joint committees, a small proportion of which are relevant to major county policies being forwarded for determination to the county planning committee and/or the county council. Such decision systems are often associated with a subdivision of the staff of the county planning department either at headquarters (as in the case of Durham for example) or in outstation 'divisional' offices (as in Lancashire and, until recently, in Cheshire). *Delegated* systems are common and involved the formal transfer of planning powers to one or more district councils. These powers vary greatly in scope and effect.

> 'At one end of the scale they are equivalent to statutory delegation. At the other end of the scale there are agreements which require that the county should make a recommendation to the district on every application and that the district may decide a limited range of applications only if it agrees with this recommendation. Other agreements range between the two extremes.' (M.H.L.G., 1967a, p. 49)

One of the biggest problems and disadvantages of delegation is the great difficulty of providing staff resources of even minimal adequacy and the consequent reliance of the districts on the county staff for advice.

The special case of Greater London

Within Greater London, special arrangements exist by virtue of the London Government Act, 1963, which replaced the old London County Council, Middlesex County Council, Croydon, East Ham and West Ham County Boroughs by the Greater London Council and thirty-three London Boroughs at the second tier (for an excellent general account see SELF, 1971). The G.L.C. was made the 'strategic' planning authority with responsibilities including overall planning of population, employment, the main land use structure, transport and communications systems. These and related issues were to be considered included in a Greater London Development Plan (to be known as the 'strategic plan' for Greater London) and each borough was to prepare a 'Borough Structure Plan'. Detailed plans could be prepared by both the G.L.C. and the boroughs, development control functions being shared between the two levels according to the nature of the application. The regulations governing the procedural aspects are somewhat complicated and fortunately these details are not essential to our purpose (see MINISTRY OF HOUSING AND LOCAL GOVERNMENT, 1965a and 1967c). We can simply note that in some cases (those without any 'strategic' significance in general – see below) the borough is the local planning authority and receives, considers and determines all such cases; certain details are forwarded to the G.L.C. for purposes of research and intelligence. In other cases, the application is classified as having 'strategic' significance and falls to be determined by the G.L.C. The criteria by which applications are classified as 'strategic' are as follows:

First of all, the G.L.C. is defined as the local planning authority for all applications (other than those relating to changes of use) within certain Comprehensive Development Areas and Supplementary Town Map Areas (see Chapter 5 which follows) in order to give continuity of treatment in these areas which had been 'inherited' from L.C.C. days. These included:

The Bermondsey C.D.A. and S.T.M.
The Bunhill Fields C.D.A. and S.T.M.
The North-West Stepney C.D.A. and S.T.M.
The Stepney and Poplar C.D.A., and S.T.M.
The Elephant and Castle C.D.A.
The Knightsbridge Green C.D.A.
The Lambsth Walk C.D.A.
The South Bank C.D.A.
The West Bethnal Green C.D.A. and
The Piccadilly Circus area as defined in a map schedule.

Also, throughout Greater London (other than in the Temples area) the G.L.C. was defined as the local planning authority for:

erection or alteration of buildings for public assembly and which could accommodate over 2,500 persons;

the use of land for sports, games, etc. involving the assembly of over 2,500 persons;

university, college, institute or similar developments;

development of all forms of transport terminals including monorail and hovercraft developments;

mineral extraction from any site of more than five acres in Greater London outside the City of London.

In addition, the boroughs and the City were required, before granting any application, to refer it to the G.L.C. if it related to:

erection or alteration of shopping floorspace of more than 250,000 sq. ft.;

erection or extension of buildings over 150 ft. high in Central London and over 125 ft. elsewhere;

erection, alteration or extension of an industrial building if that would result in over 5,000 sq. ft. of floor area and of an office building if that would produce over 3,000 sq. ft.;

any development within 110 feet of a British Rail or L.T.B. passenger station (except extension within the curtilage and for the same purpose as the existing building resulting in a floorspace increase of less than 50% or 5,000 sq. ft. whichever is the less);

any development within 220 ft. of the centre of an existing or proposed 'metropolitan road' which involved a new or altered access of increased use of the access road, new building for the same purpose outside the curtilage of the existing building or within the curtilage if it would add over 50% or 5,000 sq. ft. whichever is the less or *any* building work (irrespective of the floorspace constraint) which would advance the building line towards an existing or proposed metropolitan road;

any development which in the receiving council's opinion ought to be developed together with adjoining land in order to restrict the number of access points to a metropolitan road;

any development which might increase the amount of traffic using a metropolitan road;

the provision of a car park for over fifty cars;

any non-agricultural development in the green belt;

any development affecting a building of special architectural or historic interest.

Furthermore, the City and the boroughs, if inclined to grant permission to any application inconsistent with the 'initial development plan' (i.e. the L.C.C. and other authorities' development plans in the area forming Greater London and 'taken over' by the G.L.C. in

1965/6) or the Greater London Development Plan should refer the application to the G.L.C. In these cases, the G.L.C. may consider that permission should not be granted or only subject to conditions and they may direct the second-tier authority accordingly. If the application to which they wished to grant permission was inconsistent with a local development plan (i.e. for any borough or the City) they should refer the case to the Minister. As usual in British planning law such referrals should be made only if the resulting development would (in the local authority's opinion) involve a 'substantial departure' from the relevant development plan.

Similar provisions apply to the G.L.C. itself which shall in all such cases of inconsistency, refer the application to the Minister if they wish to grant permission.

These minutiae of development control procedure in Greater London provide us with further examples of the essential language of the operation. We can see clearly that the substantial criteria for deciding who does what and what is 'strategic' or otherwise involve questions of *location*, class of *activity or use*, the *intensity* of use, floor *area*, *height* of buildings, *precise location* (e.g. in relation to a road or railway terminus) and the amount or intensity of *road traffic* which might ensue. We should also note that certain abilities to calculate or estimate are implied in phrases like 'in the opinion of the authority . . . would be likely to result in . . . a material increase . . . or . . . a substantial departure'. In fact these dry legalistic documents raise almost all the questions about the relationships of development control to detailed, localized physical planning on the one hand and broader, area-wide 'strategic' land use and transport and socio-economic planning on the other.

In this chapter we have tried to set out the administrative and management context in which development control occurs and we have referred to the departmental and committee structures of local planning authorities and put the development control section into such a context. In Chapter 4 which follows we focus on the case and the caseworkers.

4 · Cases and Caseworkers

Form and content of cases

The cases which come before planning authorities for determination take a variety of forms. Sometimes the first point of contact is a letter or a personal visit from an intending applicant or his adviser which explores the possibility of planning permission being granted. Reference may be made to a particular site and a specific use of land or form of development or it may be cast in more general terms. Usually in such cases a dialogue will ensue between the caseworker and the applicant in which each of them tries to obtain more information from the other. For example, the applicant may try to find out what policies are in operation which may affect his proposals in order to clarify his own intentions and the officer will encourage the applicant to be more precise about his intentions or wishes. Each party is thus operating in a state of some uncertainty and the officer will often tell the enquirer that the best way of resolving this is to submit one or more formal applications for planning permission or, in some cases, an application to determine whether or not planning permission is required. Typically also, the applicant will try to extract, either verbally or in writing, some degree of commitment by the authority with respect to policies for say, density, road alignments, housing redevelopments, shopping proposals and their various programmes or timings. (Towards the end of this chapter we discuss the role of caseworkers in providing an informal information service to enquirers of all kinds.)

Cases of a special kind arise under various forms of procedure for dealing with the development intentions of government and local government agencies, nationalized industries and so on; a wide variety of these is dealt with, for example, by the 'Circular 100 procedure' (MINISTRY OF TOWN AND COUNTRY PLANNING, 1950). In such cases, there will usually be a letter from the agency concerned, followed sometimes by a meeting between their officers and those of the local planning authority. In complex or controversial cases, a series of meetings and exchanges of correspondence may ensue and build up into a substantial case history and documentation.

Another specially important kind of case arises when an applicant is 'aggrieved' by a refusal, or by conditions attaching to a permission, or by the failure of the planning authority to issue a decision within the specified time and accordingly exercises his right to *appeal* to the Minister. The Minister may decide either to consider the appeal by means of written representations from both parties or (most commonly) by holding a local inquiry, presided over by one of his Inspectors. The preparation of the authority's evidence and arguments forms a small proportion of all the cases considered by caseworkers, but appeals are particularly time-consuming and add to the pressure under which development control staff work. Because of their particular relevance to questions of policy, we shall consider them in more detail in Chapter 7.

But in general, development applications which form the great majority of cases arise from a straightforward *application for planning permission* and it is these that determine the pattern and content of the caseworker's daily task. The 426,000 applications made to the 145 local planning authorities in England and Wales during 1968 were made on at least 145 different kinds of forms. The Management Study (MINISTRY OF HOUSING AND LOCAL GOVERNMENT, 1967a) recommended that these forms be rationalized, simplified and as far as possible standardized throughout the country. Certainly it seems odd that since development control is a statutory requirement (like the need for driving licences and notification of infectious diseases) there should be such a variation from one authority to another. But the differences are of detail and there are broad similarities in their form and content. Thus one example (which is cyclostyled on two sides of foolscap) is headed by the name of the Statutes, the General Development Order and the name of the local planning authority. The applicant is then asked to state:

1. Whether this is an outline application*
2. The applicant's and/or his agent's name and address

* Defined by article 5 (2) of the General Development Order 1963 and 1969. The idea of an outline application is to seek approval for development *in principle* i.e. without details of size, form, building materials, etc. so as to avoid possible abortive expenditure on a detailed application when the authority

81

3. The (land) owner's name (if different)
4. Whether the owner's consent has been obtained*
5. The location (parish, ward, name of road)
6. The applicant's legal interest in the land
7. A verbal description of the proposed development
8. The materials and finished colour of the walls and the roof (if a building is proposed)
9. The area (acres/square feet) of land and/or buildings
10. A verbal description of the present use of land and/or buildings
11. Details of any highway access required – name of road
   – width of proposed access
   – pedestrian or vehicular
   – nature and position of existing access
   – alterations to existing access
12. Details of any layout plan already approved by the planning authority
13. In the case of residential development – number of habitable rooms
   – total floor area of non-residential use
14. In the case of industrial or commercial proposals
   – nature (processes etc. described)
   – total floor area
   – Industrial Development Certificate No.
   – provision for loading/unloading vehicles
   – disposal of trade refuse and effluents

would refuse on principle (e.g. because it was contrary to land-use policy or on the line of a proposed road). The system has been abused, however, by authorities asking for too many details – see *Ministry of Housing and Local Government (1967)*.

 * Section 16 of the Town and Country Planning Act 1962, requires that applicants must supply one of four certificates:
   A – certifying that the applicant is the freeholder or tenant of all the land involved; or,
   B – certifying that he has advertised his application, invoking the owner's representations; or,
   C – certifying that he has notified the owner of the land; or,
   D – certifying that he has made all reasonable efforts to locate the owner but failed.

15. Sources and particulars of any proposed or existing supply of
  - water
  - gas
  - electricity
and particulars of any proposed or existing drainage of
  - surface water
  - sewage

In another example (this time printed), the information asked for is broadly similar with this but in addition the applicant is asked to say:

1. What he proposes to do with any existing buildings on the site
2. What provision is to be made for planting and preservation of trees
3. The number of on- and off-site parking spaces to be provided
4. The type and colour of materials to be used in boundary walls or fences
5. The approximate number of *new* employees in the case of industrial or commercial proposals

In Greater London, application forms for both the boroughs and the G.L.C. are much more complex. A partial reason for this is the existence of a joint G.L.C.-and-boroughs 'Decisions Analysis Scheme' which collects, collates and analyses the incidence and outcomes of all applications within Greater London. For example, one of the boroughs, in addition to the kinds of information illustrated above also asks for:

In the case of industrial or commercial development:
1.   - the site area
  - the total floor area
  - the production area
  - the office area
  - the stores area
  - the area of other uses
  and with respect to each of the last four areas, the amount of additional employment, male and female jobs, which is expected.
2. Similar information with respect to all of the applicant's other existing premises in the Greater London area, if any, including those of associated or subsidiary companies
3. Which, if any, existing buildings would be vacated when the new development is completed

83

4. The goods to be made in this building (if none, the proposed use)
5. The type and horse-power of the machinery to be used
6. The number of 'keyworkers' and the nature of their work
7. Details of any processes sub-contracted and the location of sub-contractors
8. A list of the materials used, their source (within Great Britain or their port of entry) and the transport used
9. The approximate percentages of turnover to markets:
    (a) in Greater London
    (b) elsewhere in Britain
    (c) exports through London docks
    (d) exports through other (named) docks or airports
10. If the firm would be interested in a site outside Greater London state the district or county preferred
11. Full reasons for wanting to be in Greater London or on the proposed site

and *in the case of office development* the applicant must give, in addition to the usual information already mentioned:

1. Details of the Office Development Permit*
2. Details of premises and staff of proposed occupants
3. The gross floor area (including ancillary accommodation)
4. Details of location, male and female staff and floor area of existing premises occupied by the intended occupants

The application forms of the Greater London Council were almost identical but in addition asked for a considerable amount of data on proposed mineral workings – including the likely number of vehicles in and out of the site, their routes and so on, the proposed methods and sequences of excavation, deposition of top-soil, restoration and after-treatment.

All of this written and numerical information must be accompanied by *a drawn plan or plans* and once again, there are wide variations in different authority's requirements. Some are very vague and one suspects that the applicant is given verbal instructions and guidance. Others are very specific and require (for example)

1. A site plan at 1:2500 or 6 inches to 1 mile 'as appropriate' with the site in pink and any adjoining land in the same ownership in blue

* Control of Office and Industrial Development Act, 1963. *See* CULLING-WORTH (1972) p. 66.

2. A block plan at a scale of not less than 1:2500 showing:
   - the boundary of the land
   - existing and proposed trees
   - hedges and other natural features
   - existing and proposed roads and footpaths within and into the site
   - existing and proposed buildings clearly differentiated
   - the position, if known, of sewers, electricity lines and other services
3. Building plans of at least $\frac{1}{8}$ inch to 1 foot (except for very large schemes) showing plans of each floor and the roof, elevations on all sides, sections through the building showing levels; the plans should indicate the materials and colours of all external surfaces; in the case of alterations, the new work should be identified clearly.

Another authority wants three site plans, two sets of block and building plans and two layout plans. Another wants contours at 10 foot intervals; some authorities give a general indication that drawings should be on 'durable material' whilst one specifically demands drawings on *linen* and another specifies *indian ink*.

Most authorities give notes for the guidance of applicants in completing the form, some of which seem designed to confuse and dismay; some notes are brief and helpful whilst others are long-winded and marred by bureaucratic jargon. (We shall learn later about the extent of face-to-face help many applicants need simply to fill in the forms.) All authorities point out that only the more general plans are needed for outline applications.

Analysis of a sample of forms shows that the information asked for by the local planning authority falls into a number of broad groups. Firstly, there is information about the *location and extent* of the proposed development whether by postal address, Ordnance Survey map 'parcel number', site plan, block plan, floor area, or otherwise. Surprisingly little use is made of the National Grid referencing system in giving unique and unambiguous indications of location. Secondly, there is information about *activity* (or 'use') both of the existing land and buildings and the proposed development. This can range from a bold generality like 'residential use' or 'warehouse' to a fairly complex statement of industrial and commercial processes and

85

from descriptions applied to the development as a whole to details of individual parts and floors. Thirdly, authorities seek information (on all but outline applications) on a wide range of *physical details* not only of the building, engineering, architectural and landscape design aspects of the proposal, but also its relationship to existing roads, footpaths, buildings, trees and so on. Several authorities ask the applicant to provide information about the location, size and capacity of sewers, water mains, electricity lines and so on; this seems hardly fair or equitable since private individuals are being asked to provide at their expense information which should surely be available and paid for through the public purse! Fourthly, legislation requires that the applicant state his *legal interest* in the land. Finally, there are *miscellaneous* groups of information which vary widely between authorities. For example, one authority in Scotland asks applicants to estimate the commencement and completion dates and the cost of the works. The outstanding exceptions occur in Greater London and concern information about '*linkages*' e.g. transport and other functional relationships between the applicant's proposal and any other activities under his control, his estimates of *employment* to be generated by the development and the *power* demands of any machinery he may install (in the case of industrial proposals) and the estimated *vehicular trips* (in the case of proposed mineral operations).

These are exceptional and we shall have reason to discuss them later in the book; the information on application forms for development is dominated by questions of *location, activity and physical details*. This tends to be true of all kinds of cases – i.e. appeals, 'Circular 100' notifications, building preservation and advertisement cases as well as run-of-of-the-mill applications. All of this represents a considerable amount and variety of information 'input' to the consideration of each individual case and to all cases on aggregate. How much use is made of it and how relevant it is for its purposes we shall discover as we go on later to look at the information caseworkers seek and obtain from all other sources.

But it will be more convenient now to give a brief sketch of the typical path followed by a case after the applicant has filled in the forms and delivered them to the appropriate receiving authority. In this way we shall erect a simple network which we can then elaborate with details of what events and considerations affect the way in which a recommendation and a decision are reached. Also we will then be in a better position to discuss the caseworker's role, his personal attributes, his attitudes to his work and its place in physical planning and local government.

The pathway followed by a case

It will be obvious from preceding discussions that authorities operate different administrative and technical procedures for dealing with development control. Nevertheless there is a good deal in common as far as the route of a case is concerned. First of all, the application is either received through the post or by personal delivery. In counties the application will be delivered to the district council offices and in county boroughs directly at the planning office. Where the application form for planning permission is designed jointly for use in development control and in building regulations (for bye-law permission under the Public Health Acts) copies will be sent to the building inspectors also. In the smaller planning authorities the chief planning officer may have a quick look at all incoming applications at this stage to keep himself informed but this is not usual in the larger offices; there the application will go either directly to the development control section for clerical processing by their own 'admin.' staff or it will go first to a centralized 'admin.' group serving the whole planning department and then on to the development control section. In either case the 'admin.' group will check that the application has been correctly completed by the applicant, and will then either ask for the missing information or will make up *a case file*. This is usually a standard printed manila folder and varies in sophistication from a simple folio to quite elaborate affairs with built-in pockets for plans, printed boxes for checking procedural details, inserting notes, dates, even sketches and photographs. Certainly the admin. staff will have recorded carefully the date of receipt of the application and given the case a numerical or alpha-numerical code, which may or may not contain a geographical reference, e.g. to a kilometric square, ward, parish or district council area. At the same time the application's essential details – location, proposal, date, code number – will be entered in the register of planning applications which authorities must maintain for public inspection as a statutory duty, and the location and extent of the application will be plotted on an Ordnance Survey

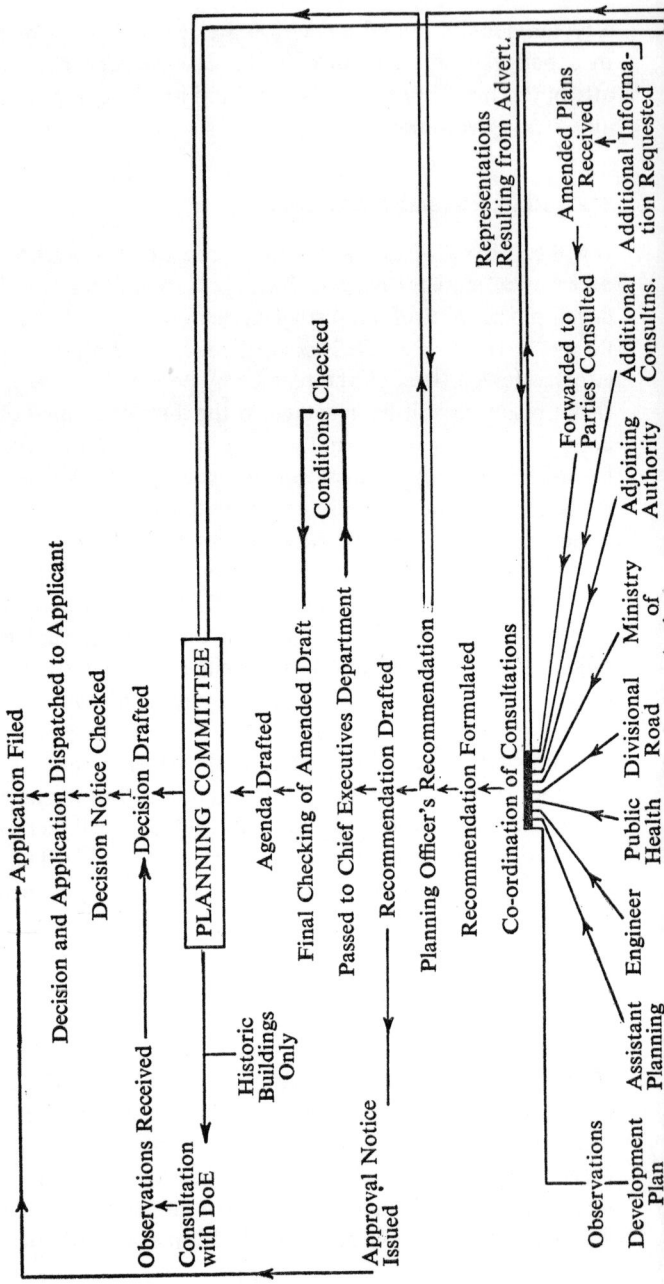

Application Filed

Decision and Application Dispatched to Applicant

Decision Notice Checked

Decision Drafted

PLANNING COMMITTEE

Agenda Drafted

Final Checking of Amended Draft — Conditions Checked

Passed to Chief Executives Department

Recommendation Drafted

Planning Officer's Recommendation

Recommendation Formulated

Co-ordination of Consultations

Observations Received

Consultation with DoE

Historic Buildings Only

Approval Notice Issued

Representations Resulting from Advert.

Forwarded to Parties Consulted — Amended Plans Received

Additional Consultns.

Additional Information Requested

Adjoining Authority

Ministry of

Divisional Road

Public Health

Engineer

Assistant Planning

Observations

Development Plan

Preliminary Consideration of Application
Consultations Determined

Meeting with
Applicant

Site Visit

Advert. Draft Preparation

Advert. in
Local Paper

Application Acknowledged

Ploted

Coded

Entered in Register

Building
Regulations
Applications

Completed Application made into File

Application Checked for Correctness

Passed to Development Control Section

Passed to Planning Officer for Preliminary Consideration

Application Received in Post – Date-stamped – Entered in Post Book

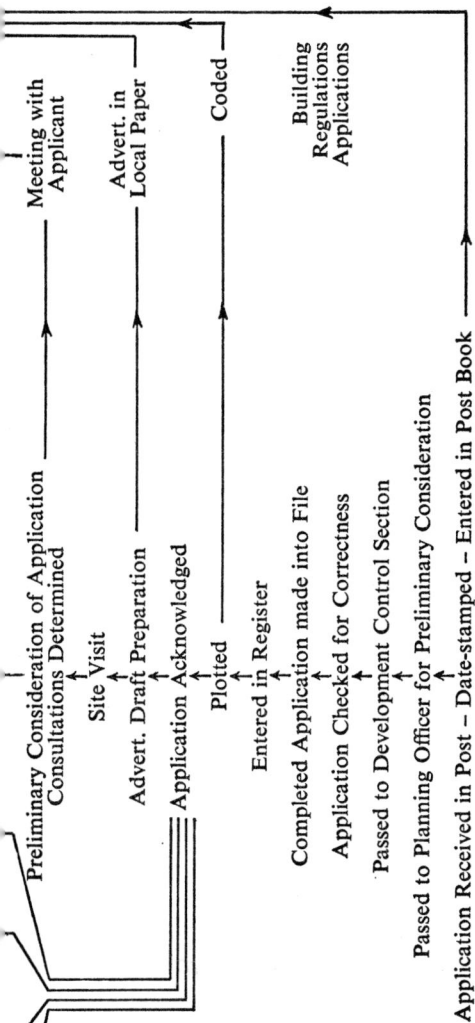

Figure 4.1: The pathway of a case file

(based on the system used by an Urban District Council with delegated planning powers)

map of suitable scale. This first stage in the case's journey is completed when the admin. staff send an acknowledgement of receipt to the applicant or his agent.

It is at this stage that the caseworker usually receives the file for the first time and begins his work. The case will remain in his care until the decision is issued to the applicant – anything up to two months or more later. Some few classes of application must be advertised – e.g. those for bingo halls, amusement arcades, public houses and nightclubs – and at this stage the advertisement will be drafted, perhaps with the co-operation of the clerk's department, and issued to the press.

The next stage is the longest and fullest in the processing of an application and is often called the 'consultations stage' for it is occupied very largely by seeking facts, interpretations, opinions and advice from a wide variety of sources. Some are mandatory and others almost so, depending on the nature or content of the application. In some cases a small number of internal (i.e. within the department or the authority) consultations occur on every application and so are put in hand immediately – those with the department's development plan, research and design sections and with the engineer's highways section for example. The determination of which other persons, departments or authorities should be consulted will now have to wait further examination of the application by the caseworker.

This fourth stage is occupied by two major steps – the 'history' and the site visit. The former is the collation of information about any previous applications, decisions, events, council resolutions and so on relating to the site of the application, its vicinity or surroundings. The latter is a personal visit to the site by the caseworker. These actions together help the caseworker to decide on the full range of consultations which should be undertaken. He, therefore, issues consultation memos. and letters asking for opinions and observations and adds to the growing case file his notes on the site 'history' and visit.

As a result of his preliminary consideration and study he may decide to seek an informal consultation with the applicant or his agent. This is done for two sorts of reasons: first to clarify any doubts about the applicant's intentions, to seek more detailed explanations of them, to find out what particular constraints or problems the applicant may have; secondly to put to the applicant that in the caseworker's opinion the application is unlikely to gain approval in its present form and to invite the applicant to submit amending details or a revised application. Such revision may be relatively minor such as roofing materials or an access detail and simply require a note of amendment to the drawings. Occasionally the revision will be substantial, however, and the applicant may agree to withdraw and submit a fresh application. In either case all those originally consulted will now be sent details of the amended or fresh application.

When all observations resulting from consultations have been received they can be collated with the caseworker's site visit notes and impressions, the views of his colleagues and so forth. This allows him to proceed to the crucial stage of drafting a recommendation. In small authorities he will submit this directly to the agenda clerk but in larger authorities a senior colleague, typically the section head of development control, will advise, guide and check his formulation.

The form and wording of the draft recommendation may then be checked by a legal officer in the clerk's department (or attached to the planning department) and the whole case will then be added to the agenda for the next meeting of the committee which deals with development control work.

The whole process of consultation in counties is qualified by the arrangements adopted for involving the district councils in control work and by the presence or absence of area committees; we discussed the various systems of 'centralization', 'decentralization' and 'delegation' in Chapter 3. There is another factor which effects the path of an application in detail at this stage and that is the extent to which councillors may be involved in looking at cases *before* their formal consideration in committee. Many planning authorities have arranged for some kind of 'call-over' procedure by which the majority of straightforward, non-controversial cases can be looked at briefly by the chairman of the planning committee, sometimes with a small number of his colleagues, before the meeting. The committee may have delegated authority to the chairman to reach and issue decisions on such cases. It has been estimated that such routine, minor applications form between 70% and 90% of all cases (MINISTRY OF HOUSING AND LOCAL GOVERNMENT, 1967a). Some authorities have gone further and delegated to named senior planning officers the formal power to take such decisions. All of these various arrangements are sought in the interests of smoother, more efficient administration so that by this 'cutting of the red tape' the public get swifter decisions

91

and also that officers' and councillors' time in technical work and debate can be concentrated on the minority of more substantial cases which require deeper study because of their greater complexity or the controversial policy issues which they may raise.

In the seventeen authorities studied, ten of them always discussed the agenda beforehand, five of them did so sometimes and only two had no prior discussions. Officers were responsible for classifying the cases and identifying which, in their opinion and their knowledge of the councillors' views, were likely to be regarded as routine or otherwise. Four of the authorities – G.L.C., Camden, Manchester and Ross and Cromarty – had schemes delegating some powers of decision-taking to their officers.

The climax of the case's journey then, is the meeting of the committee responsible for development control whether this be the main planning committee or a sub-committee. This will be attended by one or more officers from the planning department, sometimes the chief or deputy, but most usually by the section head of development control with or without the caseworkers directly involved. Often too there will be a member of the clerk's (or solicitor's) department present acting as committee clerk and able to advise on legal aspects or implications.

After the meeting all the case files, including those on which decisions have been deferred for various reasons, will come back to the development control section so that from there, directly, or via the clerk's department, the planning authority's formal decision notice can be issued.

Having described the typical path through the local government machine taken by a case we shall now turn to look in detail at all the kinds of information the caseworker uses in order to come to a view and frame his recommendation and the various sources which he taps for such facts and guidance.

Information used for framing the recommendation: the 'input' to development control

It was found in the examination of the work of seventy caseworkers in the seventeen authorities tested earlier that there is a remarkable consistency in the sources and types of information which they seek in order to frame their recommendations. This consistency is with respect to the whole set of caseworkers. We could not find any significant differences between the seventeen authorities; minor differences in the pattern were between the caseworkers rather than reflecting on the problems or backgrounds of the planning authorities or their administrative areas. This may suggest two things: first the influence of statutory requirements which are universal; secondly, that caseworkers may share a common ideology or set of principles and attitudes to their job, irrespective of their employing authority. With obvious minor variations, the approach of caseworkers to their task seems broadly similar in areas as different as Ross and Cromarty, Manchester, Camden and Lincoln.

Each caseworker interviewed was asked in part of the questionnaire to respond to a list of questions (prepared as the result of a pilot study in Manchester planning department) asking about the sources and types of information he used in making his recommendations. With respect to each source or type he was invited to indicate whether it was used 'frequently', 'sometimes' or 'never'. In appropriate cases the reply 'always' was admitted. A graphic summary of the results is shown in Figure 4.2.

We chose to use questionnaire-based interviews for the purpose because pilot studies had confirmed that case files themselves contain a bare minimum of documentation which is of value. Typically they contain the application forms themselves, copies of essential consultation letters and memos. Very rarely do they contain the caseworker's notes on visits to the site. Hardly ever does the case file contain notes of meetings with the applicant, discussions with colleagues, telephone conversations and so forth. Yet, as we shall see, these are often some of the crucial sources of information for a recommendation. The direct method of the structured interview was, therefore, adopted. We asked caseworkers to indicate their information inputs under a number of broad headings and we discuss the results obtained for each major category in turn – both scheduled and unscheduled meetings with colleagues in 'plan' and 'control'. If we give weights of 2 and 1 to the answers 'frequently' and 'sometimes' respectively, and arrange the replies from the seventy caseworkers in the resulting rank order, we have the following results:

By far the most important documentary source of information was *other case files* and information about *precedents* generally – gathered for example by informal conversations with colleagues who had

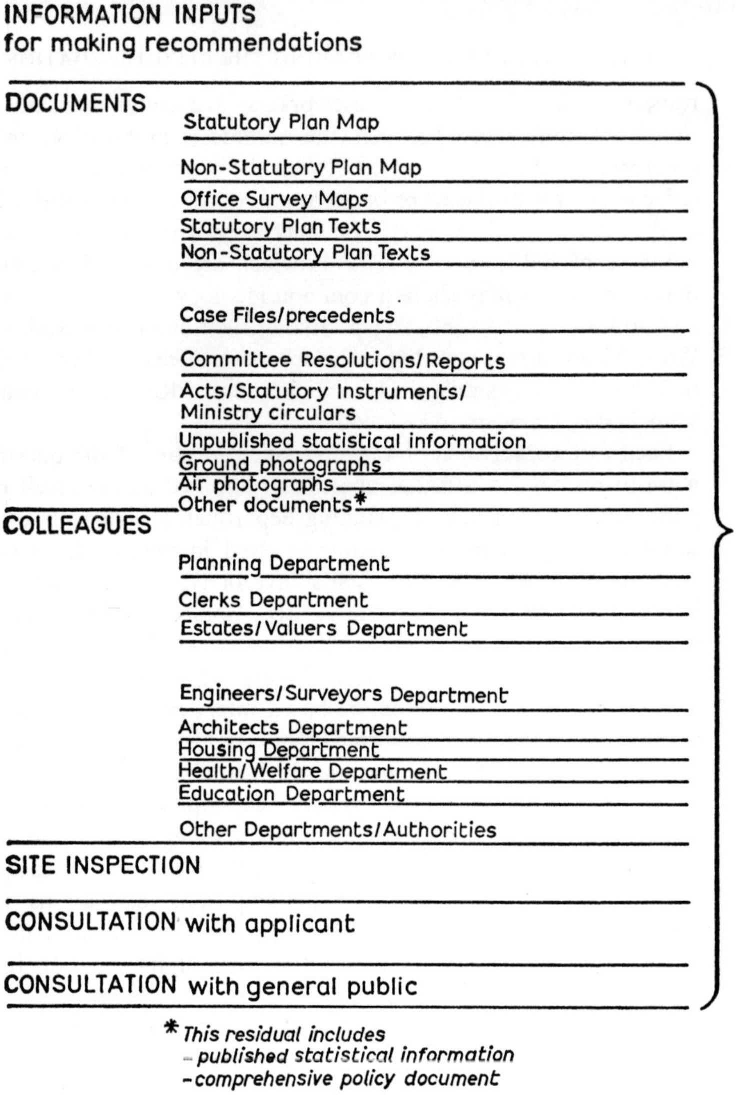

INFORMATION INPUTS
for making recommendations

DOCUMENTS

Statutory Plan Map

Non-Statutory Plan Map

Office Survey Maps

Statutory Plan Texts

Non-Statutory Plan Texts

Case Files/precedents

Committee Resolutions/Reports

Acts/Statutory Instruments/
Ministry circulars

Unpublished statistical information

Ground photographs

Air photographs

Other documents *

COLLEAGUES

Planning Department

Clerks Department

Estates/Valuers Department

Engineers/Surveyors Department

Architects Department

Housing Department

Health/Welfare Department

Education Department

Other Departments/Authorities

SITE INSPECTION

CONSULTATION with applicant

CONSULTATION with general public

* This residual includes
— published statistical information
– comprehensive policy document

Figure 4.2: Information input

dealt with similar applications or cases in the vicinity. Next in importance come the various *maps associated with the statutory development plan* closely followed by the relevant *Acts, Statutory Instruments and Circulars.* Of somewhat less significance were *non-*

94

	Professional help/advice to applicants	HELP AND ADVICE
	General Public	INFORMATION REQUESTS
	Students	outside
	Research Workers	public
	Solicitors/Estate Agents	service
	Clerk's Department	INFORMATION REQUESTS
	Estates/Valuers Dept.	inside public
	Engineers/Surveyors Dept.	services
	Architects Department	
	Housing Department	
	Health/Welfare Dept.	
	Education Department	
	Development Plan colleagues	REQUESTS
	Elsewhere	

CASE WORKER'S DECISION

REQUESTS for development control statistics

FREQUENCY OF USE/OCCURRENCE AS PERCENTAGE

0
50 % respondents
100

put of caseworkers' decisions

statutory plan maps, that is the physical plans produced for various purposes but which for a variety of reasons have not been put into statutory form and thus are kept in a 'bottom-drawer' status (see Chapter 5). Very often such schemes are prepared especially for the

95

guidance of development control. A major problem is that whilst they ensure consistency between different cases and caseworkers, (e.g. by indicating the limits of a shopping area or the alignment of a future road improvement) such 'bottom-drawer' plans sometimes have no legal force in that they have not been formally adopted by committee or council resolution, let alone by the Minister. Also of moderate significance were committee resolutions and reports. Other sources of documentary information of moderate significance included office survey maps (e.g. of the age and condition of buildings) and statutory plan texts (e.g. the 'written statement' required by the 1962 Act). Of rather low significance were the texts accompanying non-statutory plans, unpublished statistics (usually compiled in the planning office itself) and ground photographs. Aerial photographs and published statistics were hardly used at all.

Colleagues in other groups provided a great deal of information to help the caseworkers. The importance of contacts in the *planning department itself* and in the *engineer (or surveyor's) department* was overwhelming. The most frequent contacts in the planning department were with fellow caseworkers and officers in the 'design' section, i.e. those working in detailed physical planning; very little contact was maintained with 'plan' colleagues, i.e. those working on broader, strategic matters of policy for the area as a whole. Contact with the engineer's/surveyor's department was almost exclusively with highways personnel and the building inspectors. The highway officers provide information on road construction and programming or give a formal view on the road access implications of the case; building inspectors usually provide information on the extent of physical development on the site in question and adjoining areas of land. Of much less significance were contacts with the clerk's department (on legal matters) and the estate and valuer's department (typically on the extent of council property or interests in land). Contacts with the housing, welfare, education and other departments were minimal or non-existent; some caseworkers had more contact with other agencies (e.g. the Divisional Road Engineer, the River Authority, the Gas Board) than with such colleagues in their own authority.

One of the most important sources of information for the case-worker is the *site visit or inspection* and ranks alongside the use of other case files and contacts with the applicant, planning and highways colleagues as a formative influence on the recommendation. In

96

some authorities it is the policy of the development control section to visit the sites of *all* applications unless it is judged that sufficient is known in detail to make this unnecessary. Even where this 'blanket' coverage is not the rule, a very high proportion of sites is visited and such activity occupies a considerable proportion of the caseworker's time. Also, it gives him opportunities, whether deliberately sought after or not, to talk to people in the locality and gain impressions of their views about changes in the area and to hear something about their problems concerning the physical environment. This, of course, is especially true of urban areas. By far the most common reason for inspection of the site of applications was to judge or estimate 'the effect of the proposal on its surroundings', but gaining information about the site itself and gathering material which had been omitted from the application (e.g. the location of trees on the site; the height of adjoining buildings) was also significant. Clearly, these operations can vary drastically in the demands they place on the caseworker. It is a relatively simple matter for a qualified and experienced person to imagine a new bungalow or an extension on a suburban plot of land and to fill in a few details missing from the applicant's block plan. But to do similar things in the case of a major industrial proposal or a new shopping centre is an entirely different matter involving large quantities of information (e.g. about utility networks, soil structure and stability, effluent disposal problems, vehicular movements) and the problem of 'judging the effect of the proposal on its surroundings' is not only bigger but *far more complex*, extending well beyond visual considerations into dimensions such as traffic, utility, retailing, employment, educational and many other systems of public concern.

Consultation with the applicant is another very significant factor on framing a recommendation. Very rarely is this done merely in order to obtain complete factual details; these can be obtained by letter, telephone and the site visit. Usually a meeting with the applicant, with or without his architect, surveyor or other advisers, is in the nature of a *discussion and negotiation* about aspects of the application. Usually discussion centres on the layout, the elevations, materials, landscaping, road access and similar physical details. The caseworker (who will sometimes be joined by colleagues from 'design' and 'plan' sections and from the highways section of the engineer's department) will point out to the applicant certain requirements of the planning authority and seek the applicant's views about

97

the possibility of modifying his application in order to meet these problems. The applicant, of course, may be able to show the difficulty or impossibility of such modifications and if he is convincing in this the caseworker may well 'climb down' if no matters of principle or legal requirement are at stake.

In the majority of cases which are simple and straightforward one such meeting will usually suffice to enable the caseworker to make progress. But a minority of applications are much more complex and may raise issues of considerable technical complexity (e.g. air traffic control technology, soil mechanics and noise measurements if an airport extension is being proposed). Long series of meetings are often required, extending over months, sometimes a year or more. Such cases are not only very complex and demanding of specialized knowledge on both 'sides' but obviously may raise, immediately and directly, *issues of policy* for the area as a whole, or even a region. Such development control activity is clearly quantitatively and qualitatively different from dealing with run-of-the-mill applications for lock-up garages and small residential estates. We shall discuss the relationships between control, detailed planning and broader policy matters in the chapters which follow.

Consultation and contact with the general public was of moderate importance to caseworkers. We have noted that some informal opportunities arise to meet and talk with people when the site is visited. In a small minority of cases the authority will advertise the application and invite comment from members of the public.* Practice varies between authorities in this respect. Luton, we found, advertised *the complete list* of planning applications regularly in the local newspaper but the majority of authorities are not so generous with this information. Manchester caseworkers would sometimes print a leaflet inviting comment on a particular application and post this through the letter-boxes of properties in the vicinity of an application which they felt required some localized public knowledge and response. In other authorities the caseworkers would sometimes call in person and seek informal reactions about an application.

However, by far the most usual kind of contact between the general public and the caseworkers arises from specific questions and

---

* We are referring here to *voluntary* actions of this kind by the authority over and above the *statutory requirement* to advertise certain classes of application.

complaints concerning rumours or knowledge of an application. In these circumstances householders and others in the vicinity call at the planning office to seek information or express concern. In some cases this may result in community actions such as the organization of a petition or meetings to mobilize and express protests. The outcomes of such actions, if timely, will be taken into account by the caseworker along with all the other information concerning the case. The most common issues raised in all these ways – advertisement, posting leaflets, knocking on doors and individual or community action – were *visual intrusion* by the proposed development, noise, traffic and parking nuisances and the fear of *lowering property values*.

Caseworkers, as we have said, rely heavily on information from their immediate (departmental) colleagues. They rely overwhelmingly on contacts with officers working in 'design' i.e. on detailed physical plans and their contacts are largely unscheduled and informal. Only in a few authorities did we find regular, scheduled meetings at which development control staff had discussions with those working in other sections. Such regular contacts usually took the form of a 'post conference' i.e. a meeting – often daily – to inspect and discuss the morning's mail and would be attended (as in Herefordshire for example) by the chief and the section heads of 'plan', 'control' and 'design'. But the typical mode of contact between development control and 'design' was informal movement between offices, along corridors, over the internal telephones or by sharing working coffee-break or lunch. And as we have seen, the substance of such contacts would be relating the application details to a statutory or 'bottom-drawer' detailed physical plan.

There are two ways of trying to summarize or gain a general impression about the information input to a development control recommendation. First, we have the caseworker's own expressed views in answer to the question 'What in your opinion are the most important factors in making a recommendation?' And secondly, we can look at the results obtained in the research project on this topic by taking all questions relating to information for casework together.

Taking a consensus of all the caseworkers interviewed, the *development plan* was held to be the most important factor in making a recommendation and *local policies, the site and its surroundings, precedent, 'experience and common sense'* and *'personal judgement and philosophy'* were all of equal secondary importance. National standards and planning law were rated very low in their significance.

Our own analysis of replies to all the specific questions about information for recommendations reveals that the most frequent (which is not, of course, the same as 'important') factors were *detailed development plan and highway information* (gained largely from immediate colleagues), *other cases and precedents,* the details of the *application and its relation to the site and environs* (gained from discussions with the applicant and visits to the site). Of lesser significance were Acts, statutory instruments, etc., consultations with other departments of the authority, other authorities, committee or council resolutions, comments from the general public and the written matter of development plans. Information and advice from the social service, education and housing departments, the use of ground and air photographs and statistical material were of very low significance in terms of frequency of use. When such departments were consulted it was usually to check on their land development requirements generally rather than on the social significance or effects of the particular case in question.

Caseworkers try to formalize the basis of their view to the greatest extent possible. In other words, they seek *decision rules* in the form, for example, of a development plan map, a precedent such as an appeal decision, a land requirement by another department, a proposed road alignment, a national or local standard applicable to the case in question, and so forth. The amount of guidance available in these forms was inversely related to the degree of verbal, informal consultation with colleagues. In other words, caseworkers look for the most readily available reason or set of reasons which would 'swing' a decision one way or another and these are most often in the form of standards including statutory requirements. Beyond this, caseworkers were strongly inclined to look to their colleagues either directly and informally over a cup of tea, or more formally via a memorandum. With the decline in relevance of the old development plan map it is not surprising that non-statutory or 'bottom-drawer' plans have risen in importance. But such plans, especially local detailed plans, which are of the greatest help to development control, take time and skill to prepare and most parts of the authority's area will not be covered. In these circumstances, caseworkers rely heavily on informal guidance and opinion from their colleagues, seeking some sort of consensus or collective wisdom.

Information arising from casework: the 'output' from development control

It is clear from our empirical studies that development control caseworkers are an important source of certain kinds of information, not only for their colleagues in the planning department and elsewhere in local government, but also to applicants, intending applicants, their advisers and to certain groups in the public at large.

Applicants themselves (and their advisers) are the groups who command most of the attention of the caseworkers. The sort of help and advice applicants receive takes various forms but mostly it is concerned with revising the layout details of the application, revising elevations of buildings and helping them in general with the completion of the application form. As we have already noted, forms in general seem devised for each individual authority's procedural convenience and are often complicated and confusing. Ill-educated and inarticulate people often find considerable difficulty in filling in the form and it falls to the caseworkers to help those who choose not to have (or are too poor to afford) professional help. Clearly this is unsatisfactory from several viewpoints. When public authority imposes a legal requirement on people (like obtaining a driving licence or filling in an income tax return) the onus is on the authority to be as clear, simple and direct as possible. Secondly, the valuable time of the caseworker who operates under considerable pressures, is wasted by his having to make good his authority's laxity.* Finally, it is doubtful if employees of the public service should provide advice and help which is available from professional sources. Apart from these sorts of help, caseworkers also advised on the availability of sites for development and possibilities for relocation, especially intending applicants for planning permission among the general public, and solicitors and estate agents who themselves advise on such matters. These groups of people dominate those receiving information from development control officers. The topics most frequently raised include housing development and redevelopment programmes,

* Caseworkers could, of course, be more forceful in pressing for standardization and clarity in application forms. Standardization on a national basis was advocated in the Management Study on Development Control.

highway building and improvement proposals and the availability of
sites and buildings for industrial development – especially by small-
scale entrepreneurs. As compared with their colleagues in 'design' and
especially in 'plan' sections, caseworkers see little of students and
research workers. However, by contrast, development control
personnel deal fairly frequently with building-trade salesmen and
representatives wishing to find out the location and details of forthcoming developments of all kinds.

Information is provided by caseworkers to people in the public
service. A great deal of it goes to their immediate colleagues in 'design'
and to staff in the highways section of the engineer's department,
reinforcing relationships we have already stressed. Usually this
involves pointing out informally what is happening physically in the
area, what changes are imminent, what others may be expected to
arise in time by virtue of planning permissions granted and so on.
Caseworkers thus count on their 'design' and highways colleagues to
'keep tabs on' the evolving details of physical form in areas on which
they are currently working or help them to identify areas where their
design and development skills may shortly be needed. A considerable
amount of information is provided to the clerk's department of their
authorities – usually about the recommendations likely to be included
on a forthcoming committee agenda, but also about the likelihood of
planning permission being granted to various public-authority proposals. Similar information is often provided to the estates or
valuer's department. A great deal of information is given to the
clerk's departments as a result of legal 'searches' under the Land
Charges Acts. Very little information is passed to the other departments of authorities and the low frequency of this with respect to the
social services, housing and education departments emphasizes the
low significance of this relationship.

Development control caseworkers are thus deeply involved in the
information web of contact, information, advice and help provided
by local government and are an important part of the whole 'interface'
between the bureaucracy and the public. The evidence reviewed here
confirms the view expressed by the Management Study (MINISTRY
OF HOUSING AND LOCAL GOVERNMENT, 1967a, p. 16) that

'the informal enquiry service meets a public need and . . . tends to
improve the quality of the formal proposals.'

But this whole question of an interface across which public servants meet their clients face to face is so important as to warrant discussion in another context which we shall be doing in Chapter 10 below.

A portrait of the caseworker

An adequate understanding of development control casework cannot be gained without some knowledge of the caseworkers themselves. This point has especial force because of the dominance of face-to-face relationships in the caseworker's daily routine, particularly his direct and regular contacts with applicants, their advisers and members of the general public. About one-third of all 'professional' (i.e. not administrative or clerical) planning staffs work on development control, the great majority of them being caseworkers. Anyone who has direct informal contact with caseworkers in British planning offices quickly realizes that they believe themselves to be significantly different from their colleagues in several ways. The overriding impression one receives is that caseworkers as a group regard themselves as the 'Cinderellas' of the planning operation, something akin to a 'second-class citizen' feeling. This is not only their self-image but they also feel that others regard them in this light. At the same time many of them are proud of their work and point especially to its contact with the 'real world' of events and people. They believe they are able to observe and understand with much greater clarity than their colleagues the need for and the effects of policies and the constraints which must be accepted if policies and programmes are to be both credible, feasible and relevant.

In the seventeen-authority research project we were so impressed by these views that we decided to seek additional information (after the fieldwork programme) not only on the caseworkers but also on other kinds of planners in order to afford comparisons. This postal questionnaire study covered such matters as age, professional and academic qualifications, salary, job mobility and so on. In addition to this factual information gathered from sixty out of the seventy caseworkers originally interviewed in the field we had qualitative information from answers to an 'open-ended' question about the implications of structure plans under the 1968 Town and Country Planning Act for the principles and practice of development control. Similar kinds of information came from questionnaires returned by thirty-four of the forty-one 'plan' and 'design' officers interviewed in the field.

103

The factual information which emerged from all this is summarized in Figure 4.3 on facing page.

Only about half of the control personnel had any professional qualifications, less than a third in planning. But almost two-thirds were graduates (or diplomates) predominantly in planning or geography; surprisingly, there were only two architects. Very few people had worked in more than four authorities and the great majority had served in only one or two; 60% of them had spent over 60% of their careers in development control work.

The thirty-four officers who replied from 'plan' or 'design' jobs were significantly different in many respects. First of all they were distinctly better paid; very few earned less than £2,000 and most earned between £2,500 and £3,500. Only one-seventh of them were 'students' or 'trainees' and of these a good proportion were in fact studying for a *second* professional or academic qualification (e.g. planners studying landscape architecture). Almost all were professionally qualified, overwhelmingly they were Chartered Town Planners, but a quarter were members of the Royal Institute of British Architects. Surprisingly few had a double qualification. 85% were graduates and a considerable number had a higher degree or diploma – very common combinations were geography with planning (26%) and architecture with planning (24%). These latter groups, we suspect, correspond quite closely with 'plan' and 'design' work respectively. Less than one-fifth had a 'straight' planning qualification by first degree or diploma. They had moved around even less than their caseworker colleagues for only one in seven had been with more than three authorities. Also, they were very much 'plan' and 'design' people in that three-quarters of them had spent less than 20% of their time in control. The majority may well have no experience of casework at all.

About half of the development control staff were under thirty years old and about one in five were over fifty. Most people earned between £2,000 and £3,000 a year (in late 1970) but there was a significant number of students and trainees earning less than £2,000. It may be that the reason for control having 47% of its staff under thirty (compared with 33% in 'plan' and 'design') and 20% under twenty-five years old (compared with only 3% in other groups) is the large proportion of trainees and recent graduates who are allocated to this work – partly because it is unpopular because of its routine and

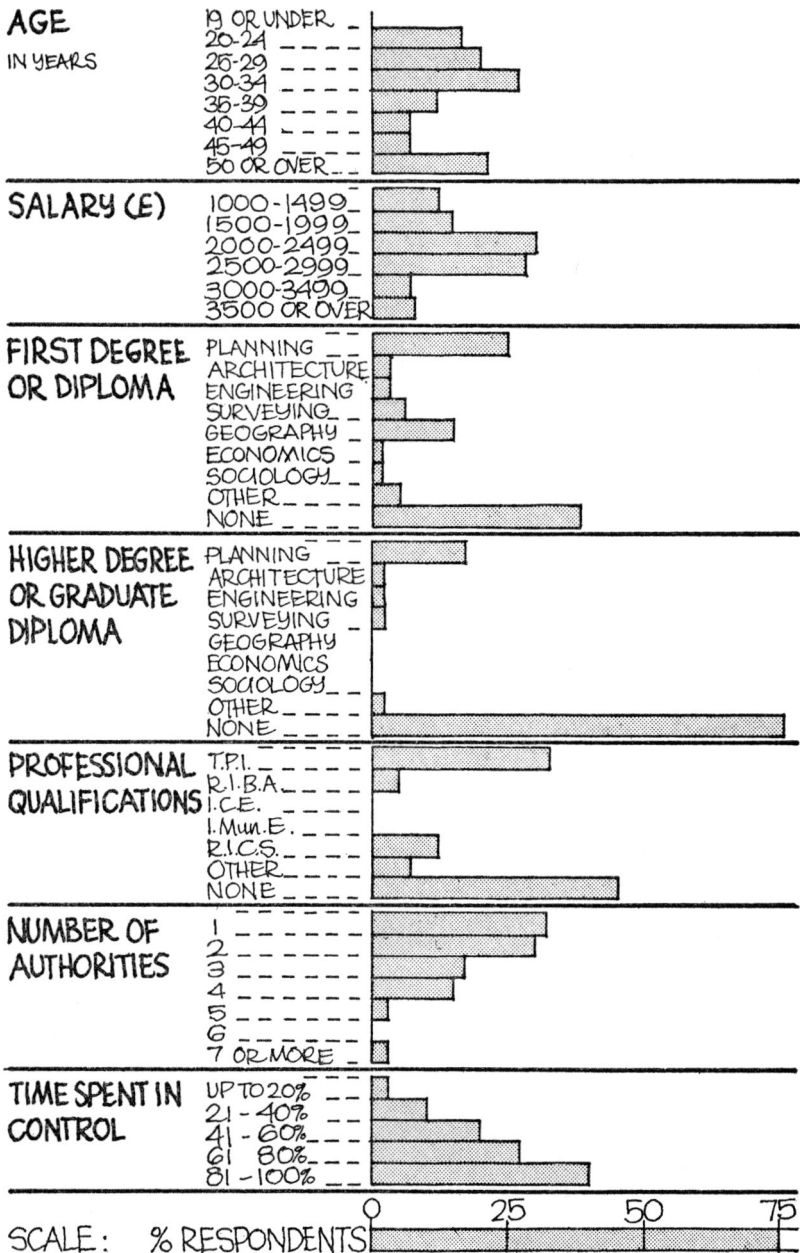

Figure 4.3: Age, qualifications and experience of caseworkers

pressures, partly because the Royal Town Planning Institute's experience requirements for aspiring entrants require a varied 'mix' of types of work, including development control.

So the 'development control folklore' including the Cinderella image, is to some extent borne out by this limited evidence. Case-workers do indeed seem to be less qualified and less well-educated in a formal sense. Certainly they are worse off financially than their colleagues in 'plan' or 'design' sections. There are more young people (including students and trainees) in control but also more people well into middle age; the thirty- and forty-year olds are a little thin on the ground. And whereas 'plan' and 'design' people stick fairly close to their trade, a fair proportion of caseworkers have had more varied experience, whether by the 'exigency of the service' or by their own desire.

But it is the expressed attitudes and values of caseworkers and their colleagues in development control which are even more revealing of themselves and of their rôle in British planning. These not only help an understanding of the present scene but must surely be useful and necessary in making speculations and suggestions about the future shape of the planning function in local government.

Attitudes and values of caseworkers

It would be oversimplifying to say that all caseworkers regard themselves as bureaucrats with hearts of gold. They vary so much in education, age and experience that obviously there is a great deal of diversity among them as a group. But they do tend to resemble other routine workers in local government – people in *other* departments – much more than their colleagues in other sections of the planning department.

Their self-image can be related to this. They are similar people doing a similar job to, say, building inspectors, senior clerical workers in the taxation office, 'land charges' clerks, school attendance officers and so on. Of course, these tasks differ a lot and require varied levels of skill but, nevertheless, they are *routine* jobs dealing with *cases* and to a greater or lesser extent *dealing with people* face to face. At worst such jobs depress officers with their humdrum sameness, their red tape, their perpetual stress, their distinct lack of glamour; at best, officers are proud of their rôle as public servants and keen to provide those services in an effective and understanding way. They are conscious too of their contact with the 'real world' of people and their problems. At the same time, this consciousness of being like many other routine caseworkers in the local government service makes them aware of the differences which exist between them and their planning department colleagues. People in 'design' and 'plan' seem to lead hard-working yet much less pressured lives, preparing development schemes, carrying out mineral surveys, studying problems of outdoor recreation and sub-regional growth strategies for areas beyond the authority's boundary, often looking speculatively some distance into the future. A very different world from next Tuesday's agenda, the petrol-filling station appeal next Thursday and five sites to visit before lunch-time.

The steady growth and diversification of design and (especially) plan work, the emergence of research and intelligence functions within the planning department has steadily over the years brought in more graduates with better pay and prospects than many development control workers. The resulting deepening contrasts and cleavages have surely helped to sustain and enlarge the 'second-class citizen' or 'Cinderella' self-image of development control people.

The attitude of caseworkers to their colleagues in 'design' varies a good deal. As we have seen, they come into close contact with such people and in some authorities design and control are formally integrated because of their close inter-relationships. (We shall develop this theme fully in Chapter 5 which follows.) On the one hand caseworkers find detailed plans very helpful and make considerable use of them. In doing so they develop relationships of mutual respect with designers. On the other hand, some design work is undoubtedly a little unrealistic and pie-in-the-sky and its perpetrators earn the scorn of the development control men.

There is a considerable detachment of caseworkers from 'plan' work and especially from its higher-level 'policy and research' manifestations. We interviewed some caseworkers who had not spoken to such colleagues inside six months or more. Often regret was expressed on both sides. People felt that there *should* be more interaction and were puzzled why this did not occur. (We shall develop this theme in Chapter 6 below.) Feelings were often sharper from the development control workers' side, however. For it is in plan, policy and research that the 'whizz-kid' young graduates are

107

believed to reside. Sometimes their work is felt to be too detached and unrealistic by caseworkers. A senior development control officer in the G.L.C. remarked:

'We have to brief policy people as to what is feasible. They may have grand ideas but often lack a reasonable footing. This branch [i.e. development control] has to confront the public at enquiries and, therefore, we have to face the acid test of justification in public. Anybody can write airy-fairy vapourings in a locked room.'

Most attitudes were more moderate, however, but many caseworkers could not find anything useful or relevant to their work in the generalized plans and policy studies produced by their colleagues in such sections. Mixed feelings ranging from animosity and perhaps jealousy to vague puzzlement and disconnection characterized the caseworkers' attitudes. They increasingly doubted the usefulness *for them* of generalized plans and policies; they wanted much more specific guidance and advice.

Attitudes to the general public were predominantly helpful and considerate. Caseworkers realize the trouble, expense and anxiety which applicants must bear and realize that (apart from architects, builders and so on) for most people a planning application is an unusual experience. They need help and guidance. Some authorities employ a person whose job is designated 'enforcement officer' or 'investigating officer', the essence of which is to check on possible infringements of planning law (e.g. development without permission, or without compliance with conditions attached to a permission). A number of such officers are retired members of the police force. Far from being some kind of plain-clothes spy, we found these officers extremely helpful, persuading people to comply with the law, explaining it to them, helping them to fill in forms, and so on. But moreover, as one of them put it:

'These country folk can be completely befogged by local government and red tape. Often they don't know their rights or are too scared to take matters up. A lot of my time is spent in being a kind of local "ombudsman" because folk who know me personally ask me to deal with their problems. I can point out such things to my colleagues back in the office.'

Younger caseworkers, often graduates 'doing their time' in development control, have taken this theme up more forcefully and some are beginning to act as 'evangelistic bureaucrats' (DAVIES, 1972); this is particularly noticeable in the poorer parts of larger cities. Many caseworkers felt that *even more* helpful contact would be necessary in future. A more articulate and less deferential general public would need more explanation and justification of planning attitudes and decisions. Development control could evolve into one important element of public participation and some officers positively relished the prospect. Others were doubtful, even cynical. Public participation would be another demand on already precious time and most members of the public:

> 'don't know what they want anyway. All they're interested in is their own house.'

The officer quoted seemed unaware of the irony that it is the applicant's house which development control affects! A considerable number of caseworkers, not only the younger ones, believed that contact with applicants and the public could be very valuable in providing feedback in a system for monitoring the effectiveness, relevance and impact of policies.

Attitudes to councillors fell into two broad categories. On the one hand we see the 'technocrat' view which regards the advice and recommendations coming from the caseworker and others as 'value-free' and based on purely professional and technical considerations. This view, in its extreme form, resents the councillors' 'messing about' with recommendations and will not come to terms with the perfectly proper political rôles of the councillor as representative and decision taker. Caseworkers who hold such views resent committee members coming into the office to ask questions about a case which is coming up and about which the councillor may have been approached by a constituent. They are even cynical when discussing the presence on the planning committee of local landowners and builders who 'upset' recommendations because of their vested interests. Councillors, in this view, are not fit to make decisions about land development because of their lack of professional understanding:

> 'Why, they even try to read the plans upside down!'

Such extreme views are rare and it is more common to find considerable respect for councillors for a number of reasons. Prominent among these is the recognition by the caseworker that the councillor too has an intimate knowledge and understanding of the 'grass-roots' in the area – especially his own ward – and his knowledge of people, problems, motives, opportunities and the 'art of the possible' complements that of the caseworker. In terms of subject matter and detail, they are often talking the same language though from different standpoints.

Caseworkers were generally sure of the value of development control. Without it, the physical environment could be worse, even 'chaotic'; with it, much of value had been maintained, even in some cases enhanced. They were almost unanimous in believing they should have far better support in the form of administrative, clerical and technical staff and ready access to good information sources to help with their recommendations. Junior support and trainee staff could well deal with most of the 70% to 90% of routine, uncontroversial cases and with such support, better qualified and more experienced caseworkers could give far better consideration in depth to the minority of complex, difficult cases which demanded close analysis (see MINISTRY OF HOUSING AND LOCAL GOVERNMENT, 1967a).

A widely held view was that caseworkers had a special place in planning because of their direct contact with the public and the benefits which would accrue to the public *and* to policy work by formal recognition of this rôle and its extension.

Whilst there were certainly those, particularly younger planners, who conceived of development control as part of a much wider public service, many professionals saw it in strongly traditional terms, i.e. as one of several means of carrying out land-use plan and civic design schemes. The specific emphasis then varied from authority to authority depending on its 'ideology'. The dominant set of values which control then helped to sustain would sometimes depend on the nature of the area, sometimes on the personality of a senior officer, sometimes on both.

For example, some development control officers in the Peak Park saw the maintenance of the traditional stone-built village and rural scene as their prime function. Similarly in Aberdeen, the granite townscape was a guiding light of the caseworkers' attitudes as were the low-density, bosky, suburban, residential areas in Bromley. It may be that these traditional justifications for development control are being strongly challenged by the younger entrants to the public service, not so much for what they represent but for *their seeming isolation from other factors of public concern*. In other words, there is

110

nothing wrong with trying to have pretty villages, tidy suburbs and safe vehicular access as long as these had been thought out within a much wider spectrum of problems and priorities. A Peak Park officer, commented that policy, plan and project work had 'gone over to a management model but development control hasn't'.

Nevertheless, the distinction was several times made between comprehensive thinking at the strategic (sub-region, city-wide) scale for the formulation and review of policies on the one hand and a comprehensive understanding of community problems at the neighbourhood or street level on the other. Several officers suggested that there might never be any direct connection between these two 'levels' of planning. 'I don't see why I should be bothered about conservation policies in a back garden,' said a Leicester caseworker. She added that 'somebody in the public service should be concerned about micro-*social* as well as micro-physical problems. . . . We need some sort of micro-problem Ombudsman.'

Here we can see one aspect of an ambiguity which has long plagued discussions of planning – is one talking about physical plans (land-use patterns, layouts, civic design schemes) or ways of proceeding in a more general sense such as in corporate planning or the 'strategic' level of local government as a whole? (HALL, 1970). This ambiguity may help to resolve what at first sight appears to be contrasted views amongst our respondents. For there are those who said that development control should be much more closely associated with 'plan' work and those who said either that it could not or would not be. Obviously it is much easier to relate development control work (as now understood and practised) to detailed physical plans than to broad social and economic strategies.

The distinction often appeared in a slightly different way. There were those caseworkers *who welcomed the 1968 Act because of its flexibility* and the scope it gave them for 'treating each case on its merits'; but equally there were many planners who said that *control would be very difficult without* detailed plans and hoped that district and especially 'action area' plans would be prepared as quickly as possible.

There was virtual unanimity about *the need for 'better' people in development control* in the future. This was expressed in a number of ways. Development control 'will require a new sort of person' we were told in the Peak Park, whilst in Camden the feeling was that in future there would be the need for 'highly qualified, responsible and articulate staff'. Many officers believed that caseworkers would have to be drawn from more able and intelligent sources in future because of the great changes already apparent in the quality of their plan and policy colleagues. It was, therefore, another perspective on the 'gulf' between plan and control which should not be allowed to widen. Thus in Durham a caseworker said that 'the specialist groups (e.g. county map, urban plans, landscape) are very able and well-informed' and this required that development control people 'would have to be of higher quality in future'. If they were 'more positive thinking would ensue'.

One officer in Luton thought that it was the system not the people in it which needed changing and that the same sort of caseworkers, given 'superior liaison with research and policy' could do a better job. But the great majority of our respondents felt the need, as did one in the G.L.C. for 'a higher level of intelligence' mostly because of the increasing brainpower available to the policy and intelligence arms of the service. Even the liaison was not automatic, of course, and had to be learned. The considerable analytical power possessed by the G.L.C. was underused by caseworkers 'because of the inertia in their . . . skills, backgrounds and attitudes'. Another officer in the G.L.C. said that 'the planners don't seem to realize that they have any problems' and that the decisions analysis scheme – a potentially rich link between policy and control – had been initiated 'by the data bank lads, *not* the potential customers in development control'.

This widespread demand that control should have at least a fair share of the increasing amounts of brainpower in planning raises problems for educators because it was a common view that the control skill could not be taught in any formal way but was ideally learned by apprenticeship. Presumably what our respondents were implying is that much on-the-job learning must in future be preceded by a higher level of formal education, perhaps of first-degree level. But the education and training of future caseworkers cannot be divorced from the needs of many other kinds of planners and local government officers; these are questions we take up in the final chapter of this book.

5 · Detailed Physical Planning and Control

Purposes

There is a multitude of purposes for detailed physical planning. Many of these can be traced to the origins of the planning movement and to the beginnings of governmental involvement in the physical environment. At first, as we saw in Chapter 1, physical 'planning' was confined to the setting of standards by which public health and safety could be ensured. The medium for doing so was the bye-laws created under the powers of the 1875 Public Health Act and similar legislation and operated by the local health authorities. But the real beginnings of the modern tradition of detailed planning is marked by the *planning schemes* which were brought into being by the 1909 Housing and Town Planning Act.

The operation of the building bye-laws in controlling ventilation, daylight, street widths and so on was found to be of limited value and a demand grew up for a more comprehensive approach to controlling urban change and growth. Health continued to be a principal concern and reformers were mindful of the need for a healthy proletariat to man industries and the army (ASHWORTH, 1954, Chapter VII). In addition, concern was being expressed at the costs of street widening in existing residential areas. Moreover, there was a growing public interest in the aesthetic qualities of the urban environment so that the ideal of the City Beautiful was added to those of the City Sanitary and the City Economic. The writings and views of William Morris and Ebenezer Howard, the designs of Raymond Unwin and Barry Parker, the growth of preservation societies and the National Trust are all in their different way reflections of this aspiration for a more seemly, harmonious and beautiful physical environment.

This multiplicity of purpose – sanitary, efficient and beautiful – characterized the objectives which lay behind the earliest town planning schemes. But they were caught up in an overarching view

which believed that health, efficiency and beauty together were contributory factors, even essential elements in the life of a civilized
society and its individual members. Much of the work in promoting
and pursuing such causes was done by private initiative in forming a
multitude of political, social, educational and cultural societies both
nationally and locally. But governmental action was deemed necessary
for a number of reasons. First of all, certain national interests were at
stake – most obviously in the health of the population and in public
spending on such things as streets and utility services. Secondly, the
power of the law was necessary in order to provide effective controls
and sanctions over physical development and its effects. Furthermore,
government had to be involved since most of the problems arising
from urban growth and change were what economists call 'externalities'; that is, they are the sorts of things which do not enter the
balance sheets of the private firm or the individual entrepreneur –
traffic congestion, water pollution, visual disfigurement, the smoke
and fumes emitted by a factory. The only effective way of dealing
with such externalities and with the *co-ordinative* problems arising
from their interactions was to secure public, i.e. governmental,
control over physical development.

The 1909 Act aimed in the words of John Burns, the President of
the Local Government Board, in the House of Commons at 'the home
healthy, the house beautiful, the town pleasant, the city dignified and
the suburb salubrious' (in what ASHWORTH (1954, p. 183) calls 'a
lamentable literary flight'). In terser legal language, the 4th Schedule
of the Act listed the actual physical content of town planning schemes
as:

(1) Streets, roads, and other ways, and stopping up, or diversion
    of existing highways
(2) Buildings, structures and erections
(3) Open spaces, private and public
(4) The preservation of objects of historical interest or natural
    beauty
(5) Sewerage, drainage, and sewage disposal
(6) Lighting
(7) Water supply
(8) Ancillary or consequential works.

How did the promotors of the Act envisage the outcome or form of
the town planning scheme? What would a scheme *be* rather than

merely contain? Frequent approving reference was made to private British development planning schemes and to overseas examples. Both sides of the House of Commons referred to the excellent qualities and success of Bournville (Birmingham), Port Sunlight (Merseyside), New Earswick (York), Hampstead Garden Suburb and similar philanthropic enterprises in town (or garden suburb) planning. Though on a somewhat grander scale, the planning schemes in Düsseldorf, Vienna and above all, Paris, were cited. The Parliamentary Secretary to the Local Government Board continued:

'The least we may demand . . . is that we should bring our level of civic development, controlled by the State as a whole, up to the level of other countries of Europe.'

The planning scheme would then be an exercise in *civic design* i.e. it would transcend the design of single buildings as by an architect, the subdivision of land with development plots as by a lawyer or surveyor, the layout of roads and utilities as by civil and municipal engineer. It would co-ordinate and integrate these elements into a whole which would be more than the sum of parts. It would serve social and community ends of health, safety and beauty. It would be backed by the power of the law (though lacking any real 'teeth' concerning private ownership, betterment in values and related matters as several critics pointed out). The planning scheme would co-ordinate and integrate public and private actions – something which 'market forces' could not do. It also implied the need for a new kind of civic design or town planning skill encompassing but perhaps transcending aspects of those of the architect, engineer, surveyor and lawyer; but that is another story which we shall take up elsewhere.

Over the years since the beginning of the century the precise content of the detailed physical plan and its statutory basis have changed a good deal. But in broad outline its purposes and content have changed remarkably little. The biggest and most significant change was first of all the extension of the *statutory* application of the planning scheme to cover all land whether or not it was in course of development. This came about in part from the 1919 Housing and Town Planning Act but more fundamentally from the 1932 Town and Country Planning Act. The second important class of statutory extensions to the original idea dates from the post-war period in which the 1947 Act and other legislation (notably the 1946 New

115

Towns Act) gave extensive powers of land purchase, land development and much tougher development control and compensation powers to local planning authorities. These changes to the 1909 planning scheme formula rendered the whole operation of physical planning much more widespread and powerful.

In detail, changes in the content of planning schemes* reflect the major issues of the period (e.g. war damage), the impact of technology (by highways, car parking) and social changes (e.g. university areas, holiday caravan sites). For example, during the 1920s and 1930s the predominant content or use of the town planning scheme was still the control of suburban residential development and associated activity – schools, shops, roads, open spaces – within design frameworks which attempted to restrict 'sprawl', 'ribbon development' disfigurement of the urban/rural fringe and to conserve fine groups of trees and buildings. The 1930s 'Special Areas' legislation called for the establishment of new industrial estates as locations for factories and workshops to provide increased and diversified employment. These estates – such as Team Valley and Jarrow on Tyneside – involved factory buildings, offices, storage space, roads, loading bays, canteens and restaurants, recreational spaces (e.g. for industrial sports clubs) all of which required physical co-ordination of the actions of central and local government, private investors and others.

Although the scale of such operations was increasing, the mode of organization remained much the same. Manchester City Council's garden city development south of the city at Wythenshawe was large by any standards and involved complex procedures of land development. A similar exercise at Speke, just outside Liverpool and involving a greater proportion of decentralized industrial as well as residential development was a comparable exercise in land purchase, assembly, preparation, layout, design and excavation.

It is sad but true that some of the most rapid advances in human skill and ingenuity occur because of wars. The Second World War gave rise, directly and indirectly, to the need for further developments in the scope, content and statutory basis of planning schemes. Directly, the war resulted in large areas of destruction by aerial bombardment and during the war itself the need to prepare the way for peacetime rebuilding became apparent. It was also realized that

* We shall retain this neat term to apply generally to the whole class of town centre plans, redevelopment plans, comprehensive development areas, etc.

116

widespread devastation in London, Plymouth, Coventry and other cities which had suffered presented an opportunity to plan for improvements in the layout and arrangement of adjoining areas. In some cases this led to an almost complete overhaul of the physical systems and structure of the central and industrial parts of the town.

The notion that areas could and should be planned for development and redevelopment as a whole was given statutory form in the 1943 and 1944 Town and Country Planning Acts. These were extended and consolidated by the definitive 1947 Act which provided the crucial vehicle of the *Comprehensive Development Area*. A 'C.D.A.' was defined as:

'an area which in the opinion of the local planning authority should be developed or redeveloped as a whole, for any one or more of the following purposes, that is to say for the purpose of dealing satisfactorily with extensive war damage or conditions of bad lay-out or obsolete development, or for the purpose of providing for the re-location of industry or the replacement of open space . . . or for any other purpose specified in the plan' (TOWN AND COUNTRY PLANNING ACT, 1947, SECTION 5 (3)).

Very wide powers of compulsory acquisition (following on those given by section 1 of the 1944 Act) were given to local authorities to help them implement their C.D.A. schemes. Extensive and varied use was made of these powers in the late 1940s and throughout the 1950s. These included not only comprehensive schemes of reconstruction and redevelopment in war-damaged areas like Stepney-Poplar in London's east end, Plymouth, Coventry, Manchester, Salford, Hull and elsewhere, but also university and cathedral towns such as Exeter, Cambridge, Oxford and Durham.

The planning scheme *par excellence* was surely exemplified in detailed proposals for 'neighbourhood units' and small development project areas in the new towns established (mostly around London) by the provisions of the New Towns Act of 1946. Here, of course, the planning scheme could trace unbroken lineage back to Bournville and New Earswick by way of Unwin and Parker's designs for Howard's original garden cities at Welwyn and Letchworth. The co-ordination, programming and control of roads, utilities, houses, schools and shops, – in fact all the physical equipment of localized daily life – required among other management aids a properly worked out physical plan.

117

But one of the biggest *new* demands for planning schemes arose from the very extensive nationwide powers of development control given by the 1947 Act. *All* land use was now subject to control and so were most kinds of private and several sorts of public development. In granting or withholding permission as well as in other matters such as revoking existing permissions or referring a case to the Minister the local planning authority had to:

> 'have regard to the provisions of the development plan, so far as material thereto, and to any other material considerations' (TOWN AND COUNTRY PLANNING ACT, 1947, SECTION 14 (1)).

This firm statutory linkage between plan and control, and the ubiquity and power of control gave added stimulus to the preparation of planning schemes. For (as we shall see in Chapter 6) the *overall* development plan document for a county borough and for the urbanized parts of counties was a map at a scale of 6″ to 1 mile (1:10,560) and for a county the basic plan was at 1″ to 1 mile (1:63,360); the making of development control decisions in areas of complex activity, mixed land uses, town centres, redevelopment areas, areas with special architectural character, etc. needed schemes worked out and expressed at a larger scale than those 'basic' plans provided. As a contemporary official review put it:

> 'If the development plan proposes to keep an open space permanently undeveloped . . . development control can be used to prevent houses being built on it; if the plan provides for turning a hotch-potch of commercial and industrial uses into a business centre, development control can preclude any more factories being built in that area.' (MINISTRY OF LOCAL GOVERNMENT AND PLANNING, 1951, p. 27)

Equally, development control could impose conditions on the grant of a permission to ensure that there was enough space for a road to be realigned or widened or that there would be sufficient daylight for an adjoining building not yet constructed.

As peacetime conditions returned and the economy began to revive (however haltingly) and real incomes to rise, the attendant industrial, commercial and transport and recreational developments gave rise to further kinds of demands for detailed planning schemes. The generality of the need remained much as ever:

118

'The task of securing the proper use of land falls into two parts: day-to-day control to ensure that proposals for individual development projects are properly sited, both for their own needs and in relation to neighbouring uses; and the preparation in advance of plans to co-ordinate the prospective demands for land in such a way as to result in pleasant, efficient and economical development, and to prevent the waste of land involved in a haphazard approach.' (MINISTRY OF HOUSING AND LOCAL GOVERNMENT, 1955, p. 60)

Specific problems and opportunities to be dealt with by the 'preparation in advance of plans' included many old and familiar ones but now we notice the rise of the urban transport problem. Now the planning schemes included ring roads, by-passes, new and widened radial roads, additional parking spaces and bus stations. Conflicts had to be resolved between these needs and commercial interests in Carlisle and college interests in Cambridge and Oxford. Indeed most interests in most places began to be confronted with the 'problem of the motor car'. Private housebuilding was expanding again and in order to deal with the increasing burden of development control work on residential applications, detailed planning schemes were needed especially in areas which would be developed in stages over the years by different builders, in villages of 'character' which were attracting commuter growth, in complex minor suburban areas where private and public developments had to be co-ordinated. The public sector was now faced with detailed planning for the expansion and re-modelling of existing towns to cope with 'overspill' under the provisions of the 1952 Town Development Act. Industrial investment was increasing and authorities who had hopefully designated land for industrial use in their plans often had to prepare detailed sketch layouts to help in co-ordinating the several applications of a number of different firms. Schemes were needed too for the reclamation, restoration and improvement of derelict land especially in mining and heavy industrial areas like Lancashire, Nottinghamshire, Yorkshire and South Wales.

During the 1960s the range of purposes comprised in the making of detailed planning schemes expanded in line with social and technological changes. Rising living standards brought the car problem to crisis level as far as the details of physical environment were concerned and required complete rethinking and redesigning of many existing schemes (especially in town centres) as well as many new

119

schemes to deal with underpasses, flyovers, roundabouts, car parks and all the other paraphernalia of motor transport. The holiday caravan sites erupted especially on the coasts and new powers of control contained in the Caravan Sites and Control of Development Act, 1960 required a great deal of design activity on new planning schemes for controlling the location and layout of sites. The shift towards conservation and improvement of old housing areas has altered the style of such planning schemes towards delicate 'surgery' as opposed to a clean-slate slum clearance and redevelopment approach. The Civic Amenities Act and the introduction of General Improvement Areas (EAGLAND, 1971) has made similar demands on the designers of planning schemes (TOMLINSON, 1970; PARKINSON, 1970; LEGGAT, 1968). Another response to the motor car problem has been the device of the pedestrian precinct either created *de novo* by development and redevelopment or by conversion of existing streets as, for example at Bolton (OGDEN, 1970).

The expansion of higher education following the report of the Robbins Committee in 1963 has given rise to the development of green-field sites like those for the Universities of Sussex, York and Lancaster and these, of course, required detailed schemes both from the professional advisers to the Universities and from the local planning authority with respect to adjoining areas. A splendid example of the need for an overall planning scheme to deal with a very complex situation of changes is provided by the Manchester Higher Education Precinct.

In summary, detailed 'physical planning schemes' serve one or more of several purposes:

The physical i.e. spatial co-ordination of a complex of different types of activities or uses of land;
The process of change including physical development and re-development again in the spatial sense;
The programming of such changes through time i.e. attempting to insure that the area 'works' satisfactorily through a period of complex physical change;
To provide guidance to development control casework;
To indicate in detail the planning authority's intentions to public and private sector developers and to act as a framework within which their architects etc. can work.

Statutory planning schemes

We have already touched on the origins of these in the private estate development schemes and similar exercises in the public sector beginning with those made under the 1909 Act. Also we have indicated that this tradition of working persisted throughout intervening years, for example under the provisions of the 1932 Town and Country Planning Act. More recently the definitive statutory model of the planning scheme is to be found in the Comprehensive Development Area Map and Supplementary Town Map provisions defined in the regulations the MINISTRY OF HOUSING AND LOCAL GOVERNMENT (1954) made under the 1947 Act and similar provisions made by Section 6 (1) of the New Towns Act, 1946.

The 1954 regulations, like their predecessors, provided for maps (and associated written material) to be submitted in due statutory form to the Minister, as additions or amendments to a development plan. They were to be drawn on the Ordnance Survey map as a base at a scale of 1:2500 though 1:1250 was allowed in certain circumstances. They had to indicate the major zones of 'primary' land use for all parts of the C.D.A.; the written matter had to include a table which showed in more detail what uses of land and buildings would or would not be allowed in each 'primary' zone. Thus for example, a primarily industrial zone might, according to such a table or matrix, be allowed to include storage and warehousing uses but not shopping and residential uses; some shopping and open space uses might be allowed in a zone 'primarily for residential use' but industry would not be permitted. It is clear that such a map and table would provide a firm guide to development control decisions. Where extensive alterations to the road network were intended as part of the comprehensive development scheme a 'Street Authorization Map' was required by the regulations.

The *intensity* with which land and buildings were to be occupied was already required to be shown on a C.D.A. map. These measures of intensity were of two forms. Firstly, for residential zones it was the 'gross residential density' in persons per acre calculated on the basis of all the (nett) residential of houses, gardens and adjoining minor roads *plus* small open spaces, small groups of shops, community centres and primary school sites i.e. all activities directly related to daily domestic life. The resulting numbers (e.g. thirty persons per

121

acre) were to be shown on the map related to each main residential zone. Secondly, for industrial and commercial use zones the Floor Space Index had to be indicated; this is a ratio which relates the maximum permissible floor area of buildings to the site area *plus* half the width of adjoining streets. Thus for example, if a site is 10,000 square feet nett and if half the width of adjoining streets is added to result in a gross area of 12,500 square feet, then a F.S.I. of 4·0 would mean that the maximum floor space allowable in the buildings in that zone or on that site would be (4·0 × 12,500) 50,000 square feet. Whether this took the form of five floors of 10,000 square feet or ten floors of 5,000 square feet was not normally determined in the C.D.A. documents but would be decided by development control casework on specific proposals in relation to such criteria as height, daylighting and sunlighting, visual aesthetics and so on.

Supplementary Town Maps, as their name implies, were essentially meant to perform the same general functions as the basic Town Map (see Chapter 6 following) but at a larger scale and, therefore, were used almost entirely to show the planning authority's proposals for town centres where the 6″ to 1 mile (1:10,560) scale could not cope. Like the C.D.A. map, the S.T.M. was to be drawn up at 1:2500 or 1:1250 scale. A S.T.M. could be and often was combined with a C.D.A. map. Typically, a S.T.M. would cover the whole of a town centre or other area of complexity and may have one or more C.D.A.s contained within its area. The difference between the two, in essence, was that whilst the S.T.M. set out the planning authority's general policies with respect to the use and development of land and buildings, the C.D.A. map implied or stated the intention to take physical action in the form of public development or redevelopment, usually backed up by proposals for *compulsory purchase*. Areas already defined as subject to compulsory purchase were to be indicated on the C.D.A. maps and referred to in the written statutory documents which accompanied them.

In general, both S.T.M.s and C.D.A. maps indicated the programmes of development intended by means of separate but concurrent Programme Maps which distinguished areas subject to action within the first two quinquinnia (0–5 years and 6–10 years) and the remainder (11–20 years) of the twenty-year period (or less) to which development plans applied.

There were several serious disadvantages and shortcomings associated with these statutory forms of planning scheme. First of all, they were for many purposes *not detailed enough*. They showed use zones, road and car parks, open spaces, etc. in broad terms but the prescribed statutory form and content did not extend to such important – often crucial – details such as the height, mass, orientation etc. of important building elements, means of ingress and egress for vehicles, traffic management measures, planting and landscaping proposals, and so on. Thus they were lacking in their ability to act as management tools relating the work and ideas of public and private developers, development control caseworkers, users and occupiers of buildings together in a complex series of operations over a number of years.

Secondly, several kinds of detailed planning problems could not be caught up in the C.D.A./S.T.M. net. There are always a number of parts of a town where changes may be expected or intended and where co-ordination and control of day-to-day and year-to-year actions is needed and where the public needs to know in some detail and with some precision what the local authority's intentions and attitudes are. Changes in isolation may be quite modest – a small road widening, some new traffic lights, a new block of shops, the provision of rear access away from the main highway, land purchase to provide a better-shaped site for a local authority depot and store, clearance of a small number of unfit houses and rehabilitation of others. But in combination within a small area and over a limited period of time these can result in substantial change and affect many interests (whether or not in land tenure). The formality and limitations of the statutory detailed plans often militate against dealing effectively and responsively with such common situations. In rural areas the need to provide detailed physical plans for villages and very small towns was not adequately met. By definition a Supplementary Town Map could only be drawn up in areas covered (or intendedly so) by Town Maps, i.e. in the major urban settlements of the county. A large number of settlements, say in the 500 – 2,500 population range could be covered only by the statutory County Development Plan at a scale of 1:63,360! Areas of large-scale mineral working or derelict land reclamation, of holiday chalet and caravan development, of smallholdings, airfield, utility and a host of other complex situations had no statutory physical plan to apply to their particular needs within a general class of problems.

123

'Bottom-drawer' plans

It is hardly surprising that urban and rural planning authorities began to prepare informal, i.e. non-statutory detailed plans to deal with these and a host of similar situations. Urban planning authorities set up or expanded their 'design' or 'redevelopment' sections and got down to the continuing job of drawing up plans for areas of complex physical change; counties prepared village plans to guide developers about the authority's attitude and to help their development control caseworkers. The larger counties with bigger staff resources might have special sections dealing with 'village plans', with 'landscape and reclamation' or in certain areas with 'tourist and holiday development'. The critical output of their work and the medium of their connection with colleagues and the public was (and is) the detailed physical plan. Lacking statutory prescription and blessing such documents became known as *'bottom-drawer' plans*.

Bottom-drawer plans have advantages and disadvantages. They can be drawn up at any scale to suit the particular situation – 1:500 if necessary to show considerable detail; they can show intended use of buildings and land in any way unconfined by statutory classification; they can show trees, levels of ground, bushes, underground utilities, caravan standings, overhead wires and pylon positions, the proprietory names of factories, warehouses, shops and so on. The maps can be annotated to show intentions, hopes, reasons or possibilities for negotiation as necessary thus cutting out cross-referencing between the drawings and a separate written document. But if written documents are necessary their form and content again is unconstrained by Ministerial requirements; they can be as outspoken (or as evasive) as their authors wish. But this very flexibility of scope and content depends in large measure on their *non-statutory* basis and this can mean that the degree to which they represent the wishes and reflect the needs of the community (rather than the whims and fancies of their bureaucratic authors) can vary greatly. Some planning authorities took most, if not all, such bottom-drawer plans to the planning committee or the council to receive views and eventually formal adoption as official policy. Other authorities, whilst stopping short of a formal resolution adopting, say, a village plan would nevertheless relate them in their deliberations about a water main, a road widening, improvement grants and development control cases to a formally adopted village or 'settlement' policy. Thus the latter would indicate which villages were chosen for major development and expansion, which for more modest growth, which were to remain unchanged and which should decline for all sorts of reasons; Durham and Caernarvonshire among many other counties have formally adopted such settlement policies in their development plans. Planning committees may then use, formally or informally, individual village plans or the more detailed and specific vehicles of policy to apply to particular cases requiring decision. But this variation in practice between authorities and areas means that it is difficult for the public and their advisers to know just what degree of formal backing a bottom-drawer plan has. Their very ambiguity can be used by less scrupulous authorities to make bottom-drawer plans seem all things to all men.

Nevertheless it gradually became apparent to planning authorities, developers, the general public and to the Ministry that the advantages of the best of the bottom-drawer system should be embodied in new kinds of *statutory* plans. In 1962 the Town Centre Map was introduced to do just that and to try and overcome some of the drawbacks of the old C.D.A. and S.T.M. system.

The Town Centre Map, as the Bulletin (MINISTRY OF HOUSING AND LOCAL GOVERNMENT AND MINISTRY OF TRANSPORT, 1962) explains, was a means whereby the local authority and the planning authority could make a 'broad and relatively quick assessment of the problems and possibilities of the town centre' as a basis for more detailed decisions. It was *not* a plan suitable for statutory submission to the Minister but rather a document 'which reflects the processes of survey, analysis and policy formulation which lies behind any planning decision or formal proposal for amendment of the development plan'.

The emphasis of the Bulletin is clearly on a new sense of the need for comprehensiveness in problem recognition, analysis and policy design but without the rigidity of statutory procedures. On the other hand, day-to-day decisions, whether arising in the public or private sectors, could not be held back until fully detailed proposals were ready and in statutory form. At some points, the Ministry seems to be close to admitting that statutory procedures for making *plans* can jeopardize the need for flexible and responsive *planning processes* to shape environmental change in the interests of the community (see for example paragraphs 26–32).

There is recognition also of the rôles played in complex change by organizations outside formal government – especially private enterprise – and hence the need for collaborative and complementary rôles which all parties understand. The content of the Town Centre Map was, however, still firmly oriented towards the physical factors of land uses, redevelopment, densities, traffic circulation and the special needs of pedestrians.

Further advances in the statutory forms for detailed planning were discussed and advocated by the Planning Advisory Group in 1964/5. They found that:

> 'the development plans have not provided an adequate instrument for detailed planning at the local level ... they do not convey any impression of how the land will in fact be developed or redeveloped or what other action may be taken in the area to change its character or to improve the environment ... They make no contribution to the quality of urban design. ... The same applies in rural areas covered by county maps, where policies are even less specific.' (PLANNING ADVISORY GROUP, 1965; para. 1:28)

Moreover, the centralized control of the Minister on what were essentially local matters was inappropriate and led to serious delays, affecting public confidence and producing out-of-date plans. The existing system also required the submission of detailed plans often 'where no substantial growth or change is expected' (para. 1:29).

The new local plans

The P.A.G. recommended the introduction of statutory *local plans* of two kinds. Firstly, the '*district plan*' to link between broad strategy and detailed execution, providing broad guidance for development control and giving a context for the most detailed plans – the '*action area plans*' (see below). Traffic and environmental management could be dealt with in a co-ordinated way. The Group admired the Town Centre Map idea (see above, p. 125) and wished, in their district plan suggestion, 'to extend this useful technique to other parts of the town' (paras. 5: 15 – 17). Secondly, the objects of *action area plans* were to provide for a detailed exposition of policies in 'areas which are to be planned and developed, redeveloped or improved in a comprehensive manner over the next ten years or so'. They were to be nothing less than 'the main programme of action for the town'. (5:9) The Group saw the action area plan not just as a means of specifying detailed intentions for controlling change in the short run but as a 'catalyst' to positive planning and a framework for positive development control. It would give guidance to developers about details of layout, including pedestrian and vehicular access, the programming of public investments and provide 'the maximum freedom for the individual designer' (para. 5:12). It would require more imagination and 'a far greater architectural contribution' in planning authorities; it offered great scope for new ideas and techniques in large-scale planning. (5:13 and 14.)

The 1968 Act reflected the almost total acceptance of the P.A.G. report by government and particularly so with respect to action area plans. Section 6 of that Act provided for action areas in *any part* of a local planning authority's jurisdiction and for the need for such plans to be kept under review. They were to be primarily maps supported by written statements. But there would be different plans for different purposes in the same area (subsection 4), which represents a dilution of the comprehensiveness implied by the P.A.G. report. The Act also makes it clear that action area and district plans are to be adopted *locally* after giving publicity to survey results and draft proposals (5:7(1)). The Minister is sent a copy of the plan and he requires to be told of what representations have been made about the draft of the plan and how the planning authority have responded. The Minister still retains some formidable reserve powers, however, and clearly had no intention of handing over detailed planning powers entirely to the local planning authorities. For instance he can require the local planning authority to do better in the way of publicity and consultation before allowing them to adopt a plan (7(4)). Furthermore, objections must be considered at a local inquiry by 'a person appointed by the Minister' or by the authority themselves. When everyone is satisfied (or has given up the struggle for the time being) the local planning authority can adopt the local plan 'by resolution'. But in the last resort the Minister can, in effect, 'call in' the whole of a local plan, either by requiring its formal submission to him for approval in the old fashion of the 1947 and 1962 Acts (1968 Act, section 9 (3) and (4)) or in default make the plan himself (1968 Act, section 12).

The district, action area and subject plans (the latter introduced in addition to the other two recommended by the P.A.G.) between them

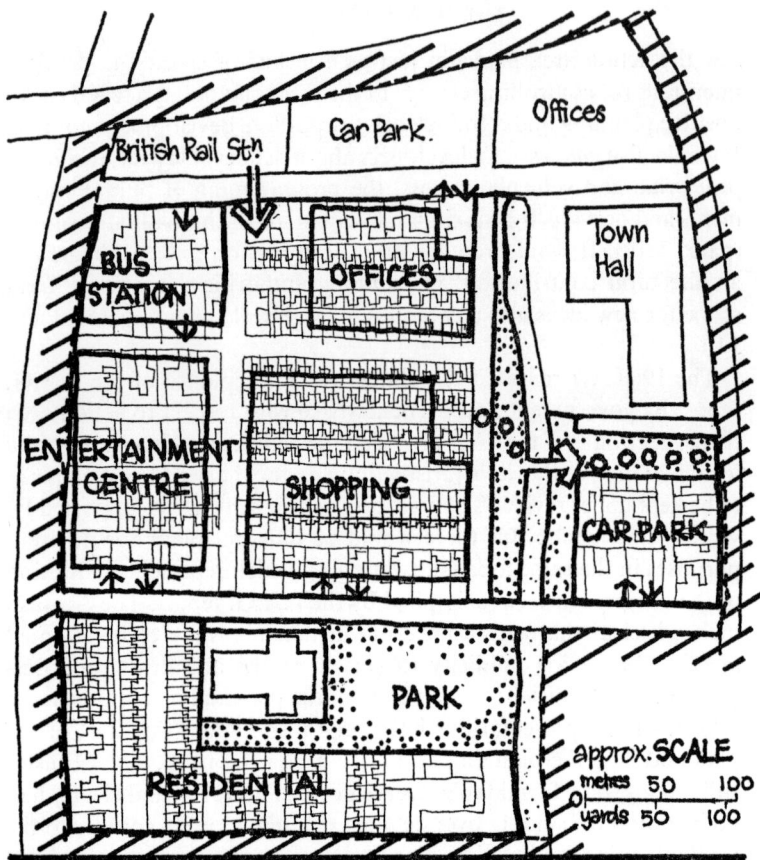

KEY: ⁄⁄⁄⁄⁄⁄ boundary to action area

Proposals:

• predominant uses shown by lettering thus:
  PARK
• public open space
• footpath
• pedestrian bridge
• vehicular access. position and number to be determined

Existing:

• buildings to be retained in existing use shown by lettering thus: Offices
• other existing buildings, to be demolished
• river

Figure 5.1: An 'action area' plan for a redevelopment scheme

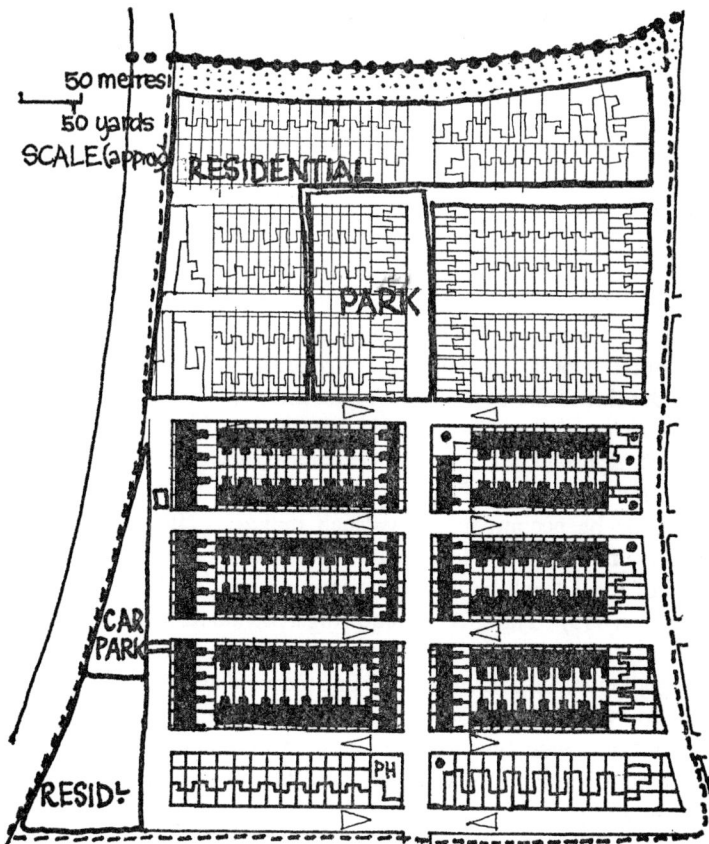

KEY:

- - - - - boundary of Action Area
• • • • boundary of District Plan

Proposals
- predominant uses shown by lettering thus: **RESIDENTIAL**
- houses selected for improvement policy
▷ - one way street with parking arrangements.

Existing
⠿ · district distributor road.
· to be retained as existing shops
• buildings to be demolished

Figure 5.2: An 'action area' plan for a residential area

are thus intended to deal with almost any conceivable situation of short and medium-term complex change in urban or rural areas. They will be the main implementative (public sector) and controlling (public and private sectors) devices for planning in local government. Not only will they depend upon the structure plans for their legal basis (1968 Act, section 6 (9)), but they will be one important means of testing and if need be, modifying and qualifying the broader policies of the structure plan (see Chapter 6).

Local plans 'are designed to enable the local planning authority to formulate in appropriate detail, their purposes for implementing or filling out the policy and general proposals of the structure plan, within the time scale of that plan'. (DEPARTMENT OF THE ENVIRON-MENT AND THE WELSH OFFICE, 1971, para. 19). Local plans will be essentially *drawings* based on the Ordnance Survey map at any scale suitable for their purpose (usually 1:1250 and 1:2500) but they can contain, or be accompanied by 'such diagrams, illustrations and descriptive matter as the local planning authority think appropriate' and all of these 'shall be treated as forming part of the plan'. (1968 Act, section 6 (5)). The effect of requiring a formal resolution to adopt the plan following publicity, representations and an inquiry, and of treating all material drawn, written or otherwise as legally part of the plan is to sweep away most of the worst features of bottom-drawer plans; at the same time the new system embodies most of their undoubted advantages of versatility and ability to be specific about details in an appropriate way.

Since the days of the P.A.G. and the 1968 Act the realm of detailed planning has continued to be the subject of discussion and more ideas about its versatility and range of possible applications have been put forward. In statutory terms, the 1967 Civic Amenities Act created *Conservation Areas* and the 1969 Housing Act brought in the concept and form of the *General Improvement Area*. Conservation Areas, although not wholly negative in intent, are primarily set up by local planning authorities to provide for the extension of the strict controls they already possessed concerning 'listed' buildings of 'special architectural and historic interest' to whole *areas* including trees, water, etc., as well as buildings. In other words, the 'townscape' message preached for so long and so eloquently by CULLEN (1971) and others had at last been given statutory form and 'teeth'. The General Improvement Areas empowered by the Housing Act were

130

much more positive in intent and method and come again as a long delayed reaction to growing concern about the physical, economic and social effects of wholesale clearance of poorer housing. Especially it allowed the housing and planning authorities to be much more selective than before in distinguishing between houses which were so far gone as to be truly 'unfit for human habitation' and those which if improved, by e.g. the addition of a bathroom, hot water, internal W.C., repointing, roof repairs and repainting could usefully be conserved and provide accommodation for a number of years to come.

Intellectual and political debate had raged for a time over the *economic* criteria of improvement *versus* replacement (see, for example, NEEDLEMAN (1966), SIGSWORTH and WILKINSON (1967) and NEEDLEMAN (1968)) and more recently the *social* and political aspects of the problem of areas of 'multiple deprivation', especially in the oldest inner suburbs of our bigger cities, has been recognized. The urban crises in the United States beginning in the late 1960s which gave rise to the Model Cities Program and parallel developments here in the 'community action' movement are examples of this growing awareness. Action Areas, Conservation Areas and General Improvement Areas, the Educational Priority Areas and the Home Office Community Development Projects are related one to another in the changing political and intellectual climate surrounding the urban crises. Some people see in such legislative developments yet more attempts by complacent bureaucrats to paper over the cracks; others see them as hopeful vehicles on which truly redistributive policies and programmes might be mounted.

These issues have not passed unnoticed within the planning profession. ANSON and SHELTON (1971) writing of the 'social aspects of improvement' note the wider approach to local physical environment problems afforded by the 1969 Housing Act but that the 'social condition requires equal attention for a truly comprehensive approach'. Action areas which involve extensive improvement to dwellings, their physical *and* social environment will then require 'a considerable effort in co-ordinating housing, planning, and social action, not only at the local authority level, but also in Whitehall'. We shall turn again to look at the possibility and desirability of new styles and forms of organization in the closing chapters of this book.

Skills and methods in detailed physical planning

In Chapter 3 we saw how detailed physical design (beyond the individual building) was a function of the planning department in British planning authorities. Some authorities continue this function into broader strategic planning. In a few others it is integrated with the development control function but in most there is a separate section of staff dealing with all levels of detailed physical design. In larger cities, like Manchester and Leicester, their work is dominated by town centre redevelopment schemes and redevelopment and improvement of the older residential areas. In rural counties they will be concerned with small town centres and village plans, in holiday areas with caravan sites and chalet developments. In the largest authorities with a diversity of problems, such as County Durham, there will be some specialization of the detailed design function into town centres, village plans, derelict land reclamation and so on, each with its own staff of skilled officers.

There is a lack of adequate information about the persons employed in British planning offices, their age, qualifications, academic and professional backgrounds in relation to the job they do and their sectional affiliations. The following paragraphs are, therefore, impressions gained from the author's experience *in* local government itself and *of* local government via two major research projects as well as impressions gained by reading advertisements for posts in local government. Such limited evidence suggests that the largest single group of professionally qualified people in 'design' sections doing detailed planning are architects. If we add in people who are architects studying for a planning qualification and those qualified both in architecture *and* town planning, we should have accounted for the great majority of the staffs under consideration. There are also small proportions of people qualified in town planning alone, a few landscape architects (some with a town planning qualification too), a few engineers, economists and sociologists. But these groups taken together are far outnumbered by the architects and architect-planners.

Other skills are sometimes consulted (rarely integrated into the designer's work). The design group responsible for, say, a town centre redevelopment plan or a housing rehabilitation and redevelopment scheme often consult other departments in their authority and other authorities, partly for reasons of bureaucratic and statutory procedure (e.g. the statutory duty to consult the District Valuer about the price to be paid for property acquisitions by local government agencies) and partly in order to use the intellectual and professional resources of e.g. lawyers in the clerk's department, chemists on the River Board's staff who are experts in pollution and toxic waste. In very large and complex exercises such as the plan for the Manchester Higher Education Precinct (mentioned above, p. 120) a large range of skills were involved at meetings and in informal contacts with the main consultants responsible. But the focus of the job – the preparation of a detail scheme for promoting programming and controlling physical change – was clearly in the heads of architects and architect planners. Although this last example was the work of private consultants the same holds true for jobs done 'in-house' by large local authorities. So strong is the architect's hold over this kind of work that in some authorities housing redevelopment design is entrusted not to the planning department but to the architect's department. Relationships between them vary from authority to authority, ranging from open warfare to creative co-operation.

Detailed planning has been a feature of British public life for a long time. From small beginnings in the Edwardian decade it came into prominence after 1945 with new towns, rebuilding the bombed cities, clearing and redeveloping the slums and remodelling town centres to try to cope with the motor car. As we have seen, detailed plans will be used in the future as one among a number of vehicles of public policy embracing a widening spectrum of purposes.

Despite all this we know next to nothing about *the actual process of producing the plans themselves.* We have some considerable understanding of the 'input' side, of the need for the plans, the powers available, and the agencies responsible for planning and implementation. We have very extensive reportage of the 'output' side in the form of articles, sketches, photographs and models of the schemes themselves. The *Architects Journal,* the *Journal of the R.I.B.A.,* the *Journal of the Town Planning Institute,** Official Architecture and Planning†* and the *Architectural Review* are perhaps the leading periodicals to have provided month by month, over the years, a continuing account of detailed physical planning in Britain. Between input and output is a process hidden from view; it is concealed in a 'black box' which is all

* Since 1971, 'Journal of the *Royal* Town Planning Institute'.
† Since 1971, renamed 'Built Environment'.

but impenetrable. A number of public service professions have tried to set down in books, articles and conference papers how they go about their jobs. Research workers in social administration, government and management science have provided perspectives and detailed accounts of the jobs done by health visitors, school inspectors, and town clerks. Of late the 'strategic' physical planners have tried to explain clearly not only their recommendation but how they actually went about their jobs (for examples see THORBURN, 1971; WANNOP, 1972; and BUCHANAN, 1966). But the working methods of the detailed planner and designer remain largely a mystery. Why should this be so?

One likely answer is precisely because they *are* designers. Traditionally architecture was regarded as a beaux-arts skill. It was pointless and vulgar to inquire into a process of personal creativity. Architectural education has become more and more associated with universities and undoubtedly this has encouraged architects to become more self-conscious about 'design method' and to talk of 'seeking optimal solutions to multi-dimensional problems' as well as the more traditional 'commodity, firmness and delight'.

Traditional concepts die hard and so do traditional methods in education. Architectural teaching, or more strictly the teaching of *design*, has always been based on the master-pupil relationship, face to face in the studio, at the pupil's drawing board. The pupil is given a problem to solve in the form of a set of given requirements (e.g. of accommodation, access, overall function) and constraints (e.g. of site, location, cost). His job is to 'solve' the problems by means of design but to transcend a merely functional solution by being creative. The creativity refers to physical forms and their spatial relationships to colour, texture, light and shade.

Much experimentation is now going on in architectural education and no doubt much change has already occurred and more is under way. But it would also be true to say that even now the face-to-face, verbal, demonstrative, trial-and-error, master-and-pupil relationship in the studio environment persists. And because of the way in which town planning education has slowly evolved from architectural schools, the studio method dominates too in the teaching of how to *make plans*. Unlike economists, historians, linguists, physicists and most other scholarly people, architects and other designers are possessors and guardians of a *mystery* in the mediaeval craft guild sense. Design as a process was not susceptible to critical examination and intellectual enquiry. One may examine its products and seek to improve upon them but the process itself was regarded as being not susceptible to rationality. There are hardly any books on how to design or how people have actually carried out specific designs.

In the early 1960s a few people began to think otherwise and some of them called a conference in design methods (JONES and THORNLEY, 1962) which sparked off debate and research which has continued and expanded (see GREGORY, 1966). But this is a recent phenomenon and such research has only just begun to influence the current generation of student architects and planners. The qualified professionals working during the last ten years had inherited the craft mystery outlook; no articles or books by them explain the design process in general or with respect to a real problem. A joint working party of the R.I.B.A. and the T.P.I. set up 'to examine the techniques of district and action area plans' ended up by discussing and reporting on everything *except* techniques! (see TOWN PLANNING INSTITUTE, 1970). The report provides a good example of what designers *begin* considering or what they need in order to perform their tasks.

First and foremost they must have an overall sense of the purpose of the design – redevelopment, rehabilitation, extension of a resi-dential area and so on. Also they need to know constituent sub-objectives, e.g. realign this road, provide for 600 dwellings in various categories, allow for 500,000 square feet of shopping floorspace. Equally important are constraints of several kinds, e.g. on land availability, areas of flooding, legal constraints. Standards of all kinds need to be known: e.g. daylighting, sunlighting, road width, ramp slopes, clearance for double-decker buses, commitments made by the authority, especially by extant planning permissions.

Much of this can be transferred to the designer's working matrix, the ordnance survey map, and its tracing-paper overlay on his drawing board. Others will be recorded as notes or underlined in desk-side reference books. The essence of the designer's skill from here onwards is to manipulate spatial arrangements in the two dimensions of the drawing board whilst conceiving the real-world results in three dimensions and respecting all constraints and satisfying all standards, by trial and error with pencil and eraser, to produce a result which is 'efficient, functional and aesthetically pleasing'. It is as

ALEXANDER (1964) has said, a process of trying to match form and context by a process of successive approximations.

We have noted that designers work alone in one sense – in their 'mystery' at the drawing board – but are surrounded by many other people who provided them with facts and opinions about requirements, standards and other 'input' criteria as well as help, criticism and guidance about implementation or specialized interpretations of their work on complex planning schemes. In the last decade or so new specialists have arisen with skills which are contributory to the design process and which are increasingly regarded as indispensable in some cases. An obvious example is the application of cost-benefit analysis in evaluating alternative schemes (LICHFIELD, 1966), the use of linear programming in order to optimize the 'mix' of house-types in a development and the use of 'critical path' techniques in controlling the programme of implementation for a large and complex project.

The constantly increasing complexity of the design of planning schemes has a number of aspects. In part it is the realization that there is much more to it than 'civic design' in the traditional beaux-arts sense and the explicit admission of social and economic issues in their own right. In part also it is the division of labour within the design and construction professions and the addition of new techniques and people possessing fresh knowledge and capability. It is probably fair to say that so far we have failed to provide training of the most appropriate kind for detailed physical planning. Many professions and their associated educational programmes would claim to do so – principally the architects (R.I.B.A.) and the town planners (R.T.P.I.), but to some extent also the chartered surveyors, the municipal engineers and others have also staked claims to this field. The architects have a strong claim in as much as a great deal of expertise in handling three-dimensional construction and design problems is undoubtedly needed. But the architect's traditional education, by emphasizing physical design, the individual building and its immediate surroundings, does not deal at all well with large-scale compositions of many buildings, roads, open spaces, and so on nor with the social, legal, economic, programmatic and other aspects involved. Town planning courses do this job rather better but it is doubtful if in general they are able to develop the same degree of skill in purely physical design as architects. This is especially true of planning courses which aim to create the all-rounder who is equally competent in planning at regional and urban scales (although individual courses and especially versatile students may well turn out really good 'urban designers'.) Attempts to provide the education necessary for detailed physical planning include the R.I.B.A.'s own Urban Design Diploma and new courses such as the graduate pro-gramme in urban design at the University of Manchester. Currently the R.T.P.I. does not encourage the development of such courses within its own framework of 'recognized' courses but allows for a 'local planning' emphasis as one of four within its basically 'generalist' scheme both for its own examinations and for evaluating courses provided by academic bodies. But although the needs and problems of local areas need study, analysis and action in a wide number of ways within an integrated set of frameworks and whilst the physical framework is undoubtedly necessary and important, it is only *one* relevant framework alongside, say, financial, legal and organizational means of achieving integration. Improved training in the skills of physical integration is urgently needed (*si argumentum requiris* . . .) but it cannot stand alone or pre-eminent. But we are digressing from detailed planning *per se* to questions of education and professionalism which will be dealt with in their own right in the closing chapter.

Design, development control and planners

At several points in the book so far and especially in Chapter 4, we have mentioned the close relationships between detailed planning and development control. We close this chapter with a review of the attitudes of planning officers to these relationships and their views on how the situation might evolve in future. The evidence, one again, is drawn from the S.S.R.C.-sponsored research project mentioned before.

In general 'design' personnel welcome the local plans – the district action area and subject plans – introduced by the 1968 Town and Country Planning Act. They praise them for their greater firmness, for their ability to show both precisely how physical change is to occur and what the local planning authority's hopes and intentions are. They welcome them as a basis for furthering and improving the close links between design and development control. They also hope and believe that the new statutory detailed plans will enable better communication with other departments (engineer, parks, public transport) and agencies (district valuer, water authority, hospital board). Officers also believed that far better communication could be achieved with the public because, unlike the old statutory plans, they could actually see the physical proposals the council had in mind. Developers and landowners too would have a vastly better impression of the authority's 'wholesale intentions for an area' and yet the plans would be 'flexible at the same time' (as a Camden officer put it). One wonders just what the overworked word 'flexible' means, but certainly the greater explicitness and the more appropriate 'language' of the new local plans won general approval.

The 1968 Act and the Development Plans Manual require that local plans be drawn up within the framework of the structure plan. This is a hierarchical view in which wider and broader considerations govern the narrower and more specific. Ideally the former is produced *before* the latter. But several people in planning offices had a different view. They believed that the local plans had much to *contribute to the structure plans.* They did not imply a reversal of the usual linear dependency in which the local and specific led by generalization to the strategic; rather they stressed the *interdependency in a continuing sense* between local and structure plans. Thus, the preparation of a structure plan would require some testing for feasibility which would, in part, be done through local planning exercise. For example, a broad intention for population distribution in the structure plan would need to be examined in relation to housing and housing land capacity in local areas. But at the same time the local planning studies and designs could suggest problems, priorities, opportunities and constraints which should be taken up in the structure planning process.

This idea of continuing interdependency was not universally held, however. A Durham County officer suggested that 'development control will find structure plans useless and will have to wait for local plans to be prepared.' A senior officer in the same department felt that planners faced a dilemma; there was so much of immediate value in the new local plans that in focusing effort on them they might 'lose sight of the objectives of the 1968 Act', i.e. a greater focus on policies and their social and economic relevance.

The new local plans were especially welcomed in rural areas such as Herefordshire where the greatest need was for village plans which

138

were more soundly based than hitherto. One officer wanted all physical matters of *local* concern – such as public health, building inspection and development control – carried out in a single agency.

A slightly different view from that which would integrate local planning and development control sees the new local plans as a vital intermediary between strategic considerations and the rôle of control i.e. as a 'translator' in both directions. An officer in Leicester believed that their greatest benefits were in areas of considerable change and that in relatively stable areas (physically), development control would only be helped if district plans 'were expressed in terms of population and so on'. This view was echoed by an officer in the Peak District National Park who said that in leisure areas the problem was to make decisions in relation to the possible 'numbers of cars and picnickers and so on' for which physical-form plans were of limited use. District and action area plans were to be welcomed but more effective planning and decision-making could equally well arise from controlled experiments in recreational areas like the Goyt Valley, where the Board were studying the effectiveness of parking, pricing, free minibuses in 'no-car' zones, etc. in order to discover 'how effective we could be in intervening in the system'. So local physical plans may need to be developed alongside *other* kinds of plans. Another officer in Leicester believed that the district plan should become the 'lowest' level of work in a planning department and that anything more detailed – physical design at the action area scale, development control and all other micro-physical and micro-social activities – should be in 'an integrated agency outside the planning department altogether'.

6 · Strategic, Comprehensive and Structure Planning

The evolution of the British statutory planning system has been discussed from a number of different viewpoints in previous chapters and especially in Chapters 1 and 5. One feature of that evolution is the gradual increase in the scope of policy matters which the statutory system tried to embrace. We have seen that at its origin the statutory plan or 'scheme' was a detailed, physical, mapped representation which derived from the surveyor's plans for land development and the architect's growing interest in 'civic design'. During the 1930s, 1940s and 1950s the need for and the use of the 'scheme' remained basically unchanged but increasingly it was being asked to act as a policy vehicle for wider and wider policy issues – recreation, traffic congestion, the distribution of employment, travel to work and so on. The ideal of 'comprehensiveness' had taken on new forms. No longer did it mean a *physical* overview and statement of policy for an area; in the post-war period, plans made under the 1947 and 1962 Acts were trying to be comprehensive in a wider sense, i.e. to touch on *most if not all* major policy problems.

This chapter begins with an account of the bifurcation of the statutory plans. The 1968 Act formalized what had been evolving informally for some time. In the last chapter we saw how the Act converted the *de facto* bottom-drawer plans into *de jure* local plans; in this chapter we begin by tracing the similar process in which the structure plan emerged as the formal equivalent of a host of policy-oriented studies of population, housing, employment and so on in many planning offices.

In 1964, in what were to be the last days of the thirteen-year Conservative administration, the then Minister of Housing and Local Government, Sir Keith Joseph, appointed a Planning Advisory Group to carry out 'a general review of the planning system' which was not concerned to look at planning policies themselves but was rather to consider 'how the planning system can be made a better vehicle for planning policies. The Group focused on the Development Plans which they called the 'key feature of the system'.

In the Group's opinion (PLANNING ADVISORY GROUP, 1965) plans had acquired 'an appearance of certainty and stability' that was misleading since land-use allocations 'permit a wide variety of use within a particular allocation, and it is impossible to forecast every land requirement over many years ahead'. They recalled that the 1947 Town and Country Planning Act – which, of course, created the Development Plan – when in its drafting stages had put much more emphasis on *principles* whereas when it finally reached the Statute Book it stressed land allocations. This had produced plans which were difficult to keep 'forward looking and responsive to the demands of change', plans that were technically inadequate and which 'do not reflect more recent developments in the field of regional and urban planning'. Activity had been divorced from movements; local government boundaries had added to the difficulties; and, finally, inadequate provisions had been made for the detailed planning of local areas where change was necessary or imminent.

As we now know, the outstanding feature of the P.A.G. report was its proposal to distinguish between the strategic and the tactical, the broad-brush and the detail, the longer-term and the near future. This distinction was also to be reflected in the way responsibility for policies was allocated:

> 'It is in our view essential to recognize and promote two levels of responsibility in plan making – the central responsibility of the Minister for policy and general standards, and the local responsibility for detailed land-use allocation and environmental planning The Minister must retain effective supervision of the policy or structural elements, and the local planning authorities must assume full responsibility for matters of local detail and local interest.' (1:35)

These different levels of planning, with different seats of responsibility and differing *content* would logically take on different *forms*. In the words of the White Paper* which set out the (Labour) Government's response to the P.A.G. report, the forms proposed consisted of:

* Cmnd.3333 of 1967.

'(1) a "*structure plan*" submitted for ministerial approval: this would be primarily a written statement of policy, accompanied by a diagrammatic structure map for counties and major towns only, designed to expose clearly the broad basic pattern of development and the transport system. These structure plans would form the main link between policies on a national and regional level and local planning. They would indicate "action areas", i.e. areas where comprehensive treatment (development, redevelopment, improvement or a mixture) was envisaged in the ensuing ten years.
(2) "*action area plans*" to be adopted locally, showing the shape of development in those areas; and
(3) other "local plans", to meet local needs, again to be adopted locally.'

The White Paper went on to discuss several other matters and pointed out that both kinds of plans would have to take account of government policies by means of full consultation during the process of preparing plans with relevant departments and, where appropriate, with 'the regional planning machinery so that account can be taken, at a formative stage, of regional policy'.

The 1968 Act and the 'Development Plans' manual

The White Paper of 1967 led via the usual parliamentary procedures to the Town and Country Planning Act of 1968 – which embodied procedures for giving statutory force and effect to the new types of planning we have been discussing – and above all to the crucial distinction between structure plans involving government policy and local plans which, whilst extending and amplifying the policies contained in the structure plan would also deal predominantly with local matters.

Another important distinction between structure and local plans is that the former are *essentially written expressions of policies* supported and illustrated as necessary by diagrams which are not related precisely to terrain via a map base, whilst the latter are *essentially physical, cartographic and drawn expressions of policies* supported and explained by a text, figures and so forth. Now concern for the physical environment is one of the cornerstones of British planning ideology (FOLEY, 1960) and we would, therefore, expect the institutions, the procedures, the professional organizations of planning as practised currently to enjoy a very easy transition to the making and implementation of local plans. A full and detailed examination of this milieu forms a major part of our concluding chapter.

But what of structure plans? On what ideology do they rest? Are they comprehensive in the sense of embracing every conceivable facet of social policy or are they limited to the broad physical, geographical and land-use aspects of such policies? In any case what procedures, institutional forms and personnel deployment do structure plans imply? Most important of all, what is their function and status within the whole realm of social policy-making? (See MCLOUGHLIN and THORNLEY, 1972.)

We may hope for some answers to these questions from the 'manual on form and content' produced by the MINISTRY of HOUSING AND LOCAL GOVERNMENT (1970) and the Welsh Office in order to give the local planning authorities advice on the new system. The manual emphasizes that both structure and local plans are to be thought of as

'decision documents relating to those matters over which planning has control or influence ... whether those changes are to be carried through by public agency or private interest' (2.9, p. 7).

But what does 'planning' mean in this context? The statutory ambit of 'town and country planning' or a wider local government, 'corporate' or 'community' planning? How far has 'planning' been widened to take account of the ideas put forward by the P.A.G.? Some guidance is forthcoming in the next few paragraphs:

'Many decisions will be taken by the local planning authority or the local authority which will effect the *physical environment* of parts of their area but which will not be implemented under planning procedures. Such decisions will be particularly relevant to local plans, though some may also find their way into structure plans. As in the past, decisions of this kind will be recorded in the appropriate part of the development plan where they represent the authorities' policy. The scope for their inclusion has been enlarged since *plans under the new system are not confined to matters of land use*; decisions that have been made, for example, to secure the improvement of homes or to establish smokeless zones will thereby be integrated within the framework of the plan.' (2.12 pp. 7–8, *emphasis added*)

143

Authorities are warned against excessive detail which would require formal amendment every time conditions changed. Thus they are advised to exclude details of traffic management schemes (which night need frequent alteration) – these should be dealt with in informal documents or in 'the traffic and transport plan' (presumably under the Transport Act of 1968). Here is a possible weakness of the new plans; that anything of significance must be put in formal, statutory terms and that, therefore, authorities may be tempted (as before) to put things in 'bottom-drawer' form which cannot legally be challenged nor publicly scrutinized.

The functions of structure plans (3.10) are to: interpret national and regional policies; establish aims, policies and general proposals; to provide guidance for development control, a basis for co-ordinating decisions and a means of bringing main planning issues and decisions before the public. The policy *status* of structure plans is here reaffirmed but still there is no clarification of the policy content or ambit. What then does 'structure' mean?

As used in the manual 'structure' means:

'the social, economic and physical systems of an area, so far as they are the subject of planning control and influence. The structure is in effect the planning framework for an area and includes such matters as the distribution of the population, the activities and the relationships between them, the patterns of land use and the development the activities give rise to, together with the network of communications and the systems of utility services.' (3.6, p. 18)

So it seems fairly clear that the structure is a physical structure – a gross urban and sub-regional geography of distributions of activity and the related network of channels. But, and this is crucial to the interpretation, such matters are only germane *'so far as they are the subject of planning control and influence'* i.e. so far as they result in an 'output' of physical development – buildings, land, roads, sewers, changes of use and so on.

Does this really mean that the content of structure plans is essentially defined by the ambit of development control and 'positive' actions relating to physical matters? Perhaps we should look once again at the policy/control relationship, this time as seen by the Development Plans manual.

Certainly the structure plans will contain 'general development control policies for items of structural importance' but they will not include detailed standards, these being 'a matter for local plans' (3.14, p. 21).

> The form and content of the written matter should include a statement of 'the aims, as derived from a study of the national, regional and sub-regional policies for the area and from an examination of the existing structure as revealed by the results of the survey'. (4.11, p. 28).

Physical aims may be in conflict and the tension between 'efficiency' and environment will be a common feature of such conflicts. The written material of the structure plan will indicate how the conflict was resolved, i.e. how aims have been ranked in importance, e.g. that accessibility by private car has been ranked above the architectural qualities of the shopping area of a town.

> 'A statement of aims will be valuable as a broad indication of what the plan is trying to do and the direction which should be taken by the changes it proposes; it will serve to secure the co-ordination of the policies and proposals in the plan. Without this statement, the authority, the public and the Minister will have difficulty in judging the value of individual decisions that make up the strategy.' (4.11, p. 28).

How firm are structure plans? That is to say, how often will they be reviewed, either in whole or part, either in their aims or in the means for realizing them? The 1947 Act had a statutory period of review which was 'at least once in every five years' but, in practice, this requirement was more honoured in the breach than in the observation and the Minister was never inclined to press a point which would have inundated his civil servants with even more work. Under the 1968 Act,

> 'the frequency of reviews is at the discretion of the local planning authority, informed by continuous monitoring of change affecting the area which may call in question the assumptions upon which the plan is based.'

and the Minister may *direct* a review if he feels that a structure plan is significantly affected by e.g. a change in national policy (3.21 and 3.22, p. 23). There is thus much greater fluidity in the formal arrangements than hitherto and maybe they are now more in line with the facts of planning life in local government.

145

This raises the question of how firm major policies can ever be in a world characterized by uncertainties of several kinds. Although uncertainties can be reduced in many ways in order to assist in strategic choices (FRIEND and JESSOP, 1969) there will always be areas where uncertainty cannot *for the time being* be reduced and yet where *a decision must be made quickly*. The new structure plan procedures allow this to be admitted so that:

> 'where proposals are provisional, having had to be made upon incomplete evidence, this should be made clear. If, later, new information calls this proposal into question or suggests how a previously unresolved planning issue should be dealt with, there may be a case for an alteration to the approved structure plan.' (4.17)

The questions which arise here are: how often is this likely to occur? Is not this the rule rather than the exception? The manual seems to imply that the world is a place characterized by complete evidence, timely information, logical sequences of related policy areas and so on – where uncertainty and ambiguity are exceptional. We are inclined to think, with Friend and Jessop, that various degrees and types of uncertainty are of the essence of planning and any planning system must be designed so as to confront that and accept it.

At several points the manual says that local plans are logically dependent on the structure plan for the area. It is, therefore, important to understand the 'policy realm' of the 1968 Act planning system *as a whole* – taking structure and local plans together.

Local plans should apply the strategy of the structure plan, provide a detailed basis for development control by prescribing areas and standards, provide a basis for 'co-ordinating development' (e.g. between the programmes of public and private agencies) and bring local and detailed planning issues before the public (7.3 and 7.4, p. 40).

A little later we are told that district plans are intended to be 'comprehensive and take all planning factors into account' and in particular to apply the structure plan policy for *environment planning and management in urban and rural contexts* (8.6, p. 48). Thus a district plan will deal not only with broadly based policies and longer-term intentions over smaller areas and at a larger scale, but also with more specific and shorter-term proposals and with

146

'development control criteria – the means towards the ends'. For example, such a district plan could relate to a sizeable market, commuter or holiday town of, say, 25,000 people. The district plan would have to

> deal with (the town's) functions in all their complexities as well as with the detailed allocations of land for specific purposes and the choice of sectors in which specific development control criteria should apply.'

Earlier the manual made it clear that structure plans (which imply and are in a sense comprised of, district plans) related to things which were 'subject to planning control and influence'. At this point we are told that the district plan's environmental management rôle will include indicating environmental areas and associated policies. Now we learn that

> 'management includes action that does not fall within the definition of development and is not under planning control'

– for example a civic-trust type paint-up and clean-up scheme (obviously involving the *voluntary co-operation* of shopowners and others). Again, a district plan could state how a general improvement area programme would be a means of encouraging self-help among home owners and

> 'the co-ordination of these actions will be best achieved within the comprehensive framework of district plans.' (8.8, p. 49)

Action Area plans are essentially physical, detailed and short term and may deal with any set of circumstances from city centre development, residential area renewal, shopping and recreation to derelict land treatment and the design of a county park. They should help to co-ordinate the work of several agencies, public and private, large and small.

Structure planners at work

At the time of writing (May 1972) structure planning is still in a state of evolution in British planning authorities. The government's intention is to introduce the new procedures gradually by the issuing of 'commencement orders', under section 105 of the 1968 Act, to planning authorities (or groups of authorities) which in effect apply

147

Part I of the Act to areas so specified (DEPARTMENT OF THE ENVIRONMENT AND THE WELSH OFFICE, 1971). A number of local planning authorities have already begun work on structure plans in anticipation of a formal commencement order – e.g. on Merseyside, in Greater Manchester, Leicester and Leicestershire and in the Brighton area. One of the most (chronologically) advanced exercises is in South Hampshire where the county has joined forces with Poole, Dorset, Portsmouth and Southampton to prepare a structure plan. As we have remarked already, in many respects the Greater London Development Plan, though unique in a strict sense (having been prepared under the London Government Act 1963), nevertheless, closely resembles a structure plan for the metropolis and can be studied as such.

But even as early as the summer of 1970 when visits were made by the author and his colleagues to seventeen local planning authorities in Britain (see Chapter 3), the spirit if not the letter of structure planning was abroad. There was a considerable amount of work going on to prepare the ground for structure planning, even in those authorities which had not been notified informally that they would be invited to submit structure plans. Thus in the London area, we had the opportunity of studying some aspects of the Greater London Development Plan in the G.L.C. itself, and in Bromley and Camden we heard of some of the implications of the G.L.D.P. for local planning and development control in the boroughs.* But Leicester, Manchester, Newport and Southend among the other authorities visited were all at that time pressing on with structure planning exercises (all of them in collaboration with neighbouring authorities) having been included in the 'first wave' of intended commencement orders.

From these first-hand experiences, from formal interviews, from documents, from informal conversation and discussion, we were able to form some impressions of how the new plans were affecting the authorities, how the plans were likely to be prepared, by whom and using what techniques. Furthermore, we were able to record the views of planners on the implications of structure plans for planning

* At the time of our visits the London boroughs were required to prepare their own structure plans within the framework of the G.L.D.P. and in consultation with the G.L.C.; the 1971 Act repealed that requirement so that now the boroughs will prepare *local* plans only, regarding the G.L.D.P. as the structure plan for their areas.

and other policies and their relevance for implementation, detailed planning and development control.

The fact that structure planning is in its earliest stages makes it difficult to evaluate with any sureness. An atmosphere of speculation and improvization surrounds its inception. We have seen so far in this chapter that the *purposes* of structure planning are far from being clear and so it is understandable and perhaps right that cautious experimentation should be the order of the day. We shall be equally exploratory in the sections which follow. First we shall look at the skills and methods which are implied by structure plans and then we shall look at the limited evidence on the methods and skills actually being used.

The most recent regulations (DEPARTMENT OF THE ENVIRON-MENT, 1971) specify 'the matters to which the policy formulated in a structure plan is required to relate'. Broadly speaking these are the same as those listed below (on page 173) when we examine the Development Plans manual. These matters – including employment, housing, transport, shopping and education – are again required to be considered in the written statement of the plan in several ways, i.e. in relation to:

The existing structure of the area, current needs and opportunities for change;
projected or likely changes and their effects;
the possibility of new town development or town expansion;
the size, composition and distribution of the population, and the state of employment and industry', the assumptions on which estimates are based both currently and 'at such future times as the local planning authority think appropriate for the purposes of the plan';
regional economic planning considerations;
social policies and considerations;
'the resources likely to be available';
broad criteria for development control;
the relationships between policies in the plan;
policy relationships and the extent of agreements with adjoining authorities;
any other relevant matters.

These statutory requirements, the evidence of the G.L.D.P. and the sub-regional studies (JACKSON, 1972) suggest the range of skills and aptitudes which will be needed by the local planning authorities. Studies of population size and composition cannot be divorced from the economic prospects in terms of industrial and commercial activities. In addition these imply analyses of labour markets from both the supply and demand sides. Studies of income and expenditure, household size and composition, will be needed for formulating policies about housing and shopping provision. The skills needed here include demographic and economic forecasting and statistics including multivariate techniques.

All or most of these policy fields need to be studied from a spatial viewpoint too since land is a resource which must be managed and distance is a deterrent to interaction which affects many policy fields (e.g. journey to work and transport planning, the working of the housing and labour markets). The present and especially the future distributions of population, households, incomes, motor cars and so on must be studied in a suitable mesh of small areas which constitute the area as a whole. The skills involved here include urban modelling, usually by mathematical methods, and significant parts of urban sociology, urban economics and urban geography.

All of this work will go on in a vacuum unless the people involved possess insights derived from many sources – the public, their elected representatives and various interest groups. Beyond the statutory requirement for 'public participation' built into the Act (sections 3 and 7) and the regulations (Parts II and VIII *inter alia*) there will be a need for good intelligence systems, social surveys and a conscious effort to interpret the policy significance of daily routine administration and the provision of various services such as housing, development control, education and the social services. Skill in social survey, data, information, intelligence and administration will need to be allied with political aptitude and awareness and the ability to communicate with many different people in appropriate ways.

In order to do all this, structure planners will need skill in building inter-departmental, inter-authority, authority-to-public, authority-to-government and many other bridges in order to explore, discuss, persuade and respond. John POWER (1971) calls the possessors of these networking skills 'reticulists' and recalls that American political parlance has long recognized such people as 'fixers'. The planners will need to consider questions of implementation very carefully. Thought about *who* will implement the plan, through what *powers*, with what *sanctions* and *resources* will be vitally necessary. A little later we consider the experience of the G.L.D.P. Inquiry and show how this lesson has had to be learned by the Greater London Council and its planners. Forethought for implementation brings in central government departments, nationalized industry, private industry and commerce and a host of other groups and instructions both public and private. In a reformed system of local government in 1974 the rôle of the district councils in the counties and metropolitan areas will be crucial since much implementation of structure plans is likely to occur via local plans and development control, both of which are to be operated largely by the district councils. The structure planners will need a sound understanding of how government and the private sectors work in general and how certain parts (e.g. the local education department, the construction industry) work in more detail. In particular an understanding of local government finance and other sources of public capital and revenue will be vital.

To discharge all these responsibilities adequately, the skills of social and public administration, local authority management, the 'fixer' and communication skills will be needed.

Monitoring the day-to-day and year-to-year *outcomes* of structure planning will not occur for some time. But during the preparatory stages it is important to consider how these outcomes (in terms of services, public and private investments, regulatory actions and key variables like population, housing, jobs, incomes) will be monitored, who will collect the data, who will transmit it, process, store and analyse it, who will respond to such intelligence and how policy makers are to be alerted to the results of all this effort. Once again skills in survey, data and information techniques, and an understanding of intelligence systems will be required. But so much depends not just on building *stocks* of information but in making it *flow* in the right form and to the right people so that action may result; for these reasons, the structure planners must again possess aptitudes of political awareness and skill in communication.

Even a rapid (and no doubt inadequate) forecast of some of the skills, methods and aptitudes that structure planning implies reveals a wide diversity of intellectual disciplines and professional domains. It includes mathematics and statistics for modelling and much else, the social sciences of economics, social and public administration, the spatial and environmental sciences of geography, ecology and land

151

resource management. Some skills do not exist as formal acaedmic or professional fields, e.g. the fixers, the intelligence-system operators.

This speculative view of the human capabilities likely to be needed in structure planning may be compared with the contributions made by planners and research workers at a conference held during the period in question (CENTRE FOR ENVIRONMENTAL STUDIES, 1971). Forecasting and 'microprojection' techniques were featured in an account of the South Hampshire structure plan; a Lowry-type mathematical model had been developed for structure planning in Cheshire; threshold analysis was tested in a study of the Falkirk-Grangemouth area whilst monitoring procedures and information systems were being developed in order to advance the Leicester-Leicestershire structure plan. The conference was aware at several points of the need for skills which transcend the 'hard' specific techniques.

> 'The separation of parts of the planning procees should be avoided . . . decisions must be taken which relate directly to other departments. . . . At the present it is likely that many structure plans will be undertaken without proper organization for corporate planning.' (p. 41)

To what extent are these skills and qualities represented *now* amongst those engaged in the inception of structure planning? How far are they likely to be available in the foreseeable future? The evidence gained from the study of planners in the seventeen authorities mentioned before sheds at least some light on these questions.

Of the seventeen authorities studied, three had no strategic 'plan' staff as such. Crawley, being a district council, relied on the West Sussex County Planning Department staff for such work, Skelmersdale similarly looked to Lancashire (and to the consultants' 'Master Plan' for the new town) and Ross and Cromarty to the Highlands and Islands Development Board and the closely allied East Ross working group. Three authorities – Newport, Southend and Herefordshire – had integral 'plan' and 'design' sections in their planning departments. All of the others had a separate 'plan' section which dealt with strategic, broad-brush studies of the whole administrative area (or larger areas), studies of specific aspects of planning such as retailing or transport, plans for the whole area such as the county development plan, information and intelligence services and so on.

AGE
IN YEARS
- 19 OR UNDER
- 20-24
- 25-29
- 30-34
- 35-39
- 40-44
- 45-49
- 50 OR OVER

SALARY (£)
- 1000-1499
- 1500-1999
- 2000-2499
- 2500-2999
- 3000-3499
- 3500 OR OVER

FIRST DEGREE
OR DIPLOMA
- PLANNING
- ARCHITECTURE
- ENGINEERING
- SURVEYING
- GEOGRAPHY
- ECONOMICS
- SOCIOLOGY
- OTHER
- NONE

HIGHER DEGREE
OR GRADUATE
DIPLOMA
- PLANNING
- ARCHITECTURE
- ENGINEERING
- SURVEYING
- GEOGRAPHY
- ECONOMICS
- SOCIOLOGY
- OTHER
- NONE

PROFESSIONAL
QUALIFICATIONS
- T.P.I.
- R.I.B.A.
- I.C.E.
- I.Mun.E.
- R.I.C.S.
- OTHER
- NONE

NUMBER OF
AUTHORITIES
- 1
- 2
- 3
- 4
- 5
- 6
- 7 OR MORE

TIME SPENT IN
PLANNING, OTHER
THAN CONTROL
- UP TO 20%
- 21-40%
- 41-60%
- 61-80%
- 81-100%

SCALE: % RESPONDENTS
0   25   50   75

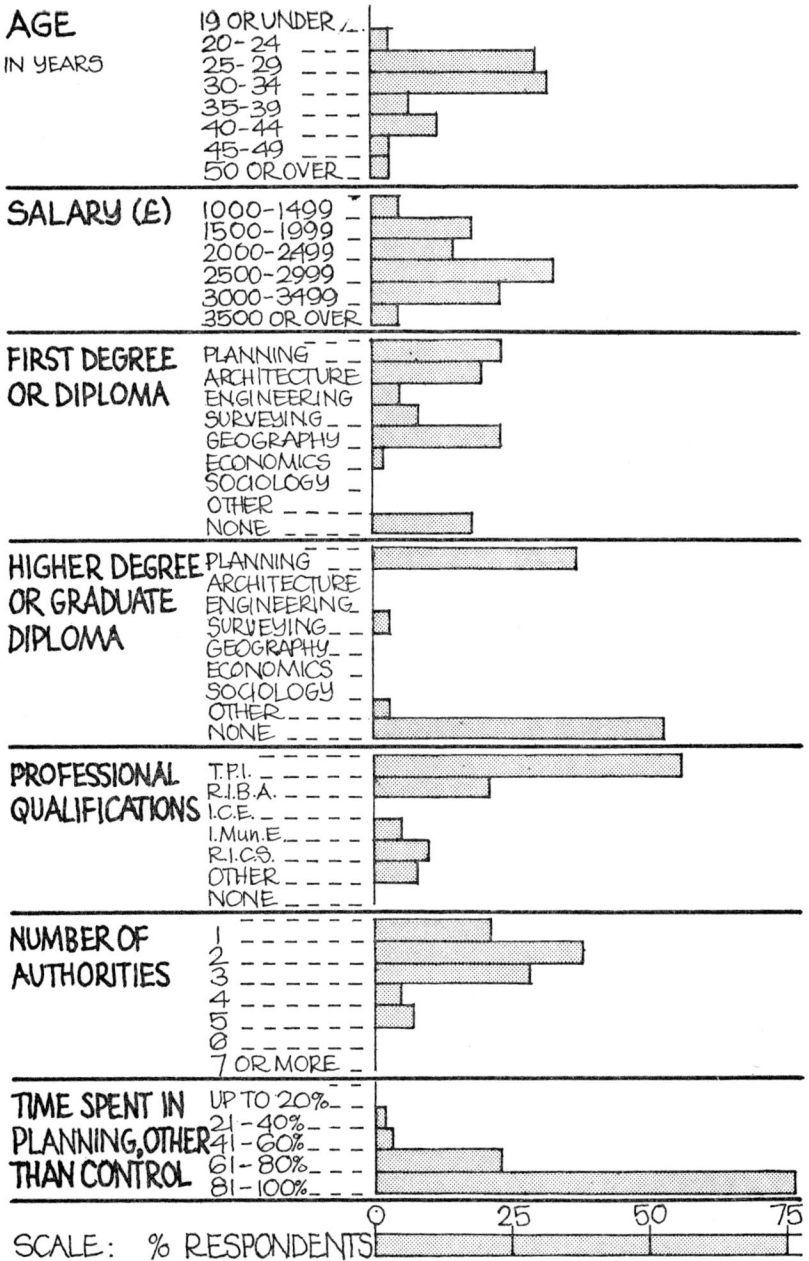

Figure 6.1: Age, qualifications and experience of 'plan' people

In some large authorities (e.g. Durham, G.L.C.) the 'plan' function was subdivided geographically or, more usually, functionally to deal with particular problems in some depth. Much of this work already approximates to the preparation of structure plans whether it is being done under a formal or informal invitation of the central government department or not.

We remarked when discussing the academic and professional qualifications of development control staff, that 'hard' reliable evidence was difficult to obtain. Our own survey was very limited both in its scope and in size. We sent questionnaires to the forty-one officers who worked in 'plan' or 'design' in the authorities we visited and we had thirty-seven usable replies. Of these officers, twenty-one worked in 'plan' and sixteen in 'design'. Such small numbers can result only in impressions about the factors in which we are interested. Nevertheless, most of our findings on this small scale seem to bear comparison with larger-scale enquiries, some with local government staffing generally (COMMITTEE ON THE STAFFING OF LOCAL GOVERNMENT, 1967) and some specifically with the staffing of planning departments (e.g. TOWN PLANNING INSTITUTE, 1964 and GOSS, 1963).

Of 'plan' and 'design' staffs taken together, 23% had a first degree or diploma qualification in planning, 23% in geography and 20% in architecture. (18% had no undergraduate qualification.) 8% were qualified surveyors, 5% were engineers and only one person in the sample (2%) was qualified in the social sciences – economics in this case. We believe it is fair to assume that the architects, engineers and surveyors were primarily engaged in 'design' work and therefore that 'plan' work is overwhelmingly carried out by people with initial academic qualifications in town planning or geography.

About two-fifths of plan and design officers had a higher degree or post-graduate qualification in planning; half of these were 'design' officers – predominantly architects – who had obtained an academic planning qualification. The other half was overwhelmingly comprised of geographers working in 'plan' sections. 56% of all 'plan' and 'design' officers were corporate members of the Town Planning Institute.

We showed in Chapter 4 that in comparison with their development control colleagues, 'plan' and 'design' staffs were better paid, better educated and qualified and tended to be more firmly wedded to their work in as much as few of them had any experience of development control. These officers were dominated by two groups with a double qualification, either academic, professional or in a combination of both, the *architect-planners* who dominate the 'design' sections and the *geographer-planners* who form the largest single group in 'plan' sections. In the latter kind of work – that which closely resembles structure plan work – there are also several people who are straightforward *town planners* either academically, professionally or both. That is to say they have a degree or diploma in planning plus corporate membership of the R.T.P.I. Sometimes the professional qualification will have been gained without academic education but these people are in a minority since 85% of all such officers were graduates.

More recent evidence gained from a current investigation (spring 1972) of the preparation of a structure plan for a northern metropolitan county tends to confirm these findings. Of the nine most senior officers, i.e. those with directive responsibility for defining broad tasks and managing their accomplishment, no less than five were geographers including the study director. One officer was an economic geographer, one a transportation engineer, one an architect and one an economist. All of these senior men save one (the traffic engineer) had a planning qualification also. We believe that detailed study of the staffing of strategic and structure planning work, including its associated research and intelligence activities, would reveal that *such work is dominated by town planners and especially by those first qualified in geography.*

Despite the intellectual domination of the field by the spatial and locational skills, a very wide diversity of tasks are currently undertaken. This applies to both large and small authorities although the bigger ones can usually achieve a greater degree of specialization and possibly sophistication in these manifold tasks. For example, at the time of our visit (June 1970), the G.L.C. had a Director of Research and Intelligence whose group provided comprehensive statistical services, library facilities, systems analysis, methodological advice, special studies of housing, recreation, environmental and community studies, population, economic, intelligence, evaluation methods, employment, health and welfare, education and children, residential studies, regional planning, services and amenities, etc. The Plans Branch included specialist direction and advice on the Greater

155

London Development Plan itself, the 'initial development plan' (i.e. the L.C.C., Middlesex and other development plans still legally current until the formal approval of the G.L.D.P.) and a section of officers dealing with problems of plan making in the London boroughs as seen from a G.L.C. standpoint. Although the G.L.C. is exceptional, the larger authorities like Durham showed similar evidence of specialization of these plan/research/intelligence functions. The new county authorities (after 1974) and especially the populous and complex metropolitan counties such as Greater Manchester, will doubtless find they need access to a wide range of specialist advice to discharge the whole range of structure plan work.

Relationships between 'plan' and development control work

We found as a general rule that whenever there was a functional division or section for broad-brush planning and intelligence work separated from the rest of the department (as e.g. in Manchester, Durham and Camden) this section had very little to do with development control casework. The opposite applied to places like Southend and Lincoln where everyone worked in the same large office, without rigid divisions of responsibility; at Crawley the policy functions are limited in extent (guidance coming from West Sussex County Council) and most of the work was in fact control. In all cases, as we have seen in chapter 5, 'design' staff play by far the greatest part in giving advice to their caseworker colleagues.

Of course, this is precisely what one would expect. Design staff deal largely with physical detail and so do caseworkers. The kinds of applications most often referred to design staffs were located in town centres (e.g. in Oxford), conservation areas (e.g. Lincoln) or other areas where large scale or complex changes were occurring. In addition, specific functional types of application were passed on according to the authority's major problems – examples are 'listed' buildings in Lincoln, advertisements and shops in Newport and large-scale residential proposals in Oxford.

The 'languages' of development control and detailed physical planning are compatible and, therefore, we find that there is considerable interaction and support between their respective staffs. Over the years town and country planning has taken on more and more concern for the social, economic and environmental policy issues which lie behind physical plans as such and the changes high-lighted by the P.A.G. report and the 1968 Act reflect this gradual development of British statutory planning. Obviously there can be no *direct* relationship between control and strategic, policy-oriented plans such as structure plans. For example, a single application for a petrol filling-station or a house extension or a change of use from cotton mill to wholesale automobile-parts warehouse has, of itself, no direct implications for the generation, or review of policy. But in aggregate development control work has considerable relevance to strategic policy from several viewpoints. Many planning authorities have found that over a period of a year or two, the granting and refusal of filling-station applications not only pointed to the need for a policy (if none existed) but could serve as a check on the relevance, feasibility and effectiveness of the current policy. A con-centration in part of a town of a considerable number of applications for extensions to existing houses may be a check (say, on population distribution) as well as being early warning of further changes which might be needed in policies for water supply, sewerage, primary schools (within its own purview) and for electricity, gas and other utility services (provided by other agencies). One change-of-use application from disused cotton mill to exhaust and tyre distributor has no policy significance at all, but a rise in the frequency of similar applications over a period of time could signify or confirm imminent changes in the demand for certain kinds of labour, the patterns of journeys to work, the need for retraining programmes, changed demands on the telephone services and so on. All of these have policy significance for the local planning authorities as well as for the Department of Trade and Industry, the Passenger Transport Executive, the Post Office and several other agencies, singly and in combination.

We found that many planning officers were aware of the great potential relevance of development control to policy. But equally we found evidence of some lack of awareness of these vital but subtle and indirect relationships and quite frequently some criticism of structure plans because they would provide no guidance for develop-ment control. These impressions received in conversation with the officers we met in our fieldwork suggested that some people at least were still unable to realize the full significance of changes introduced by structure plans. In particular there were those who seemed inclined to think of the 'key diagram' (as it has now been dubbed officially) as a new generalized kind of land-use plan rather than as *one* of several ways of indicating the policies embodied in the structure plan – which in the words of the Act is primarily 'a written statement'.

This view was expressed quite strongly by some development control officers in the G.L.C. They were not enthusiastic about structure plans which would be 'worse than useless' for developers, landowners and households. The current old-style plans enabled one to 'see a picture' and development control was a powerful tool in making this picture turn into reality. These G.L.C. officers agreed that action area and district plans would be very useful to development control work but they regretted the removal of map-based zonings or land-use allocations from structure plans. Nobody, they said, would know precisely what the authority's policies were and that included caseworkers too.

These interviews from which these impressions were drawn took place in June and July 1970. Almost exactly a year later some rather more formal exchanges (involving learned counsel at the G.L.D.P. Inquiry) were to reveal that the G.L.C. officers' regret at the passing of the zoning principle from structure plans had not prevented their using the Metropolitan Structure Diagram as if it were an old-fashioned land-use allocation map.

Counsel for objectors who raised this point following an appeal made relating to the development of a 'Trade Mart' at Osterley Park, Middlesex told the G.L.D.P. inquiry on 6 July 1971 that at the previous appeal hearing

'The Greater London Council produced an ordinance [*sic*] survey overlay which they said showed precisely the boundaries of the M4 linear park in relation to the ordinance map and, of course, to the metropolitan open space. . . . the Assistant Solicitor to the Greater London Council attempted to show me how the boundaries on this map, the Greater London Development Plan, the metropolitan structure map . . . related precisely to the ordinance survey plan.' (G.L.D.P. Inquiry, 1971, p. 3)

The debate which followed resulted in a statement by the chairman of the Inquiry Panel that such a use of the metropolitan structure diagram was mistaken and he hoped it would not be done again.

Three weeks later *The Times* (27 July 1971) said that in Mr. Layfield's opinion, if a map like this were used

'as an instrument of development control, or as the basis for a local plan in relation to any site, it ceased to be a solely strategic device . . .'.

The newspaper notice also added that

'The G.L.C. has since submitted changes to the written statement in the plan making it clear that notations on the map do not affect existing rights or permissions, and must not be construed as zoning for land-use allocations; and that its boundaries are not precise.'

This well-documented and publicized situation suggests that there may be problems of understanding the full significance of plans like the G.L.D.P. It would also seem that planning professionals themselves are not entirely clear as to the rôle of structure plans in relation to other aspects of the planning function. We reviewed the opinions of the planning officers we met during the course of our research in the closing sections of Chapter 4.

The evidence and the opinions put forward in this chapter show that strategic and structure planning is to some extent an extension of a part of the town planning function as it has existed since 1947–8. That is to say, the old-style development plans needed population forecasts, land resource inventories, assessments of housing need, spending power and so on. During the 1960s, increasing attention was paid to public and private transport in relation to land-use planning. But under the old dispensations, the resulting 'town maps' and 'county maps' were still unequivocally land-use maps expressing policies for the use and development of all land in the authority's jurisdiction.

Structure plans are in many ways quite different. They must treat social and economic issues much more directly as such and not simply in relation to spatial and land development problems. It is true that they will, still tend to have such an emphasis, much as P.P.B. (Planning, Programming and Budgetting) systems may emphasize capital and revenue, and manpower plans will emphasize human resources. But structure plans, like these other complimentary forms of strategic planning, will need close inter-relationships one with another in a policy realm within local government. As we have seen, it is folly to divorce such planning from considerations of programming and implementation but it is equally illogical to expect them to have *clear-cut and direct* relationships with day-to-day action. They are conceived and expressed in higher-level languages – the languages of *policy*. To try and translate, by means of tracing-paper overlays or otherwise, between a structure plan diagram and a specific development proposal is to be just as insensible of the language difference as to consult a table of figures in a broad financial plan to see whether or not a filing cabinet can be purchased.

The beginnings of structure planning in Britain suggest that those involved may, consciously or otherwise, be aware of the distinctions between action and policy, tactics and strategy. The lack of much contact between the policy/research/intelligence sections and development control/design in planning offices is one bit of evidence of this. But there are two main attendant dangers. First, that there may be a lack of awareness of the importance of building and maintaining rich, complex *indirect* vertical connections between say, development control and structure planning. Secondly, there may be insufficient *direct* horizontal connections being established between structure planning and *other* forms of policy work in *other* departments and authorities. We must now turn to consider the 'policy realm' in local government.

7 · Policy in Local Government

What is policy?

To ask such a question is to enter a discussion of government itself. Policies are more generic than discreet actions (such as clearing a street of unfit houses or electrifying a railway line) and more specific than broad social goals (such as raising the standards of mobility or providing decent accommodation for all). Discussions of policy involve discussions of ends and means but this takes us into difficult realms where the crucial question is likely to be what model of government are we adopting for the purpose of discussing policy in a useful context.

Government may be taken to represent a set of institutions which asserts a legal claim to take decisions which are binding on all persons and institutions within its bailiwick. Liberal models of government are based on the notion that the demands of the community are the key factors leading to responses in government; by contrast, authoritarian models are essentially based on the converse. Government should not be conceived of as a monolithic entity since it depends upon considerable and complex divisions of labour within itself. The analogy with the 'single-minded' corporate firm has many weaknesses too; it is probably better to compare government's internal structure with the set of firms comprising the whole of an industry. So government can be regarded as a set of

> 'initiating and responsive entities, conceivably independent of or regardless of information from the outside world. Reciprocally, political relationships may occur within society independently of the interventions of government.' (ROSE, 1971)

Similarly there is little point in regarding 'the community' in a monolithic fashion; it too must be seen as a set of overlapping and shifting groups with different needs, values and demands. The resulting highly complex interchanges between two sets of institutions – government and community – invokes the cybernetic model of governance or steersmanship (Greek, *kubernan* = steersman; Latin, *gubernare* = to steer). But the highly complex models which are the proper domain of cybernetics make it difficult if not impossible to disentangle causal relationships with any precision whilst maintaining a holistic approach. Ends and means are not only connected in a vast 'seamless web' of multiple feedback relationships but the relative strengths of the connections, let alone their structure, must be considered dynamically. 'Means' at one point in such networks are simply ends when seen from another viewpoint. This suggests, however, that we might identify policy as the ends or intentions as seen by the governors as a whole or some particular set of governors (ROSE, op. cit.). But to leave the matter there may result in the interpretation of policies as rather vague and abstract ideals which, by implying that everyone should 'stand up and cheer', lack the capacity to provide operational criteria to judge progress towards or retrogression from defined ends.

We would rather look on policies as being more identified with and conscious of means as well as with a broad sense of direction. In this light they would be intermediary between goals on the one hand and specific programmes of action on the other. They would enable the actions of government to be judged on the basis of rationality in at least two ways: firstly by providing operational statements about how positive ends were to be sought (or negative outcomes avoided) and secondly by affording frameworks for day-to-day administrative actions and programmes.

Policies in government are thus the basis of day-to-day administrative actions and decisions. If we regard the ongoing process of decision making as a hierarchical network then policies occur near the top. There, they serve as statements of means to provide for progress towards the goals and objectives of the organization.

Policies must, therefore, interpret goals and 'translate' them into operational form so as to include objectives which are more precise, more operational statements. Such statements can provide a framework for even more specific programmes of actions relating to a geographical or functional subsystem.

For example, a goal of government may be to improve the housing conditions of the population at large. Objectives would then be expressed in terms of *policies* to clear the slums, give subsidies to council housing, build new and expanded towns, legislate for improvement areas and conservation areas, and so forth. The presence of policies makes civil servants, local government officers, housing managers, architects, builders, investors, landlords and tenants aware of the framework within which decisions can be made and also acts as a guide to the makers of individual decisions.

FRIEND and JESSOP (1969) regard planning as a process of strategic choice 'if the selection of current actions is made only after a formulation and comparison of possible situations over a wide field of decision relating to certain anticipated as well as future situations'. Thus, local authorities are both *regulators* of the actions of all kinds of individuals and institutions as well as *providers* of the goods, resources and information to give a variety of services to the community.

They develop a conceptual model to discuss the nature of planning and this consists essentially of interactions between a 'governmental system' and a 'community system'. Both of these are recognized to be complex in themselves and, therefore, their relationships have a very high variety indeed as they cross the interface between people and officials – between 'us' and 'them'.

These interactions are typified by the emergence within the community system of a 'situation' – we might equally well call it a problem. The problem could be routine and trivial in itself, such as an application for a vehicle road fund licence; or it might be extremely complex and unusual, such as a change in the use of private transport.

In the simplest version of the Friend and Jessop model such a situation or problem crosses the interface between the community system (where it originates) to the governmental system where it undergoes 'appraisal' leading to a choice of action. When a problem is perceived by the governmental system, having crossed the interface from the community side, it is usually translated into terms acceptable or meaningful to the governmental system. Put another way, the problem as experienced and expressed by a family or a section of the community may well be interpreted in quite a different way by the public service agencies whose job it is to take note of the problem and act upon it. The problem may be very unitary and all-of-a-piece to those who first suffer it but if the bureaucratic structure is a

163

fragmented one, the problem is likely to be perceived as fragmented by the bureaucracy since they are unable to see it whole. Even an inter-agency or interdepartmental group is only a partial solution since, in almost every such case, effective *action* can be taken only within the existing structure. Working mothers have a 'keeping-the-kids-occupied-from-nine-till-four' problem but this will be percieved quite differently by (a) the education department, (b) the boards of governors of the schools concerned, (c) the head teachers and staff, (d) the school meals organizers, (e) the traffic wardens, (f) the local public transport authorities.

Sometimes a problem *cannot officially be perceived at all if there is no agency in existence to deal with it*. A good example is the 'serving the rural community' problem which is on the fringe of responsibility for the Post Office, the local health and education authorities, public transport operators, ambulance service, retail distributors and so on. The rural community is nobody's child; a current cliffhanger is provided by watching to see if the county councils will take this problem over and if so if they will they create a special agency to do so.

When government takes action it results in a change in the community system so that the *next problem arises in a different context*. Thus FRIEND and JESSOP refine their model and show that:

> 'the extent to which the context of operations change will depend on the governmental system's capacity to *learn* about the changing pressures and relationships of the community system. Through such a learning process, the appreciation of factors relevant to decision-making may gradually change, so that the range of situations covered by operational policies will either extend or diminish over time; meanwhile, objectives may gradually become modified and the ability to mobilize resources become either more or less constrained.' (pp. 105–6)

This leads to a number of important conclusions about the nature of the public planning process. First, the nature of uncertainties surrounding the appraisal of any problem or situation is 'unlikely to be fully perceived by any one individual or specialist group within the governmental system'. Secondly, for all sorts of good reasons, urgent situations do get attention and action more quickly and thus lead to more rapid processes of appraisal and choice. So that:

'the process by which the community presents situations requiring intervention by government is essentially a continuous one: it is not like the presentation of a brief to an architect an engineer as a result of which some set of related choices must be made in order to produce a "finished" design by some particular point in time . . . the governmental system must, whether consciously or otherwise, develop *predictive models* of the community system and the way its internal relationships can be expected to change and develop over future time.' (p. 109)

This is precisely the cybernetic principle of developing an adaptive control mechanism whereby it is necessary for the control device (Friend and Jessop's government system) to evolve and grow in *variety* by mapping within itself the variety of the disturbances (coming from the community system) which it has to control (ASHBY, 1956; BEER, 1966).

The origin of policies

How *do* policies originate? There seems to be a large number o different ways in which this can happen.

Let us first consider the abstract ideal embodied in the conventional model of making a plan. This, as we have seen in earlier chapters derives from a misapplication of the design methods of architecture and engineering to 'comprehensive' city planning and public policy-making. In the design process it is clearly necessary to establish the objects of the exercise at the very outset and this is called the development of the brief in architectural and engineering circles. Where projects are large and complex – e.g. a power station, oil refinery, airport terminal, etc. – the finite statement of intention must be capable of being drawn, modelled and otherwise specified. This then serves as a means of controlling the business of building and engineering works until the project is completed.

When this design-professions model is applied in government it appears as a *goal-setting* stage in which an attempt is made to thrash out by debate among professionals, elected representatives and community groups the overriding aims of a planning exercise.

At a slightly more specific level, goals may be worked out in terms of their implications for policies and programmes either as a single set of suggestions or as a set of alternative developmental or other

165

strategies (e.g. SOUTH HAMPSHIRE TECHNICAL UNIT, 1970). Here the policy worker faces a dilemma: either he must stop short and maintain a truly long-range and comprehensive view (or set of views) on which to invite debate and risk the criticism that they are too ill-defined and vague to generate useful discussion; *or* he must spell out all the details and invite the criticism that in creating a blueprint for the future he is claiming omniscience or arrogating to himself dictatorial powers with which to coerce all and sundry into fitting the Procrustean bed of his design.

It is easy to see that policies can arise quite easily out of professional views, even fashions. For some time, British planners were strongly influenced by what ASH (1966) has called 'the linear-city fad'. At the intra-urban or civic-design scale fashions have affected the design of housing areas – pedestrian/vehicular segregation, patio gardens, Radburn layouts and so on.

Perhaps the most famous example of a policy instrument arising from the views of a number of influential people in public and professional life is the green belt idea (THOMAS, 1970). Sometimes policy origins are more dramatic as for example the changes which occurred as a result of the Rachman scandal and the Milner Holland report on inner London's housing (CULLINGWORTH, 1965). More often policies arise and evolve in a less dramatic way as feelings about problems grow, as consciousness of change filters through to a larger number of people and as facts and analyses are published and publicized. Words like 'environment', 'ecology' and 'pollution' are *political* currency in Britain now – over and beyond their former professional usage. Similarly, an amalgam of better statistics, sounder journalism, professional awareness and mass communication has resulted in widespread concern for regional economic development as a policy issue (FRIEDMANN and ALONSO, 1964). Growing literacy enabled Sicilians to hear about standards of living in Milan and television viewers in Ebbw Vale could savour, vicariously, the joys of Ealing.

There is no standard or invariant way in which public policies emerge and become established. Nevertheless, there are a number of stages of growth, each one having a considerable amount of diversity, through which policies pass on their way to the statute book, the council resolution or the unspoken acceptance that 'this is the way things are done.' At the outset a problem, an event or a state of affairs is perceived by a single individual or a set of individuals.

Someone trying to telephone gets three wrong numbers in a row, a child is seriously injured on its way to school, ten more houses are built, a family is evicted for arrears in rent payments, three hundred lorries cross a bridge, someone waits two and a half hours in an out-patient clinic along with thirty-five other people all of whom were given 09.00 appointments. Most often nothing is done because either the events are not recorded, or, if recorded, they never progress from the stage of being raw data. Sometimes a person with a grievance is too shy, or afraid, or inarticulate or ineffective to start changes moving. But sometimes repercussions are felt, the vehicle count is transmitted via statisticians and civil servants to a junior Minister, the evicted family is given the 'full treatment' by the sensational press but also by the serious journals. The plight of people in 'outpatients' eventually reaches O.R. workers and via a conference paper it attracts the attention of hospital administrators.

The rôle of certain groups is critical. Sometimes it is a neighbour-hood street or community association that will bring grievances to light and to the notice of the local authority members and officials; sometimes an 'interest community' is the vehicle for giving the impetus to a situation or a grievance, as when various bodies interested in outdoor recreation created the political pressures which led to the Hobhouse Commission and the National Parks Act. Very often in British public life a Royal Commission or an expert com-mittee is employed as a means of investigating a situation, collecting data, appraising possible solutions and making recommendations; needless to say, these commissions are also classic ploys of govern-ments wishing to avoid or delay the embarrassment of a policy decision.

Occasionally, a remarkable individual, an intellectual, spiritual or political leader 'afire with faith in what people ought to want' (VICKERS, 1968, p. 46), succeeds in altering existing policies drastically or, more usually, will be instrumental in the creation of entirely new policies. The Garden City movement (and hence New Towns policy), the Leicestershire schools system and Lancashire's highway policies in the 1960s can be attributed – if not entirely, then very largely – to the flair, imagination, persistence and even eccentricity of remarkable individuals.

It is clear that policies are not always invented by politicians, nor are they thought out in think-tanks; nor is every front page story in

167

the tabloids the progenitor of a new policy; nor do policies arise every time an eccentric or crank has an idea in his bath or every time some iniquity or injustice is visited on any individual.

But it is the ongoing interaction and flux of these several kinds of events, in combination and sequence and the complex interactions they bring about as between the urban and planning systems, that give rise to policies and ultimately result in what FRIEND and JESSOP call:

'a formal commitment . . . through an assignment of resources or a public statement of intent'.

As we said earlier, our simplified view (drawn from FRIEND and JESSOP) is that policies having been stated formally in the planning system then give rise to and modify actions in the urban system. In this section we want to focus on that set of relationships crossing the interface between the urban and the planning systems and which results in or affects actions.

Most obviously, policies give rise to or modify plans and programmes. Thus a plan together with its constituent policy about the clearance of slum housing and programme for the redevelopment of a particular area will be modified by a changed housing subsidy policy. This will result in different kinds of effects within the planning system as *provider* and as *regulator*. The provider rôle may be altered so that the purchase of houses for clearance is slowed down and with it, the supply of newly-built houses and flats, new roads and schools. The regulator rôle is likely to be altered more pervasively because the attitudes taken to a multitude of public and private requests to take action – to buy, to build, to provide, to withdraw, to begin, to increase – are likely to be modified by the changes in policy.

At its simplest then we might envisage a branching hierarchy of command within the planning system which divides and subdivides its new orders and instructions. But we have already discovered that reality does not fit this simple model. For to follow this uni-directional scheme (whereby comprehensive policies are divided into sectoral policies and plans then into programmes and specific projects and day-to-day actions) is to blind oneself to the question of where and how do policies arise.

We can see that *the realm of action itself can be a rich source of information* which not only indicates whether or not policies are

168

being fulfilled in the simple sense, but also how effectively certain sets of actions serve certain bundles of programmes and policies. The action realm enables direct and continuing study of the effectiveness of policies and their degree of current relevance to problems.

But, moreover, the raw material is there, in the realms where action takes place, to provide the impetus and direction for the revision of policies and the generation of new ones. For actions do not simply depend upon policies; in certain important senses the converse is at least partly true. If we wish that policies are *relevant* to the needs of the community there must be feedback from the action level to the review of policy. If we wish policies to result in *effective* programmes the same is true. If political decisions about policies are the better for being informed about the results of current policies, the response of the public and the 'straws in the wind' giving advance notice of the need for changes, then again there must be connection between the action and policy domains. And if the design of policies or 'bundles' of policies is to be realistic in the sense of being operationally feasible, there must be concurrent study of the means of implementation. This requires a good deal of knowledge about the agencies, resources, constraints and opportunities which exist at the level of actions and programmes. The inquiry (1970–2) into the Greater London Development Plan bears exhaustive, if not always eloquent, witness to this point.

Having looked at some of the generalities of policy and its formulation and the relationships between policy and action we must now try to discuss the specific case of Britain's town and country planning system since the war. We shall begin with an examination of the ideals of comprehensiveness which is so strongly woven into planning professionalism.

Planning and policy in British local government

When the COMMITTEE ON THE QUALIFICATIONS OF PLANNERS (1950) was set up it was charged first of all 'to take account of the present and prospective scope of Town and Country Planning...'. The Committee's findings of twenty-one years ago are a benchmark from which we can establish our position and sense of direction in looking at the evolution of the development plan as a policy instrument.

They contrasted the 'positive' and 'negative' sides of British planning. They found that the negative side has been the subject of:

> 'a continuous development of laws, regulations and administrative machinery; but when the purpose changed over to one of positive or constructive planning, the planning authorities . . . found themselves charged with a function for which their organization, that had grown by a process of gradual evolution in the county boroughs and had hardly existed for executive functions in the counties, was not fully adapted.' (p. 11)

The same was true of central government where the British system of departmentalism had made the development of policies affecting the development of land arise in several different departments at the same time (e.g. in Transport, Agriculture and Trade).

The Schuster Committee (as it is popularly known) found that definitions of town and country planning in the statute book made it clear that the planning referred to was 'planning the use and development of land' but that to do so raised large questions concerning social and economic objectives, both nationally and locally, which have profound effects on the lives of people living in any area. It was this set of functional relationships between land development plans and social policies which, in the view of the Committee 'raised more than anything else the question of the qualifications required by those engaged in town and country planning' (p. 15).

They also draw attention to two of the ambiguities which surrounded the crucial notion of comprehensiveness – and still do to some extent:

> 'whether planning is to be regarded primarily as a "social" activity or as a matter of "design". And linked with this is another question on which there is some difference of view, viz: should planning be regarded as team work, or as a task for one directing mind? . . . We think that some confusion is caused by the use of the word "design" in two different senses; in the sense of setting out on a drawing board a pattern of physical factors, and also in the sense of arranging a social and economic pattern for communities. We prefer to use the word "design" only in the first sense, since "design" implies a fixed pattern. The process of arranging a pattern for communities must be continuous and constantly adapted to changing conditions.' (19–20)

170

Of course, the Schuster Committee had no power to influence administrative policies but no doubt its views evoked sympathetic echoes within the civil service and elsewhere. But what we should notice is not only the view that planning was essentially a matter of social and economic concern but that this continuous synthesizing activity of social policy could be expressed primarily in terms of physical conditions and land use. Put another way, the Schuster Committee had no doubt about the socially comprehensive nature of the *ends* of planning, but they seemed content that the *means* for achieving these ends should be a physical

'plan that is practical, economic and aesthetically pleasing' (p. 21).

A similar view of the nature of plans and their relation to policies can be gleaned from an official source (MINISTRY OF HOUSING AND LOCAL GOVERNMENT, 1955). Planning of land use we are told falls into two parts: day-to-day control

'and the preparation in advance of plans to co-ordinate the prospective demands for land in such a way as to result in pleasant, efficient and economical development, and to prevent the waste of land involved in a haphazard approach. . . . The purpose of a development plan is to give a broad picture of the intentions and expectations which a planning authority have for the development of their area, for about twenty years ahead . . . the plan must be a broad statement (which) should not go into detail unnecessarily or too soon. . . .'

One of the bases of the central department's existence was the statutory duty of the local planning authorities to submit their plans to the Minister for approval – as related policy issues such as housing were dealt with in the same department, but transport questions were in a separate and more powerful Ministry dominated by professional engineers. All of these types and others would be the subject of re-examination by the Planning Advisory Group a decade later (see SHARP, 1969).

We should also note that 'Planning' is Chapter V of the report of *one Ministry*, the other chapters dealing with 'Housing', 'Local Government', 'Local Government Finance', 'Wales' and – before the chapter on planning – 'Water and sewerage'. One looks in vain for any whiff of policy issues in the chapter, though carefully worded discussions of urgent policy issues do occur in 'the Content of Plans':

171

'A plan must allocate land for foreseeable development; must try to sort out the different uses of land in existing towns in an effort to disentangle residential, commercial and industrial development and to make adequate and convenient provision for all these; and must reserve land likely to be wanted for public needs, e.g. new roads, school sites, open spaces.'

This entails making an estimate of the future population

'within an area being planned (for which the Registrar General's figures have been used), and of the extent to which the population can be accommodated, allowing for all requirements. . . .' (p. 62)

It has taken a long time for the growth of the realization that problems dealt with in these essentially physical development plans had many *other* facets besides land use and location. The quality of housing areas cannot be divorced from the income, education and skill of the residents; nor could the growth of local economies be considered without a national and regional context involving policies for stringent control in labour-shortage areas and inducements to investment in areas of high unemployment. In short, all major social and economic and physical problems are caught up in complex webs of inter-relation, only some of which involve problems of land development and physical planning.

The Development Plans manual (MINISTRY OF HOUSING AND LOCAL GOVERNMENT, 1970) is a serious attempt to set out the function of structure and local plans. In so doing it seems to illuminate yet again one of the fundamental ambiguities in British planning. When we say 'comprehensive' do we mean taking an integrated or systemic view of the problems addressed *via* a physical framework or something wider and more complex? And does 'planning' mean the actions prescribed by eponymous statutes, the making of land-use designs whether broadly or in detail, or again, something far wider and more complex?

Appendix A of the manual gives examples of the content of structure plans worked out in some detail. Following the introductory sections on area, context, aims, strategy and so on come the substantive topics – population, employment and income, resources, housing . . . and so on. The ambiguities are now exposed clearly. Not only are many aspects of social and economic policy (e.g. income, general social policies) to be interpreted and studied almost entirely in spatial terms, but also important issues are to be included even though physical 'planning control and influence' could not be expected to play the major part or even any significant part in their implementation.

According to Appendix A of the manual the subjects which will be dealt with – including their 'complex inter-relationships' include:

population, employment and income, resources, housing, industry and commerce, transportation, shopping, education, other social and community services, recreation and leisure, conservation, townscape and landscape, utility services and 'other subjects'.

Many questions are raised by this Appendix. For our purposes the most important are four:

(1) Is the policy scope of structure planning so wide as to be virtually coterminous with the concerns of local government?
(2) If that is so, are the Development Plans, i.e. both the structure plan and its local plans, going to be the chief if not the only vehicles by which the policies of local government are developed and expressed?
(3) If there are *other* vehicles for expressing policies – e.g. educational plans, social services plans, capital and revenue budgets, recreational and leisure plans, transport plans – what are to be the relationships with the 1968 Act Development Plans?
(4) What are the implications of answers to these questions for the administrative structure, management processes and staff deployment in local government?

In a way events have outstripped the capacity of government to respond. For example, insistent pressures from some politicians and civil servants as well as from local government, the public, academics and others finally brought about the unification of the Ministry of Housing and Local Government – i.e. the land-use planning Ministry – with the Ministry of Transport within the Department of the Environment. There, at least in principle, the strong policy interactions between land-use and transport systems could be handled within the same organization and with a common set of assumptions and criteria. Similar arguments obviously would be applied to local government and indeed were when Lady SHARP (1969) reported to the government on the problem of 'Transport Planning; the men for the job'. Some of her general findings are highly pertinent in that although emphasizing the land-uses-and-movements interaction she clearly sees that such issues raise much wider and indeed all-embracing questions of social policy generally. The resources devoted to land-use and transport plans and the programmes to which they give rise represent resources *not* spent on housing services, education, public health, the library service and so on. Moreover, programmes of development for land use and transport result directly in physical development and changed transport flows but have indirect effects which lie in quite different policy realms. For example, the closure of a railway line or the removal of a fare subsidy may hasten the economic and social decline of a rural region bringing with it all the problems of closing down small schools, finding adequate farm labour and fighting to maintain a host of social organizations.

Of course, a land-use and transport organization in local government could make signal improvements in reaching sensible decisions about broad-scale land development, population distributions and the major networks provided for the movement of people and goods. But the resultant effects of development in land use and transport, though perhaps of secondary importance to planners in those fields, are in fact *primary policy issues* to planners in, say, education and social services. All such services raise matters of *financial planning and policy* to the financial officer and his staff.

What seems to have happened in British public life is that we have now succeeded in making some response to the demands for land-use and transport issues to be considered and tackled in an integrated way. But we are still at sea about the growing realization that all policy issues are inter-related. This certainly does not mean that there are no identifiable divisions or boundaries between problem areas or programmes of action; on the contrary, it will be very valuable to think *more*, not less, in terms of fairly sharply defined problems which are in principle soluble and which need to be tackled by groups of people having clear ability and knowledge which they can bring to bear on the problem. Nor does it mean that there need not be clear-cut executive or 'line' agencies performing day-to-day tasks of a continuing and routinized kind; driving licences will be issued, weights and measures checked, ambulance gear boxes overhauled, railway signal boxes manned and 92c (F) P49 will be completed in triplicate by roughly five hundred and fifty people per day, whatever one's views on the nature of social policy, its formulation and execution.

The need for the introduction of policy making

What it does mean is that local government in Britain will have to come to terms with several different sorts of realization simultaneously. First one must realize that 'everything in the city affects everything else' and no matter how much bureaucratic convenience may be served by a particular management and staff structure the problems dealt with are not neat and tidy. Secondly, although cynics will try to belittle the extent to which it is happening, there seems little doubt that a real devolution of authority has begun in which the policy functions formerly reserved by the central departments in Whitehall are increasingly to be carried out in town and county halls. Put another way, local governments are going to have the chance to *govern*. Third, these two developments are bound to have a considerable influence on such things as professionalism and job demarcation in local government including the creation of *completely new kinds of work*.

We suggest that the most significant change of all arises from the need for local authorities to develop, monitor and review their own policies. This requires fairly drastic transformations of much local government principle and practice. Since its inception in modern form in 1888 British local government has been essentially the local executive arm for central government policies. Almost without exception the policies which provide the rationale for day-to-day administrative actions have been originated and expressed centrally, i.e. at national level. The typical sequence is familiar enough: a particular problem is perceived which may be one of housing, transport, trade, morality, agriculture, pollution, food, drugs, etc. The processes of discussion, formulating opinion, disseminating news, sounding out views, etc. begins and after a time the major political parties establish their positions. The leaders of the 'movement' seek to influence the government either directly or via the civil servants and if these moves are successful a White Paper (latterly also a Green Paper for discussion) will appear setting out the problems as perceived by government, government's reactions and a sketchy outline of proposed legislation. Then the formular sequence of Bill, Parliamentary procedures and the Royal Assent.

In a great many important fields of social legislation, local government is given the major rôle to play as executive, all the major policy

175

questions being reserved to the central government. Central government – Ministers and the civil service – has a long tradition of policy thinking, a well-developed set of 'languages' and a rich set of behaviour patterns in which to deal with the whole business. Moreover, it has a set of forms in which to express policies at various stages of evolution.

Local government will have to acquire as speedily as possible the behaviour patterns which go with a policy-formulating rôle. It will have to recruit and nurture people who are so fitted and develop by trials and errors the best ways in which to move forward in many different kinds of policy fields. Some of this will be rational, analytical, deliberate and self-conscious such as the use of management consultants, developing programme analysis and budgeting systems, so as to provide for explicitly policy-oriented rôles, e.g. in jobs called 'corporate planner' or groups called 'policy advisory board'. But such deliberate action whilst a necessary condition of the move into the world of policies is probably not a sufficient condition. We suspect that a certain *style* of thinking and action is necessary but it is very difficult to define since there are no obvious formal qualifications for such rôles (save experience) and very few precedents in local government.

Moreover, local government lacks the precedents for expressing policies which are available to the central government. These include not only the White Papers, Bills and Acts but also Ministerial answers given to questions in the House, speeches made outside Parliament, the answers given (or extracted!) by interviews in the press, on radio or television. Major policy issues such as entry into the European Common Market, the law relating to homosexuality or the labelling of food and drugs – these and many other issues were widely publicized by all the news media and to some extent the background or build-up of Royal Commissions, feature articles in the press, public meetings, the statements made by professional organizations, learned societies and academics – all these means of furthering the debate were employed.

These sorts of discussions, soundings and lobbyings have been singularly lacking on the local government scene. Policy statements from local councils are conspicuous because of their rarity and often arise in response to a national policy initiative. Good examples of such policy statements are provided by the evolution of comprehensive secondary education in which the promptings of the Minister successively extracted commitments from many authorities unwilling to do so (or to follow the Government's lead).

ROSE (1971) found during the course of fieldwork investigating housing policies and agencies in local government that some officials

> 'could not answer a seemingly simple question about the objectives of their unit, because they did not think in such terms. When the question was rephrased to refer to their functions (i.e. statutory duties) their answers came readily.'

In general he considered that in many fields

> 'middle echelon public officials are not expected to define their rôle in terms of wider means – end relationships. The concentration of attention upon narrow statutory requirements does present difficulties for systems analysis, in so far as officials do not see (or are not trained to think about) statutes as means to further ends. Their statutory duty is an end in itself.'

The present author found precisely the same phenomenon in interviews with many planning officers. Policy was an alien notion to many in local government. One did what the Act laid down, in ways which were modified by local circumstances and guided by bureaucratic notions of efficiency and good housekeeping.

It is highly significant to our discussion that *one of the very few established vehicles for the formal public expression of policy by local governments is the Development Plan*. The other example is provided by the Education Development Plans instituted by the 1944 Education Act but there was no provision for their review and very little publicity attached to them. On the contrary, the Development Plans became well known and recognized as expressions of public policy. They were also easily understood because of their relationship to the ground (via the Ordnance Survey maps used as a base for the plan's indications). Perhaps because of its undoubted supremacy, even uniqueness, as a policy vehicle, perhaps also because of the professional planners' 'comprehensive' ideology, the British Development Plan has tended to become something of a catch-all in policy terms, though this has varied from authority to authority.

This is regrettable for two main sets of reasons. First, from an analytical or evaluatory viewpoint, policies need to be tested and

177

conflicts resolved along a number of important dimensions – notably their effects on budgets, taxation, rate revenues, etc., and also their effects on manpower, numbers and types of skills needed and likely to be available in the short, medium and long term. Land and location is another important dimension (e.g. where should development occur, how much land, what ecological effects are likely) but it is only one of several and not always the most important. For example, housing policies may be far more usefully debated in terms of their effects on rents and rates than in terms of acres and locations. Again, educational policy is often best developed and analysed in terms of the supply of teachers, the numbers and abilities of children, availability of special skills and equipment. There is a clear need for various means of *clear policy expression* comparable with the spatial expressions of the old Development Plans and the 1968 Act local plans. There are several signs that these lessons are being learned. The production of a 'popular' version of the Greater London Development Plan is one of a somewhat limited kind. More hopeful is the preparation by STOCKPORT COUNTY BOROUGH (1972) of a complete inventory of all its policies which, as *The Guardian* (17.5.72) said were 'not only policies set out in minute books but those in people's minds'.

If local government is to respond to the initiatives for its own development provided by such diverse sources as the Maud Committee, the Institute for Local Government Studies at Birmingham and the Mallaby Committee as well as taking full advantage of its imminent reorganization (in 1973–4) there are several important matters to be faced. Dominating these are the need to seek out the best ways of feeling for the springs or roots of policy issues; ways of helping to translate these into policy discussions; ways of informing the debate with the best possible analyses and evaluations of alternatives; ways of leading the debate towards commitments; ways of expressing these commitments so that they are intelligible to consumers and provide clear guidelines for day-to-day administration.

Our preliminary conclusions on these several points are as follows:

(1) In general, there is need for much greater attention to be paid to the interface between the consumers and providers of local government services whether these are personal, social, community or more abstract, area-wide services so as to help provide a more relevant, realistic and responsive set of policies

178

and also to help the business of foreseeing the need for fresh policies;

(2) Specifically, we are sure that development control and its associated activities in local government (e.g. building inspection, advertisement control, tree preservation, pollution control) should be regarded in that light;

(3) The local (district, action area) plans provided for by the 1968 Act and discussed in the Development Plans manual should provide adequate expressions of development policies and a clear guide to administrative actions such as development control, etc.;

(4) Structure plans could be a very valuable vehicle for the expression of policies with respect to land development, land resource conservation, environmental management and in general the physical and spatial implications of the authority's policies as a whole;

(5) Structure plans in their present, statutory form should not be treated as a unique nor as a superior kind of policy vehicle because of their inherent bias towards land development questions;

(6) Consideration should be given to the means for achieving continuing evaluation of policies including their public exposition, examination and challenge;

(7) Attention must be given to the manpower needs of broad social policy work in local government, a service which has been dominated in the past by routine administration, by functional specialisms and by a somewhat rigid professionalization of departmental tasks almost to the exclusion of thought, discussion and action about the wider issues of social policy.

We would accept the view of local government management put forward by the Maud Committee (COMMITTEE on the MANAGEMENT OF LOCAL GOVERNMENT, 1967) and conceive that the principal function of the policy group and the closely related parts of the intelligence system would be the continuous development of policies within a corporate planning framework. Departments would have specific 'line' i.e. executive functions in local government and would be shorn of their separate – and divisive – 'staff' functions traditional to British local government (GRIFFITHS, 1966; STEWART, 1971). Planning then would take on the meaning it has in the dictionary and in common parlance rather than the limited, confused and ambiguous meaning it has in 'town and country' planning and, above all, in the Development Plans manual.

But the 1968 Act is in the statute book and structure plan work has begun. How are we to reconcile corporate planning and the 1968 Act? For that is one of the biggest problems since it provides for a *statutory* plan.

Structure planning and corporate planning

One answer which we consider well-founded and desirable has been proposed by STEWART and EDDISON (1971). They point out that while structure planning is *statutory*, corporate planning is not. Structure planning, therefore, has a direct and *formal* relationship with central government whilst corporate planning would be informal and indirectly related to central government. At the same time corporate planning would be more flexible in its procedures and provide a looser, more open framework for a *wide variety of parallel planning exercises*, integrated within it, e.g. planning for transport, social services, education and housing.

But as we have seen, the poverty of policy thinking and the paucity of policy awareness in British local government is largely if not wholly accountable to the historical development of its activities as the provision of largely separate services *required by statute*. There is the danger that continued reliance on statutory (i.e. central government) initiatives will hinder, if not prevent, the necessary growth of the ability to govern in the true sense, rather than merely to carry out executive actions. At the same time, one of the greatest needs in public life from the community's viewpoint is that public bodies should be *explicit* about policies; as one interviewee put it, there is a great need for 'bureaucrats to come clean'. This may indicate the need for some statutory requirement to express policies – *all* policies – like Stockport's voluntary effort. It might be contained in a future Local Government Act and would lay down a general requirement to publicize policies in the formulative as well as the definitive stages (on the central government model of the Green Paper, the White Paper, the Bill, the Act, the Ministerial Circular, etc.).

Structure planning in the 1968 Act sense would be *one of several planning exercises going on continuously*. But truly comprehensive planning must continuously be evaluated along *several dimensions*,

180

notably capital, revenue, manpower, land and buildings. Neverthe-less, 'Land' in the classical economic sense is one of the three great resources and, therefore, constrains all corporate plans. Land in the widest sense can enable, guide, limit, qualify and initiate policies in its own right as well as having complex cross-relationships with other resource analyses.

Structure planning should, therefore, be carried out because it is vitally necessary, provided that a more conservative and realistic view is taken of its ambit. Rather than trying to subsume, resolve and express every policy area within one (physical, 'structure', land-use) framework it should come into its own as being:

(a) the vehicle for expressing *land development* and *environmental management policies* as such;
(b) the framework for testing and analysing the *land-resource and spatial implications* of policy questions and solutions in all the other policy fields of the authority.

We should seriously question whether the present arrangements are satisfactory. Structure planning is a statutory requirement but those who plan education, the social services and housing in local govern-ment can, if they are sufficiently myopic and unscrupulous, either avoid making their policies clear and explicit or avoid making policies altogether. An arrangement worth trying would be a general statutory requirement to develop a minimum range of policies and to be open about them but to leave decisions about the precise scope and content of such policies where they belong – in the hands of local authorities which are truly local *governments.*

181

8 · A Cybernetic Analysis of Planning Systems and Urban Systems

So far in this book we have been concerned with an historical review of the evident objectives of planning, with legal and procedural aspects of detailed physical planning and control, with general or 'structure' planning and with policy in local government. In general we have been looking at two sets of phenomena: on the one hand the institutional frameworks and procedures of government (particularly those concerned with town and country planning); on the other hand, but to a lesser extent, the substantive concerns of those governmental institutions and procedures. In this chapter we want to take up again a discussion of what government and planning acts *on*, i.e. of the phenomena which are its concern. At the same time we want to develop more fully the *relationship* between planning and its concerns.

In a way this discussion will be threefold: firstly with the idea of governmental and planning systems; secondly with those kinds of social and urban systems which are of interest and concern; thirdly with the conjoint systems resulting from a fusion of these two. This latter framework is necessary in order fully to explore and understand the relationships which persist and evolve between the governmental/ planning and the social/urban systems, their modes of interaction, how each may modify the other, in what ways and under what conditions. In doing so we shall have to deal amongst other things with ideas of goal-seeking or purposive behaviour.

Complex governmental systems and cybernetics

We hinted at such an approach at the beginning of the previous chapter when, following ROSE (1971), we advocated a view of government as a set of 'initiating and responsive entities' and a view of the community as a 'set of overlapping and shifting groups with different needs, values and demands'. A number of writers have suggested or used similar models to describe and to analyse such processes. For example FRIEND and JESSOP (1969) adopted a framework in which the 'governmental system' interacted with the 'community system' in the process of 'strategic choice' though, as we pointed out in the preceding chapter, their major concern was with the behaviour of the local authority as a governmental system.

A very full and general treatment has been put forward by Hasan OZBEKHAN (1969) in his notes toward a general theory of planning. First, he says it is clear that planning (as a major aspect of governmental activity) operates *on* something *for* a specific purpose, 'otherwise it would be in the order of an *acte gratuit*'. He notes, as we did in Chapter 1 of this book, the very wide range of the objects which could be the concerns of planning. This results in a need to adopt as wide a definition as possible of their range, not only of concrete objects or social structures,

> 'but also relations between such structures, interactions among them, interface phenomena and, most importantly, human activity guided by intention' (p. 53).

When the object or set of objects acted *on* is regarded as a system the whole business becomes more complex. When the governmental/ planning system is analysed in a disaggregated way at the same time, the resulting dynamic conjoint system may be highly complex. It may be difficult or impossible to identify cause-and-effect linkages for the whole of this situation though this will often be possible for small parts or subsystems which can be relatively closed for analysis. Equally, the notion of *overall* objectives which enable the study of behaviour to see whether it is rational or purposive, may be extraordinarily difficult when we deal with such highly complex systems.

Now the notions of great complexity, of interaction between systems which are extremely complex and of decision, control and purposive behaviour in complex systems are the domain of the science of *cybernetics*. In the words of KLÍR and VALACH (1967)

> 'Cybernetics is a science dealing, on the one hand, with the study of relatively closed systems from the viewpoint of their exchange of information with their environment, on the other hand with the

study of the structures of these systems from the viewpoint of the information interchange between their elements.' (section 3.5)

Throughout the 1960s a variety of disciplines were demanding both a clearer theoretical basis for urban planning and, simultaneously, a drastic shift from a 'centre of gravity' in the design disciplines to one in the social sciences. One or two writers only made specific reference to the potentialities of cybernetics in as many words though a greater number discuss the problem in terms which are readily fitted within a cybernetic approach. Thus all demands for a unifying framework which would simultaneously deal with the ideas of systems, complexity, adaptability, learning, probabilism, positive and negative feedback, hierarchical structure, information, communication, conflict resolution, forecasting, and learning may be satisfied by recourse to cybernetic models of urban systems and urban planning processes (MCLOUGHLIN and WEBSTER, 1970).

A good idea of the potential and generality of cybernetics can be gathered from ASHBY (1956). He points out that it treats ways of behaving, not what behaves, and therefore the truths, like those of geometry, are not dependent on the branches of science concerned in any particular real-world system. Cybernetics offers, therefore, a vocabulary and concepts for diverse sorts of system and may help to build 'a number of interesting parallelisms between machine and brain and society'. Planners and other 'urbanists' have become not a little alarmed at the awful complexity which the newer approaches make inevitable. For the conceptual model of traditional *design*, as ALEXANDER (1964) showed, required a relatively simple conception of the system being designed; once other decision units are admitted, (as the newer social-science models require) then the complexity of urban systems moves into the astronomical range.

However, cybernetics quite deliberately faces up to complexity. For it 'offers the hope of providing effective methods for the study and control of systems that are intrinsically extremely complex' (ASHBY). To classical science, complexity was chaos and (depending on one's religious-philosophical inclination) God or man must intervene and restore order to what was an unstable condition; chaos was an omnipresent threat. BEER (1960) calls this 'a basic myth' and subjects it to vigorous attack. Certainly the idea that urban systems are inherently chaotic and that the planners must constantly be vigilant and active in imposing order is a deeply rooted one (see Chapter 1 of this book). Without plans and other controls 'the traffic will grind to a halt', 'cities will choke themselves to death', or suburbia will 'cover the whole country from end to end'.

BEER's retort is quite simple: this is not so. On the contrary, *it is order which is usual and more natural than chaos* and the evidence for this is widespread. In particular, any existing system of human relationships in a large and complex society should be regarded as largely homeostatic (i.e. self-regulating to a 'steady state'). Furthermore, any institution probably relies a great deal more on its self-organization for its success than on the official management.

The problems of managing urban regions and of making decisions within the framework of such management processes are the practical aspects of the problems we face. It is only very recently, however, that we have bent our intellectual energies to the whole field of decision making and choice and we are still confused and ill informed. Seventeenth-, eighteenth- and nineteenth-century science was mostly concerned with understanding the physical world of natural resources as materials, machines for doing work, and with the amplification of the human muscles and sensory powers.

The greatest phase of this physical amplification has passed and with it the concern for resource extraction, transport and manufacturing. The major human problems are now concerned with decisions and choices, with the management of man and machinery and resources. We no longer need much amplification of our physical powers for nuclear weapons and rocket technology now make a plateau in energy output. What we must now be concerned with, and above all else, is with the amplification of our mental powers through the study of brain-like mechanisms which give rise to the phenomenon of 'decision and control' (BEER, 1966).

Major effects not only of intellect but also of faith will be necessary to overcome prejudice and misconceptions of the nature of scientific inquiry and especially problems in which human beings are involved. Operational research and cybernetics are together concerned with understanding complex real-world situations and deciding which principles should be invoked to institute and maintain the control of an enterprise. At present, there exists two polarized approaches to control – the *laissez-faire* approach and the mandatory approach – and both rely on partial models drawn from organic controls as found in natural systems. These are usually quasi-independent domains arranged hierarchically but very richly interconnected so that information flows with maximum freedom around the whole system. The management task (always *given* objectives) is then one of organizational design. In general; the control system should

> 'be one which operates itself, but which can be monitored from on high, and given new direction towards predetermined goals which it does not itself recognize and of which it cannot indeed be made aware' (BEER, 1966, p. 383).

Cybernetics, generalizing from the study of very complex systems, draws most of its important models from the life sciences. The goals of such systems are 'viability' which we may interpret as the ability to persist under certain conditions. It is a feature of very complex systems that to be viable they have to be highly responsive to the changes in their environment, capable of discerning and anticipating such change, i.e. learning which responses are likely to be called for and how to react favourably. This may well involve operating *on* the environment itself. In other words, such systems have the capability to respond so profoundly that they have in fact altered the conditions (or parameters) which define viability. The appropriate models from the life sciences are the processes of learning and evolution.

Cybernetics, system theory and social systems

One major concern of the chapter is to try and establish a cybernetic basis for a social-process view of planning. For if one is going to approach planning via social rather than physical-environment ideas and paths, and if one is simultaneously endeavouring to adopt a cybernetic or general-systems standpoint, then it clearly becomes necessary, indeed essential, to examine the possible basis for a cybernetic view of social systems.

Planning at the present time has three important features which make it essential to have a social view:

First, there is the shift to a dynamic social-process view which we have noted already. This requires that plans themselves must become adaptive and flexible – something which is easier said than done, partly because the professional ideology of planners is so deeply committed to the making of plans or the process of design rather than the (necessarily continuous) processes of implementation, monitoring, evaluation of outcomes, reformulation and review. The former dominant ideology of design has depended rather heavily on borrowings from the physical sciences and sometimes their applications in technological fields for the development of its core methods from their original architectural-engineering core. In the 1950s and 1960s planners were introduced to the world of social physics and its applications, to decision theory and some of the simpler decision aids such as linear programming. They also struggled hard to find the best equivalent or extension of cost-benefit analysis. But these developments were directed not at a continuous process of *planning* but almost wholly at the *making of plans*. The study of planning will require at least a study of the processes by which social policies are carried through into action as well as the generality of guidance and control found in cybernetics.

Secondly, it follows that in becoming at least as concerned with implementing as with designing plans, regard must be paid to theories of social action, to the means by which actions are carried out in the public sector and regulated by public authorities in the case of private-sector actions, to the means by which the original objectives which found expression in the policies and programmes embodied in current plans are mediated in turn by the response of users and recipiants. For example, the original plan may have responded to certain public transport objectives with a set of recommendations about service levels and fares; the public's response to these will in turn bring about a reconsideration of not only the policies themselves but also, in time, the objectives on which they were predicated. Social understanding and social research must underpin the planners' actions not only in implementing plans but more especially in interpreting responses and judging the needs and opportunities for modifying policies or taking new initiatives (DONNISON, 1972a).

Finally, there is the need for social research and social theories to deepen the planner's understanding of the world in which he operates in a general way for 'cities and social entities and their physical characteristics only gain meaning when men give it to them' (PAHL, 1968). Planners have been very slow to realize that, like all their fellow-creatures, their perception of the world around them is highly selective, particular and coloured by social and professional indoctrination. To the majority of people the

187

'environment in a real sense is composed by the individuals, families and institutions which surround and influence them and through which they operate; it is only in part (and for all we know, maybe quite a small part) the physical environment of buildings, roads and parks and the countryside.' (BROADY, 1967)

The rôle and purpose of social considerations in the development of a theory of planning have also been highlighted in the critique by DAKIN (1963) of the 'choice' theory proposed by DAVIDOFF and REINER (1963). First, Dakin emphasized that a good theory would have to be applicable to any kind of political system and 'because it [planning] takes place within human society it must be related to social theory' for

'even the most limited form of planning takes place within the social framework and no kind of planning can be envisaged which does not relate to man's activities. Planning may be regarded as a part of the social process: in the on-going business of living we plan all sorts of activities. The way in which we plan the choices we make, the measures at our disposal for realizing our aims, and our methods of effectuation are essentially generated within the cultural pattern of our society.' (p. 23)

Dakin also regards it as essential to see planning as a process to combat entropy in a world where no simple central purpose can be discerned nor social ends clearly identified.

Another major reason for the involvement of social system analysis is the weight we accord to those who like MEIER (1962) and DEUTSCH (1961) interpret the city in terms of communication theory or as a 'communication engine'. According to this view the postulates of modern information science and theory can be applied to the study of urban growth which is interpreted as a process of seeking to maximize 'contact choices'. Obviously this will be constrained by communication technology and in particular the transportation system will affect the spatial distribution of contact choices. But there can be too much of a good thing and people may experience 'information overload' which can signal nervous disorders, as well as information-system malfunctions. Information overload may be an important factor in the business of 'getting-away-from-it-all' to the low-density suburb or the week-end cottage in the mountains or more fundamentally, becoming a 'middle-class drop-out' and abandoning the high-pressure life-style for something less demanding.

Any fresh theoretical approach to planning, we are convinced, must be based upon the prior analysis of social systems. For we concur with FRIEDMANN (1967) in looking on planning as the 'guidance of change within a social system' because an adequate conceptual framework for analysing planning behaviour (such as he proposes) would cover such matters as forms of thought or ideologies in planning, institutions for political guidance and conflict resolution and types of implementation procedure.

We are not claiming any originality in proposing an attempt to interpret urban phenomena in cybernetic terms for such approaches are at the least ten years old. We have already mentioned the work of MEIER (1962) who had an early vision of the promise of general-system approaches. Some years before writing his book on a 'communications theory of urban growth' he had realized that cybernetic notions were transforming research on certain biological and engineering problems but that so far the social and behavioural sciences had either chosen to ignore (or were ignorant of) the significance of this work.

However, as social scientists gradually did become aware of it they developed a number of apprehensions about the applicability of cybernetic analysis to social systems; in one or two cases the apprehensions sharpened into downright hostility and rejection. Two words in particular – 'system' and 'control' – seem to cause perceptible distress to some social scientists (and indeed to other people too). The word 'system' to them betokens a state of affairs whose structure is well known, even completely understood, and whose behaviour, therefore, is orderly and entirely predictable. The word 'control' raises rather more sinister images of 'social engineering', the brute-force methods of totalitarian regimes or the subtler methods of Orwell's thought police.

It is not difficult to understand why these words and the concepts they call to mind should seem at best inappropriate, at worst repugnant to students of society. Human society, they say, is rich, complex, dynamic, ambiguous, full of tension and uncertainty, never completely knowable. There are very few people who would contradict such sentiments; certainly among those who are interested in general notions of system and control few would support any contrary view.

189

Where then does the difficulty lie? Almost certainly, as several writers have suggested, in a faulty and incomplete understanding of modern system theory on the part of most social scientists or, in other words, an interpretation of the concepts of 'system' and 'control' in terms of older biological and technological models – which indeed are inappropriate for the study of society.

CADWALLADER (1959) was one of the first to put his finger on some of the central difficulties:

'The fundamental theme of cybernetics is always control and regulation in open systems. It is concerned with homeostasis in organisms and steady states in organizations. Its orientation is the source of considerable misunderstanding because many of the sociologists who are interested in the subject of social change object to the use of all concepts of equilibrium, homeostasis or stability, arguing that to include such ideas as a central part of social theory is to preclude the possibility of dealing with changes. They seem to believe that stability and change are not only contradictory ideas but that the processes themselves are totally incompatible. The difficulty here is not merely semantic: some kinds of stability do negate certain kinds of change. What has been overlooked is that at least one category of stability depends upon and is the consequence of change. Just this kind of stability is of prime interest to cybernetics.' (pp. 154–5)

What seems to have alienated a very considerable number of social scientists from general systems and cybernetic viewpoints is: first, that the systems approaches with which most people are familiar were for the most part analogies with organisms or machines; secondly, that there are truly semantic problems created by the use of words transposed from their field of origin directly into social system analysis (e.g. 'machine' as used by ASHBY, 'learning' as used by GROSS); thirdly, that perhaps a considerable number of social scientists were not sufficiently versed in mathematical and statistical concepts to distinguish clearly between determinism and probabilism or between the notion of constancy as meaning something absolutely unvarying and something changing so that although detailed or micro-states altered considerably its overall or macro-state could be regarded as unchanging; finally, there is the very widespread failure to distinguish between the substantive content of an area of interest or a set of entities on the one hand and 'the principles of organization

190

per se, regardless, or what it is that is organized' (BUCKLEY, 1967, p. 36). In this way, many social scientists have turned their backs on system theory believing that because some of its concepts derived from the study of mechanisms or of (single) organisms it was, there-fore, wholly inappropriate for dealing with something as complex, quicksilver and *human* as the study of society.

We believe such views to be mistaken either because being irrational and prejudiced they are unworthy of serious intellectual inquiry or because they are based on false premises concerning the nature of system theory. We shall attempt to show how system-theoretic and cybernetic approaches are appropriate for the study of social systems; we shall also go further and suggest that such approaches hold out considerable hope for the study of several very important questions in policy-oriented social research. We shall depend very heavily on the excellent exposition of BUCKLEY (1967) who begins by showing how some of the earlier social systems models – particularly those involving the notions of *equilibrium* as set out in the work of Talcott Parsons and George Homans – break down before the persistent problems of social science. One of the biggest difficulties is that equilibrium in machines or physical systems is usually an invariant condition but this is clearly not so for a social system. It is, therefore, not possible to say when a social system is in equilibrium i.e. what are its defining characteristics. Furthermore, such a definition, if possible would have to admit unvarying distinctions between behaviour which tended towards equilibrium and that which was deviant. Also the equilibrium model cannot readily deal with the notion that social systems are open to their environment and hence subject to irreversible change.

The key to the way forward is a means for studying 'organized complexity' and it turns out that the best of the traditional disciplines for doing so was biology – and in particular its own techniques-in-chief, i.e. teleology and taxonomy. These twin supports of biological methods, the concern with purposes and with classification have been adapted in the new general-systems perspective: first, teleology has 'been made respectable by cybernetics . . . which made possible an acceptable operational definition of goal-seeking behaviour with-out true teleology' by recourse to methods of causal relations in-cluding feedback loops; secondly, 'the distinction between machines with and without the feedback loops that make for goal-seeking is a *topological* distinction, definable in terms of graph theory, a branch of topology' (BUCKLEY, p. 38).

Cybernetics, topology and decision theory together make up an integrated body of concepts for the study of 'organized complexity'. Such approaches to social science should be especially fruitful since they promise to develop a common language and a set of techniques; a view of society in terms of information and communication networks, an emphasis on relationships rather than entities and, finally, an adequate treatment of goal-seeking behaviour in operational terms.

The crucial distinctions being made are between three different 'levels' of system models. It is failure to make these distinctions which has led to most of the grave difficulties in integrating cybernetics with the social sciences and which have caused the latter to hold system theory and its apologists in something close to disrepute. The three levels of system proposed by Buckley are:

(1) *equilibrium* – typified by simple physical systems and those which lose information, organization or energy (i.e. gain entropy) in moving to the equilibrium point;

(2) *homeostatic* – typified by more complex physical systems and certain organic systems in which a relatively high level of organization is maintained in the face of external influences tending to reduce it;

(3) *adaptive* – typified by ecological and 'sociocultural' systems whose organization becomes progressively more elaborate and whose range of behaviour is correspondingly increased; such systems, far from seeking to protect themselves from environmental disturbance actually *depend on such disturbances* for their growth and evolution.

It is possible and often very useful to regard these three levels as the tiers in a hierarchy. However, we should not think that there are *always* three levels in the most complex systems. It is possible to analyse the most complex systems at a very large number of levels, depending on the purpose of the analysis and the resources which can be devoted to describing system structure and behaviour.

The three classes presented are, therefore, types of behaviour which predominate in certain levels of systems. The behaviour which gives rise to the classification of a system as equilibrium-seeking, homeostatic or adaptive seems to depend partly on the kind of interchanges which are observed between elements or subsystems within the system and between the system and its environment. Equilibrium-seeking systems are typified by exchanging materials and energy between elements and are relatively closed to any environment. Homeostatic systems also make considerable use of physical exchange but additionally they need inputs of energy and information from an environment in order to maintain the steady state. Adaptive systems are typified by exchanges of information. Although 'information' is usually dependent on some physical or energy base it is the information or *pattern*, the variations in structure which are of predominant importance.

We can now consider simple examples of systems which illustrate the three typical levels of analysis: a pile of stones is in *equilibrium* and is so maintained by the pressures which are exchanges between the elements, i.e. the individual stones themselves; a waterfall is in steady-state or, as we say, *homeostatic* since although it is (literally) more fluid and dynamic than an equilibrial system and since the molecules constituting the system are never the same individuals, the energy and material relationships between the molecules of water is so patterned as to result in a steady state provided there is some continuing input (of water) and in spite of winds, erosion, rock falls, diversions of the stream and so on; finally, a herd of animals is an adaptive system where the exchanges which constitute the key to its systemic qualities are predominantly informational, i.e. patterned variety irrespective of the physical carriers involved. Among the many criteria for the continued existence of the herd we might include: the ability to adapt to changing conditions of food supply and to co-operate in seeking it out; caring for the young; the whole process of reproduction which involves not only sexual union and the transfer via the D.N.A. molecules of genetic 'information' but also the ability to recognize, through patterned signals, the most appropriate time (of the year or of the life-cycle) for reproduction; individual and collective defence strategies against predators including the ability to detect their presence or approach; the ability to test from time to time the viability of the breeding stock through actual or ritualized combat. These and many other patterns of behaviour may contribute to the viability of a herd of animals and taken together as a complete repertory or set of behaviours constitute its capability to survive. We could emphasize once more the significance

193

of the transfer of *pattern* between members and between them and their environment. Furthermore, the ability to go on surviving or to survive better will depend on *changing and diversifying the set of survival behaviours*. This above all is the characteristic we must try to understand if we are to attempt an adequate analysis of human social systems.

Before we go on to look very closely at the characteristics of diversification, growth and adaptation we should consider some further aspects of the hierarchical nature of the various classes of system we identified earlier.

First of all it seems that we can usually discover or identify the simpler within the complex so that homeostatic systems can, if we increase the resolution level at which we observe them (KLÍR and VALACH, 1967), be found to consist of subsystems which are equilibrial and composed, therefore, of elements whose exchanges are for the most part of materials and energy. Similarly, complex adaptive systems, if observed at a higher resolution level, usually reveal subsystems of which some are homeostatic, some equilibrial.

Secondly, it appears that as we increase the resolution level of *all* conceivable systems we reach a limit (at least for systems which are directly observable) which is entirely equilibrial and composed of energy/matter exchanges; this is, of course, the molecular level at which system behaviour is *determinate*. At this limiting resolution level we always obtain what ASHBY (1956) calls a 'determinate machine', i.e. one whose transformations are 'single-valued'. KLÍR and VALACH (1967), therefore, make the point that for every system, however *probabilistic* it is at the level at which we first conceive or define it, is in fact *determinate at the limiting resolution level*.

This leads us to an important point with respect to social systems and one which is highly relevant to the doubts over general-system approaches to social science. It is that the awful spectre of a mechanistic (i.e. deterministic) model of society which many believe to be implicit in a 'systems approach' is in fact a non-problem because 'determinism' and 'probabilism' have no meaning *unless related to a system defined at a particular resolution level*; for such a defined level there is a degree of probabilism or degree of determinacy for any transformation of that system from one state to another.

A social system, like any other, can be determinate in two senses, one somewhat loose, the other perfectly strict. In the loose sense a

194

system may be described as 'determinate' if its transition probabilities are constant and this would be revealed by Markovian analysis (ASHBY, 1956, Chapter 9); for example, a demographer will say that the crude death rate for a whole population will always lie between two figures and this statement implies a deterministic view of a particular social (i.e. demographic) system. In the stricter sense a social system will become determinate if observed at the molecular level – in which case it has lost all meaning as a social system and become the constituent chemical materials. So we retreat from such absurdity and observe that human social systems when subjected to formal analysis and model-building are likely to be observed as subject to certain *constant probabilities* which will vary with the transition being described. As RAPAPORT (1966a) so truly observes, arguments about determinism *vs.* probabilism in human affairs are very 'tedious', the real question being the degree of probability at the given resolution level.

Characteristics of adaptive systems

We must now examine rather more closely the characteristics which enable us to describe a system as 'adaptive' and especially we must see how well such a general model is able to reflect what we know empirically, and what we believe intuitively about socio-cultural systems.

In other chapters, when discussing system behaviour at a very general level, we discovered that behaviour depends upon structure and in particular the way in which elements are interconnected, the nature of the couplings whether series, parallel or feedback (KLÍR and VALACH, 1967, p. 37). In this chapter we have noted that complex adaptive systems are characterized by their dependence on information transfers with their environment and between their own elements. We have gone on to recognize adaptive systems as open systems which are decreasing in entropy or elaborating their structure and organization. In this way they are at least maintaining but usually increasing their viability by constantly deriving better strategies for survival.

How is this achieved? How do systems become more elaborate? Is this what is meant by 'purposive' or 'goal-seeking' behaviour? We are now beginning to understand that the answer to questions about the source of increased organization and elaboration is that this arises through *deviations or perturbations being amplified by positive feedback* which is thus an essential feature of very complex adaptive systems. Cybernetics and system theory at first paid considerable attention to homeostatic processes in which negative feedbacks predominate and help to bring about the reduction of deviations from a norm and hence a return of the system to a steady state. But MARUYAMA (1963) pointed out the enormous importance of positive feedbacks in 'deviation-amplifying mutual causal processes' which he also dubbed the 'second cybernetics'. It is interesting that the examples he uses to illustrate his thesis are urban agglomerative processes (nothing succeeds like success), the development of biological mutations and the 'polarization' of social groups. RAPAPORT (1966) mentions the work of Richardson on the origins of warfare as an example of positive feedback acting on the views of the would-be belligerents until the deviation in values and ideologies becomes so great as to 'explode' into war. Such outcomes are, however, modified by negative feedbacks – for example the electorate may demand a reduction in military expenditure or the technological advances which had earlier helped to make conflict seem *more* probable, can later make it less probable. (All of these viewpoints can be applied to the nuclear arms race between the great powers from, say, 1950 to 1965.) Similar phenomena are the growth of racial discrimination, biological evolution and population growth.

But we still need an even more explicit account of the way in which deviant behaviour arises, how tensions grow and are dissipated, how conflicts develop and are resolved, how ideas originate and the way all of these processes enable systems to increase their degree of organization. This process as a whole is referred to as *morphogenesis* and BUCKLEY (1967) has offered an abstract model of the process.

The essence of morphogenesis is that by interacting freely with a turbulent environment, the open system – be it biological, psychological or sociocultural is able successively to 'map' the variety of the environment within itself. This is achieved by generating within the system itself a variety of states which are thus necessarily coupled to the environment. Many of these will be unsuccessful, i.e. they will *not* result in any lasting elaboration of the structure or behaviour of the system. But some of the couplings *will* be successful and will result in elaborated organization. The internal structure (connections, negative and positive feedback loops, etc.) of the system evolves so that each succeeding set of states presented for coupling with the environment is constrained in such a way that more successful and less unsuccessful states are generated.

Very briefly, the essence of morphogenesis is fourfold:

(1) constant, rich interaction between system and environment (awareness);
(2) a high variety of states to be coupled with the environment in such interaction (exploration and innovation);
(3) criteria for selecting the successful states (judgement, choice);
(4) some means of registering the characteristic patterns of success (memory).

The account we have just given (which follows comparable statements by BUCKLEY in his Chapter 3 and CADWALLADER, 1959, p. 156) is essentially about learning or evolution. We should notice particularly that the generation of a variety of states, highly exploratory attitudes towards the environment and capacities for discriminating pattern are essential to morphogenesis. In other words, innovatory behaviour depends upon the ability to generate variety within the system and this may be exemplified in part at least by what we call deviant behaviour.

It follows that a very good and useful model of the social processes wherein individuals interact largely via flows of information (which in turn is largely symbolic) and whereby institutions are formed, maintained, elaborated and reformed can be provided by modern systems theory. The emphasis in the modern theory on complex, adaptive open systems is able to overcome most of the problems associated with structural and consensus theories of society deriving from simpler system models. A very important feature of the new model is the necessary and continuous presence of tension produced by the importation of variety into the system and by the generation of 'deviation' within it.

EASTON (1966) has suggested that a modern systems model focusing on political life could take input-output form or what he calls 'a flow model of the political system'. But for him it is variety-generation which enables political systems 'to persist in a world of both stability and change'. And it seems that if a political system – defined as 'those interactions through which values are authoritatively allocated'

– is to fulfil its rôle as a regulator keeping the essential variables of cultural survival with limits – it must obey Ashby's law of requisite variety (see Chapter 9 below). By obeying this law, political systems can 'regulate their own behaviour, transform their internal structure and even . . . remodel their fundamental goals' (EASTON, p. 145).

Social change and the distribution of power are clearly interactive when viewed in a modern systems framework. Social change can increase the total amount of power by effecting technological changes, it can increase the potential sources of power by industrialization and the rise of a bourgeoisie, it can create new organizations as seats of power and it can produce ideological change by means of organized groups.

The policy decisions of those now in power tend to produce social changes which may redistribute power and the nature of the power distribution will determine the nature and likelihood of social change (GITTEL, 1966). The immediate and sharp significance of this is highlighted by the growing problems of the inner areas of American and (to a lesser degree) European cities. The problems of 'multiple deprivation' – or being at the bottom of the income, health, housing and educational piles – are now the subject of considerable research and action. REX (1968), in a carefully observed study of the differentials of income, status, race, etc. in a 'zone of transition' showed how these are related to the allocation or distribution of housing.

One possible implication of the adaptive model of social systems is to call into question the whole concept of 'institution'. For as BUCKLEY (1967) argues, once one admits deviance, tension, conflict, differential power-distributions and the consequent struggles as central and essential to one's theoretical framework then such phenomena as

'Organized crime, political corruption, economic fraud and exploitation, and other "social problems" are so pervasive, stable and difficult to root out precisely because they are "institutionalized". That is, they involve complex inter-personal and often highly organized, networks of expectations, communications, normative interpretations, interests and belief, embedded in the same sociocultural matrix as are "legitimized" structures.' (p. 161)

One of the complex outcomes of our contemporary urban problems is the way in which new institutions have proliferated usually as

198

'counter-planning' agencies, sometimes with the active support of the established authorities. Another outcome is the *challenge to the legitimacy* of the established organs of government. Yet another is the demands for consultation, co-operation, *involvement and participation*, each in its different way a challenge to current modes of government.

It may be not entirely fortuitous that several of these phenomena grew up in the 1960s concurrently with a large concern about the distribution of wealth, influence and power in modern society on the one hand and a demand for reformed governmental institutions on the other.

Learning and evolution in social systems

Learning in general is that process whereby patterns identified in its environment by a system becomes mapped within the system itself so that it is capable of responding effectively (i.e. in a way that helps to ensure viability). The more rapidly and diversely the system can explore the environment the more rapidly will this sympathetic mapping occur, i.e. the system is a better and quicker learner. Modern systems theory shows with rigour how this is perfectly general and is in no way hindered by the concept of vitalism in biology; rather such cybernetic models of learning have helped to dispel the mechanistic *vs.* vitalistic battles (KLÍR and VALACH, 1967).

Whereas *learning* refers to the individual, i.e. to an organism in biology, *evolution* refers to the species as a whole. Learning is, therefore, the process just described with respect to a central nervous system and brain. But learning with respect to a species is obviously a characteristic of the gene-pattern and takes a much longer time; it is a function of the ability of the gene-pattern to possess sufficient variety to cope with the ever-shifting variety of the environment.

What unifies both and makes the cybernetic model perfectly general is the dominant characteristic of increasing complexity; great complexity can result from quite simple elements provided they are richly interconnected. For example, the D.N.A. molecule is composed of only four kinds of nucleotide bases arranged on the double-helical core but each molecule may consist of 3×10^7 bases in all which gives an extremely high variety. PRINGLE (1956) showed how an electrical system of coupled oscillators, each one producing a very simple rhythm could, when cross-coupled into a rich feedback loop network, produce a pattern of rhythms which evolved into something more and more complex. He also showed how homologues for 'learning' and 'memory' could be found in the electrical model. BRAVERMAN and SCHRANDT (1967) produced a computer simulation of the growth of a colony of hydroids – in itself a very complex ecological process – by using simple growth rules in the computer algorithm.

We are familiar with the networks of communication which transfer food, raw materials, electrical energy and containers along physical channels or which operate electromagnetically. But we can conceive of a homomorphic network – i.e. one which is almost but not quite identical with the former – and which transmits, in the opposite direction, the money and information which must flow for the whole system to be internally homeostatic.

'Above' this information-and-money transfer network is a system of institutions which create and monitor the necessary signals or impulse patterns which activate this network. This set includes banks, *bourses*, government financial departments, legal institutions and processes, markets for various goods and services, communications systems and management institutions. A lot of these flows have given rise to information businesses which internalize the flows that were formerly scattered throughout the transfer system (DUNN, 1970).

Such a system is in steady state if its input and output are constant but this is seldom the case for reasons we have met already. Currently the big 'disturbances' with which such information systems have to cope are the direct and indirect effects of technological change. So, social systems are quite different from those typified by equilibrial machines. A social system is capable of learning, indeed, *must* be so capable not only

'because exogenous changes modify the signals affecting the control process and favouring innovative adaptations as a defensive measure. It is also true because the active creative capacity of social systems is continuously seeking ways to improve the efficiencies of internal processes and to ameliorate the constraints of external environments.' (p. 255)

This essential creative innovation is becoming organized in institutions which develop and test new patterns of behaviour for both physical and social systems and this is clearly far beyond a mere

200

(homeostatic) response to change, it is a morphogenic force *inducing* change in social systems,

> 'more than a process of evaluation of new processes in the light of old goals, it is also a process addressed to the formulation of new goals that is so much a part of the process of social learning.' (pp. 255–6)

It is so rich in variety, in ambiguity and in symbolic mediation as to be beyond the capacity of computerized information systems (as presently developed) and to depend very heavily on face-to-face contact and communication between people involved in such creative activity.

A certain amount of empirical study (BURNS and STALKER, 1968) has been accomplished on the subject of innovation and learning and organizations. WADE (1971), writing of the possibility of innovation within planning agencies concludes that innovation is likely to be significantly greater when the organizational structure of the agency is 'organic' rather than 'mechanistic'. That is to say, innovation is found to be much greater in organizations characterized by: the use of contributive knowledge and skill, the orientation of work around specific problems and tasks from the 'real world', continual adjustment and refinement of tasks through frequent 'horizontal' interaction with others, these interactions taking the form of information and advice rather than commands. WADE cites the use of *ad hoc* agencies (e.g. the sub-regional study teams) as examples of 'instant' innovative agencies, partly because it was recognized that existing local government bodies were too mechanistic to tackle the novel problems which justified the studies themselves. Lastly, he concludes that a high degree of uncertainty within institutions about the environment is likely to produce a more favourable attitude towards innovation – (c.p. the common sayings 'Any port in a storm', 'It's worth a try'). He believes that the structure and the reform of local government are combining to push British planning authorities towards relatively high levels of innovation.

Government (all government institutions) has the special responsibilities of *learning on behalf of society as a whole*. To do so it must be capable of discarding structures designed to solve old problems and setting up fresh ones. This seems to be terribly difficult because of the colossal inertia built into all bureaucratic systems. The British government has never lacked ideas for solving our persistent economic problems – whether of balance of payments, wage inflation, price stability, unemployment or sluggish investment – but it has been inordinately difficult to put policies into effect. The same is true of housing, education, transport, indeed any major problem area.

We can appreciate the government must be an information process detecting issues and problems and being aware of the consequences of action by transporting imperatives, data and views within and between its own parts. It must keep relevant records about the system it is trying to regulate (e.g. industrial productivity, prices, wages and salaries), it must also study and monitor a wider socio-cultural environment for clues about the behaviour of these systems and likely shifts in their development and thus in the effectiveness of various modes of intervention. In short, government can readily be understood within a *cybernetic model of organization* (DEUTSCH, 1961).

This is a very different business from that of a mechanistic controller of equilibrial systems by means of simple negative feedback. But one can use the metaphor of the engineer watching the needles on the dials showing the 'essential variables' which ASHBY (1956) has insisted are logically necessary for all control. VICKERS (1968) can thus observe that

> 'the indices which the political governor watches are for the most part not mere observations of the present state of critical variables but estimates of their future course, based on his latest knowledge of them (which is usually imperfect) and worked up by a process of mental simulation. A more important difference is that half his skill consists in setting the standards which he shall try to attain. For, unlike the engineer, who controls a system designed to be controllable, the politician intervenes in a system not designed by him, with the limited object of making its course even slightly more acceptable or less repugnant to his human values than it would otherwise be.' (p. 92 Pelican edition, 1970)

So in a cybernetic model of social systems, the rôle of governments, regulating by successively mapping the variety of society within themselves, is not only to see that regulatory acts (policies and programmes) are in fact carried out but essentially to look continuously at the ethical questions of what *ought* to be done, what *should* we be doing, where lies *gubernatorial right and wrong?*

At this point we seem to be drawn back to an hierarchical view of complex systems and to the notion that each level in a hierarchy is a 'meta-system' to the one below. Theoretically one can imagine an endless series of steps but in practice it is useful and necessary to identify a finite number. BEER's (1969) general model of organizational structure recognizes five major levels, for instance; we shall explore this model later in the book. But for the moment it is enough to stress the hierarchical nature of all cybernetic models of complex organization. To a very considerable extent this hierarchy is itself a result of evolution historically and is illustrated by the principle that each superior level, being a meta-system in terms of the one below, debates questions about the system it governs and to which it is linked but in a higher-level or 'meta' language.

Thus problems of agricultural society and technology were debated and mediated by manorial courts in terms of land-tenure law; a mercantile and industrial society gave rise to governing bodies such as municipal corporations, trade and craft guilds which debated volumes of product, rates of taxation, methods and skills; when the predominant or emergent problems are those of distribution and circulation of goods and services, governmental institutions must develop a new level and language to debate their distributional ethics; now that we are creating a world where *information and ideas* are becoming (at least in the economically advanced societies) the major 'commodities' and 'services' which influence power differentials and societal dynamics then the major concern of government must be the ethical questions of *policies relating to ideas and information.*

For example, questions that are likely to enter these debates are: the rights of access to information in general and to personal information in particular by individuals and groups; the right of 'news media' to ask certain kinds of questions; the relevance of a person's religious, sexual, political and aesthetic ideas to his fitness for certain kinds of jobs; the rights of one set of groups or institutions to withhold information from citizens or from each other.

The time-lags which constrain the evolution of governmental institutions (and particularly the content of their policies) results in the phenomenon so beloved of cynical commentators that governments are deployed so as to offer good solutions to problems which solved themselves ten years ago. Thus it is plain that in the technologically advanced countries, instead of being now equipped to address the problems and issues of an information-and-ideas-driven society, they are structured so as to deal with agriculture, trade, the health services and so on.

Let us emphasize – these institutions are still needed, still relevant, still indispensable simply because we are dealing with an evolving hierarchy. We still have problems of agriculture, trade and health which need agencies to deal with them. In the past we needed farms, factories and infirmaries and these persist because to a greater or lesser degree we still need them. The point is the general cybernetic problem of control that if a system evolves and becomes more complex (as all viable systems do) then the control systems integrated with it must evolve in similar fashion. So governmental institutions must develop to cope with 'post-industrial' society.

Developments in communications science themselves should

'lead us to attach due importance to the difference between systems which are open only to the exchange of matter and energy and those which are also open to the exchange of information. . . . A space satellite, a system open to information as well as energy, is clearly not to be fully explained in terms of the principles governing simpler machines which are open to exchanges of energy alone, although, of course, they are equally obedient to those principles. Personal and social systems can be shown, I think, to exemplify still higher levels of organization.' (VICKERS, 1968, pp. 20–4)

Not only is it possible to interpret social systems in terms of modern cybernetic and general-systems models, but on many counts it seems desirable to do so for the added insights which such interpretations offer in the study of certain pressing problems of our time. In particular the nature of social conflict, tension and deviance, the rôle of ideas and symbolic communications, the rôle of governments as social learning agencies and the concept of 'institution' itself come up for useful and fruitful scrutiny.

Ecosystems, geosystems and urban systems

The view which we developed in the preceeding section of an adaptive 'sociocultural' system was very wide, inclusive and general. We concluded that the notion of adaptive systems to which modern systems theory had given rise could certainly be applied to the analysis of society. But this notion of society was deliberately comprehensive so that we could later explore if necessary a large number of particular parts or subsystems of such an inclusive system. As we said at the outset of the chapter, we must identify the governmental and planning systems as being important *operators*. But at the same time one of the principal goals of this section will be to sketch out the *operands* in planning. For, if we acknowledge that planning 'represents acting on some object, defined as *environment* . . . for the *purpose* of effecting changes in the environment' (OZBEKHAN, 1969, p. 151), we must also ask what is the 'object' on which planning activity operates? Or, to use a similar concept – that of *regulation* – we can regard the planning/ governmental system as the regulators and ask ourselves *what is the object system* whose 'essential variables' (ASHBY, 1956, Part Three) are being governed?

We showed in Chapter 1 that the objects of planning are defined by the *issues and problems* which arise in society. So, in an interesting way, planning is related to the very turbulence, conflict and tension which is a necessary condition of an adaptive social system. And, as we saw in Chapter 7, *social policies* will then tend to form and coalesce around sets of issues as the government system strives to fulfil a relevant and effective rôle. It might, therefore, appear that the objects of planning, since they are problems and issues posed by the community, are so fluid as to be difficult to define with any precision. This is true at various scales of planning and governmental activity. Some problems seem particularly persistent and planning agencies must adapt in a durable way to cope – for example, with the economic problems of Scotland, Wales and Northern England or the use of the private motor car and the related pressures on outdoor recreation facilities. Others are at the opposite extreme, emerging rapidly as nine-days' wonders and equally rapidly disappearing – conversion of cinemas to bingo halls, the demand for amusement arcades.

We know that we are working within a highly complex adaptive 'sociocultural' system and it is entirely consistent with such a view that the problem addressed by a planning system will be in a state of flux. So we must define the objects of planning not only in terms of the set of problems which happen to exist at one particular time, or as they are visualized in any particular community or culture but as *the universe of entities and relations from which these particular sets are drawn*. This universe of entities and relations will be a system – smaller than the sociocultural system which envelops the whole of our concerns and our discussion but 'large' enough to include all those time-, place- and culture-specific problems and issues which people choose to regard as planning problems.

So our problem in defining the object system for planning is so to select a set of entities and relationships which is sufficiently bounded as to be recognizable and useful and yet sufficiently wide as to be able to accommodate all those situations which communities and governments from time to time agree to define as planning problems.

Now this has been one of the most taxing difficulties for all concerned over a long period of time. True enough life goes on, investments are made, administrative procedures are carried out, agencies are formed and reformed, political debates about the legitimacy and content of programmes continue as year succeeds year. But these events both contribute to and draw upon the evolving idea of what is the object system of planning – that *upon* which it operates.

A number of people have reviewed this problem or tackled it head-on. COCKBURN (1970) has shown for example how the difficulties which British planners have faced in defining educational objectives are related directly to questions of shifting definitions and considerable uncertainty about planning.

Similarly OZBEKHAN (1969) did not find it easy to define an object-system on which planning operates. Having referred to the 'entire experiential milieu of man' he readily concedes that 'so large an array of elements clearly needs some ordering if one is to talk about it meaningfully' (p. 101). In this view, planned change must concentrate on a readjustment of the ecological basis for human life and the basis for this is to be found in the relationship between two systems – the environment seen as a system and planning as a system.

It would seem that one central point of identification for the system on which planning operates is the earth's 'life-support system'. In recent years ideas drawn from general-systems theory and cybernetics have increasingly been applied to ecological problems. This is hardly surprising when, in common parlance as well as in formal scientific terms, the urgent problems we face seem to fall within the general class of problems of control. Earlier analyses (and empirical investigations) of ecological systems had used measures of energy – the calorific values involved in photosynthesis, respiration and protein-exchange chains for example. But it is possible to bring within the same framework the equally relevant, indeed the indispensable consideration of laws, religion, political power, income and expenditure of money, etc. Thus:

> 'when systems are considered in energy terms, some of the bewildering complexity of our world disappears; situations of many types and sizes turn out to be special cases of relatively few basic types . . . energy diagraming [sic] helps us consider the great problems of power, pollution, food and war free from our fetters of indoctrination.' (ODUM, 1971, vii)

In selecting from the totality of the human condition some object system on which planning is to operate it must be intelligible and relevant for the major traditional disciplines if only because the 'fetters of indoctrination' which they partly represent are sets of concepts and languages. These must be accounted for in any attempt to construct a meta-system in which they can operate and a meta-language in which to communicate.

We could now suggest some minimum conditions which a framework for defining the *object-system of planning* would have to meet:

(1) It must be capable of including the natural environment of the planet's resource endowment;
(2) It must be capable of including a typology of activities comprising and emanating from the living creatures of the earth and especially those of human beings;
(3) It must be capable of including land both as a resource (since all activity occupies land) and as a set of locations (since the deterrence of distance is relevant to interaction);
(4) It must be capable of including the multitude of artifacts which make up the artificial environment of human beings;
(5) It must be capable of including all matters relevant to the relationships between human societies and their natural and artificial environments – flows of money, men, information, instructions, orders, laws, concepts and ideas;
(6) It must allow for empirical observation;
(7) It must have a holistic quality, i.e. be a unitary yet diversified system rather than a mere assemblage of unrelated systems;
(8) It should be sufficiently adaptable and flexible as to accommodate the description and analysis of ever-shifting planning problems and yet possess sufficient constancy as to enable proper study of the dynamic processes themselves.

Planning suffers from an almost total absence of paradigms (HAGGETT and CHORLEY, 1967), i.e. 'broadly significant models of value to a wide community of scholars'. A paradigm for the object-system of planning must be wide enough to be comprehensible and useful for many people and institutions far outside the academic realm.

One way of considering the object-systems of planning is to see them as sets of attributes of the physical, spatial and socio-economic world studied traditionally by different kinds of geographers – 'physical' geographers and geomorphologists, 'regional' and 'urban' geographers, 'social' or 'human' and 'economic' geographers. One aspect of the development of geography is the search for a unified field or framework for the building of concepts and techniques. So far, despite long experimentations with regionalism, environmental-ism, human ecology and other approaches, the traditional paradigm of geography has been called 'classifactory' and judged as being 'under severe stress'. The goal which geography is urged to strive for, even if it is never wholly attainable, is in Ackerman's words 'nothing less than an understanding of the vast, interacting system comprising all humanity and its natural environment on the surface of the earth' (HAGGETT and CHORLEY, 1967, p. 39).

Our argument here is that this 'vast interacting system' which provides a goal for the development of geography can be approached in two complementary ways. The first is from the social systems perspective which we outlined in an earlier section. Through the kind of general-system insights proposed by BUCKLEY (1967) we can focus on the essentially *human* aspects and subsystems of the planet. Here the focus is on the nature of government, institutions, power, purposive behaviour and *planning*.

Secondly, by an approach to the same general goals but this time with an emphasis on the 'natural environment on the surface of the earth' we can employ the ideas of *ecosystems and geosystems* as discussed by STODDART (1967). The notion of *ecosystem* was first proposed by the ecologist Tansley in 1935 and was later defined by him as 'the whole complex of organisms . . . naturally living together as a sociological unit' and its habitat. The emphasis is on interactions through which the whole system is maintained – in line with theories of general systems. Stoddart goes on to cite Fosberg's much later development of the ecosystem idea, in which it is:

208

'a functioning interacting system composed of one or more living organisms and their effective environment, both physical and biological. . . . the description of an ecosystem may include its spatial relations, inventories of its physical features, its habitat and ecological niches, its organisms and its basic reserves of matter and energy; the nature of its income (or input) of matter and energy; and the behaviour or trend of its entropy level' (quoted by STODDART,1967).

The correspondence between the ecosystem thus defined and the subject matter of geography needs no emphasis; but equally, it is at least clear, prima facie, how fruitful it may be in defining the scope of *object-systems* for planning. The main reservation one feels at this point is that the origins of the ecosystem idea are essentially in *plant and animal* communities whose 'sociological' structure is so different in many important respects from those including man. To say the least, human social systems are maintained by interactions which involve transfers of material, energy and information which are vastly different in quantity and quality from those which bind together plant-animal systems.

Yet there can be no question of completely separate analysis; at the lowest resolution level the planet is one unified ecological system in which humans play a major – and possibly crucial – rôle. Is the ecosystem concept capable of extension without distortion to include not only the biological but also the cultural aspects of human systems? Several ecologists have done so empirically but confined their studies to situations which were possibly too simple to provide adequate tests – e.g. to coral atolls, other islands, salt marshes, etc., where the rôle and scope of human intervention was limited. Stoddart comments that more complex ecosystems including humans 'are likely to be difficult until experience is gained with relatively simple or restricted systems' (p. 529). He goes on to mention the work of Dice who reviewed ecosystem research to discover how far it seemed capable of the extensions we are seeking. Dice was of the opinion that in addition to the usual feedback controls observed such as starvation, predation, disease, migration and competition, one could add the particularly *human* interactions of:

'public opinion, punishment and rewards, wealth, taxation, supply and demand, co-operation and the democratic process [and] that human ecosystems may be conceived at successively larger scale intervals: tribe, homestead, village, town, city, national and international levels' (quoted by STODDART, 1967, p. 530).

Such a scheme would admit within its provenance many of the classic problems of 'planning' as addressed by governments in recent decades: of agricultural land conversion and urbanization, of air and water pollution, of land conservation and reclamation. But the ecosystem concept, by insisting on the specifically general-system properties in such phenomena, transcends mere description of static patterns and cross-section analysis and requires us to lay bare the functional linkages and the patterns of transmission between system elements. Of particular importance is the possibility of identifying (in the hope of quantifying where possible) the interactions in terms of negative and positive feedback connections, for it is these which give rise to the properties of growth and adaption in complex systems. Urbanization and economic and technological developments of many kinds are as much a feature of human ecosystems as of the social systems we noted before.

What we see once more exemplified in this discussion is the power of general-system analyses and the potential which it holds out not only within but also between traditional areas of study. The overlap and interpenetration we are observing now is between ecosystem and social system models whereby we are less and less concerned with the substantive content of the two kinds of systems and more and more aware of *their common general-system properties*. And yet at the same time we can identify subsystems or areas which do *not* overlap and which for the convenience of description and analysis we can say are purely 'social' and purely 'ecological'. For example, the networks through which political power flows carrying 'demands' and 'supports' (EASTON, 1966) can be conceived of aspatially; plant and animal communities exist which are so remote from and unaffected by human activities as to require no social system elements for adequate analysis.

But the more interesting and fruitful ideas are generated by the integrated model which embraces the ecosystem and social system within its subsystems. Such an extended general-system model may be termed a *geosystem* (STODDART, 1967, p. 537) and could provide us with the framework we are seeking i.e. one within whose wide confines we may define the ever shifting yet more specific object systems of planning.

How far such a paradigm, or highly general model, satisfies the conditions we set out earlier we shall go on to examine now. As far as *eco*systems are concerned, STODDART (1967, p. 524) noted that they were:

(1) unified frameworks for analysis
(2) possessed rational, orderly structure
(3) functional and hence capable of empirical study and a considerable degree of quantification.
(4) possessed of general-system properties and thus related generically to all open systems.

The geosystem framework for the objects of planning, when examined in relation to the eight major criteria listed earlier is clearly inclusive of natural environments and the earth's resources, the activities of living creatures, land as a resource and as a set of inter-related locations, (see Fosberg's definition of ecosystem, above) the artefacts of human beings, the material and non-material flows which connect the various elements and achieve their relationships. Most important for those concerned with the study, the formulation, discussion, analysis and implementation of public policies, the geosystem provides a framework for empirical observation, for description and measurement of something which is conceived essentially as a unified whole of parts and relationships.

Studies of general-system properties and especially those of complex adaptive systems, confirm that the essence of the ordering or organizing principle, homeostasis, ultrastability and morphogenic properties lies in the inter-relationships between the system elements. The structure of the exchange networks and the reaction (or 'relaxation') times of output response to input stimulus are some of the most important parameters of system behaviour (see KLÍR and VALACH, 1967).

We should also remind ourselves that it is the topological properties of the transfer networks and the patterns of the information which is transferred which is essential rather than what (material or otherwise) is transferred. We also know that the more complex a system, the more are its interchanges likely to be of coded information rather than matter or energy. Indeed 'cybernetic systems' have been defined by reference to the importance of information transfers (KLÍR and VALACH, 1967) and these are particularly to be found in what BUCKLEY (1967) calls 'sociocultural' systems and what we are here calling 'geosystems'.

A very useful 'flow network image of urban structures' has been put forward by DUNN (1970) who concluded that urban systems could be seen as:

> 'a set of interrelated activities. The interrelationships are formed by the sharing of transformation and transfer functions ... These ... (and their associated tree and circuit networks) can relate to processes addressed to the physical transformations and transfers of society, to the information transformations and transfers forming the communication dual, or the information transformations and transfers forming the process of social learning.' (pp. 256-7)

Different interactions and overlaps of the various kinds of networks result in urban areas having varied characteristics: trade, production, information/management or social learning, i.e. research and innovation. Whilst there are never (or very very seldom) any pure types, the resulting range of many different kinds of urban system in fact results from the combination of only a few basic types of flow networks extending from primary resources to the ever-growing tendrils or loose ends of the social learning networks.

The resulting mega-system or overarching set of urban systems is cognate with the geosystem paradigm. This, in turn, is shown once more to be capable of identifying and providing the empirical basis for the study of *any* kind of urban system – or what WILSON (1970a) has called 'urban systems of interest'.

Planning systems, urban systems and purposive behaviour

It is time to try and attempt a summary of the argument so far and at the same time to introduce some consistent terminology. Up to now we have tended to use the terms – e.g. 'sociocultural' system (BUCKLEY) and 'geosystem' (STODDART) – employed by the authors whom we have cited. From here on we would like to use our own terms:

> *A planning system* is a subsystem of government whose prime objective is to operate on some set of circumstances in order to

bring about future changes which are held to be improvements; it is to be regarded as an adaptive system like Buckley's socio-cultural system (though not as extensive) and Friend and Jessop's governmental system.

Urban systems form the set of circumstances upon which the planning system operates. They arise and evolve by social and political action in ways discussed previously and are subsystems of Stoddart's geosystem. Since Stoddart includes various kinds of social and political processes within his geosystem we can also say that our urban systems bear considerable resemblance to Friend and Jessop's community system.

The study of planning can be accomplished within the framework resulting from the coupling of these two systems. No simple mechanistic model can be inferred from this coupling. The two systems overlap to some extent as will be clear from the preceding extended discussions. For example, community action may be thought of as arising within the urban systems and seeking to change the kind, pace and direction of change currently pursued by the planning system. If community groups become institutionalized they may then be best understood as forming part of the planning system itself; and the substantive results of their actions (e.g. in housing, schools, traffic flows) would then be regarded as changes in the urban systems themselves.

In cybernetic terms, planning systems therefore, perform key regulatory functions on behalf of the conjoint system. Such high-level regulation is not simply coercive, negative feedback in order to iron out deviations and restore norms through such simple controlling action is necessary at lower levels in the system. Nor is it simply a matter of maintaining in more subtle ways a set of steady states, though these too are subsumed within the generality of complex regulation. To these necessary conditions of complex control must be added the sufficient conditions of adaptive control – foresight, anticipation, changing structure and behaviour.

But for what? Why adapt, why change, why control and regulate? If control in very complex systems is largely intrinsic what is the purpose or function of high-level regulation and control pursued by planning systems in urban governance? We concluded our highly empirical study of the question of what planning is *for* in Chapter 1 with the suggestion that (at least in Britain) the dominant guiding principle has been *control itself*. This surely reflects the 'basic myth' (BEER, 1960) that chaos is always threatening and that the planning system must intervene in order to restore order. A theoretical analysis of planning and urban systems confirms this view. But the crucial distinction which must be made is between simplistic, coercive, low-variety control (by e.g. land-use plans) on the one hand with complex, high-variety regulation through gubernatorial processes on the other.

When we come to discuss the ends which planning is supposed to serve we are confronted with what are possibly the biggest problems of all. They are daunting enough in corporate planning or military strategy where goals and objectives appear to be relatively easy to define and in social and political systems these problems are magnified. One reason for the extra complexity is the absence of any single goal-setting mechanism. Another is the serious problem of setting down in observable and measurable form what the objectives are so that progression (or retrogression) can be noted and acted upon within a monitoring framework. Some would argue that the most important goals of public action, 'liberty, equality, fraternity' – (DONNISON, 1970) are bound to be difficult to define.

Another problem here is that planning, lacking its own theoretical foundation, has tended to turn to other disciplines for help – to sociology, social psychology, anthropology, political science and welfare economics for example – only to find that help, where it is offered, is 'tentative and complex' (MCKENZIE, 1967).

The conventional wisdom of planning is founded on comprehensiveness and a long-range view. The rationality of seeking system-wide goals over a longer time span has been the subject of considerable criticism in the last ten years. One of the most powerful attacks comes from HIRSCHMAN and LINDBLOM (1962) who argued that attempts to define and reach system-wide optima were mistaken because complex open systems move naturally from one imbalance to another; this is the source of their dynamism, adaptability and capacity to 'learn' which an imposed comprehensiveness could stifle. We cannot simply dismiss this as verbal imagery. SCHUTZEN-BERGER (1954) was sure that unless the goal was finite and predictable 'the optimal strategy is just the simple tactic of attempting to do one's best on a purely local basis' and that where the target or goal moves randomly such incrementalism 'can be shown, by mathematical proof, to be actually the best one possible'.

It is only with relatively simple systems that we can specify a unique goal and arrange for simple controls to 'lock' on to the target via negative feedback loops. The trouble is we tend to bring to the complex world of urban social systems the concepts and techniques which are appropriate to deal with the closed systems recognized by physical sciences and simple technology. Finite design technologies often require a choice between discreet alternatives and this strategy has received much attention in planning lately. It is fifteen years since SIMON (1956) came to the conclusion that 'we should be sceptical in postulating for humans, or other organisms, elaborate mechanisms for choosing among diverse ends. Common denominators . . . may simply not exist.' This was echoed by ALTSHULER (1965), a political scientist who has made several deep studies of the urban political process, believing that the continued assumption (by planners) of comprehensive community goals 'constitute a serious impediment to the effectiveness of planning'.

It is almost certain that most of the problems associated with goals, objectives and purposive behaviour in urban-regional planning are conceptual rather than operational; we lack a properly developed 'language' for these discussions. According to GROSS (1965) we can overcome most of the problems here by using a general-systems model – especially one using the input-output form. In this one can manipulate controllable input and observe the output effects. The object-system being controlled is then a 'black box' whose structure and behaviour is gradually but never fully revealed, as the observer/ operator learns the best ways in which performance can be altered in relation to goals.

We should not assume that goals and objectives are fixed. Indeed one of the distinguishing marks of the wild-goose chase after comprehensive goals (or the Optimum Optimorum or the General Welfare Function) is that the biggest problem is its complexity.

The goals of a very complex adaptive system are not susceptible to simple analysis as are those of much simpler systems which are governed by the maximizing or minimizing of some identifiable function and are usually finite or durable unless some controlling parameter is altered by some 'outside' agency. Adaptive systems have mapped *within themselves* the proliferating variety of their environment and have thus become successively more complex (see BUCKLEY, 1967, p. 62).

We must, therefore, confront a concept as vague as 'viability' when dealing with complex systems. Rather than a retreat to the superficial and woolly this is an advance from self-deceiving attempts at bogus precision. EASTON (1966) concludes as much when discussing political systems. Viability depends on keeping 'essential variables' within a critical range and in political life these variables are those which enable legitimate authority to be exercised and accepted (p. 148). 'How do political systems manage to persist in a world of both stability and change?' asked Easton. His answer is completely consistent with those coming from a host of other disciplines which have used open-system analysis *viz.* rich interaction with the environment and the creative use of innovative behaviour to develop the 'requisite variety' (ASHBY, 1956) for adaptive behaviour.

It is intuitively obvious that the conceptual models for the very complex planning and urban systems should come not from physical, technological or design science but *from the life sciences.* And it is clear too that the concept of *learning* must be (and can be, with rigour) extended to encompass the urban and planning institutions which attempt deliberate control.

Research into problems of controlling urban systems are surprisingly rare but HAMILTON *et al* (1969) provide a very good example of exploring goals, forecasting, evaluation, choices and management problems in the Susquehanna river-basin. The essence of their conclusions is that the research-development-management sequence should be a *learning process* beginning with very simple (i.e. 'childish') models of the system of interest which are then put to work in exploring the real world. Not surprisingly, they prove too crude and make mistakes but they are successively refined by careful analysis of the outcomes so that the real-world's complexity is mapped within the models until requisite control variety is achieved together with the capability to steer towards a current goal whilst being ready to postulate modified goals.

There is a dangerous reef here on which we may founder if not careful. Self-regulation or intrinsic control is certainly a feature of complex systems but it does *not* follow that geosystems are self-regulating without any positive action by man for *the deliberate actions of man are part of the intrinsic controls* (BUCKLEY, 1967, p. 163).

At the same time, deviant and disorganizing forces may be at work;

216

the breakdown of information flows and the existence of 'noisy' channels can lead to lessened cohesion manifesting itself in social conflicts despite increased reliance on explicit (state) controls. This feedback loop is often positive and can lead to repressive police states and the ultimate collapse of law and order. BUCKLEY concludes that goal-seeking, purposive behaviour involves individuals and groups seeking to

> 'generate meanings, interaction patterns and ecological arrange-ments that are more or less temporary adjustments always open to redefinition and rearrangement.... Modern systems analysis suggests that a sociocultural system ... requires some optimum level of both stability and flexibility: a relative stability ... of interpersonal relations ... and, at the same time, a relative flexibility of structural relations characterized by the lack of strong barriers to change, along with a certain propensity for reorganizing the current institutional structure should environmental challenges or emerging internal conditions suggest the need. A central feature of the complex adaptive system is its capacity to persist or develop by changing its own structure, sometimes in fundamental ways.' (BUCKLEY, 1967, pp. 205–6)

This latter capability will include the regular building of fresh institutions and the remodelling of existing institutions in order to cope with the 'turbulance' of the geosystem environment of planning. The implications of this conclusion for government, local govern-ment, the professions and other bodies relevant to our purpose will be dealt with in subsequent chapters.

217

9 · Requisite Variety and Intelligence Systems

Introductory

In this chapter we are taking up the idea of Chapter 8 that in general the study of planning in local government can be carried on within a framework which identifies two inter-related systems – a planning system and a set of urban systems with the former acting as a regulator. On this conceptual basis, and taking account of reasonable practical constraints (e.g. local government reforms, technology, manpower), we shall in Chapter 10 aim to put forward proposals which are felt to be practicable, useful and which should lead to more effective, responsive and adaptive processes.

The law of requisite variety

In Chapter 8 we discussed several important ideas which derive from cybernetics and systems theory; for example the notions of adaptive control and morphogenesis in highly complex 'sociocultural' systems. But we omitted anything but a passing mention of one of the most important principles of regulation identified in cybernetics – the Law of Requisite Variety (ASHBY, 1956, Chapter 11). This omission was made deliberately so that the principle could be brought out fully in this chapter in a context which deals simultaneously with its practical implications. For of all the ideas coming from cybernetics which have a bearing on problems of urban government and planning (and there are many – see MCLOUGHLIN and WEBSTER, 1970) *we believe that the principle of Requisite Variety is paramount*. So important is this law that many other general-system properties which have relevant practical implications for urban planning (e.g. entropy and information) can be related to the idea of requisite variety.

Ashby's original statement holds that the variety of a set of outcomes resulting from inputs or disturbances to a system can only be

218

reduced in proportion to the variety of a regulator associated with that system. In the limiting cases, if the regulator has zero variety, then the full variety of the disturbances can pass to the system; on the other hand, if the regulator has *at least* the same variety as the disturbances then it is possible to compensate entirely for their effects on the system, i.e. the outcomes will have zero variety. In general, variety is the number of possible states which a system can assume and is a function of the number of elements in the system, the number of distinguishable states of each element and the patterns or networks by which the elements are interconnected.

Unless constraints exist (e.g. on the number of states which elements can assume or on the couplings) variety can be very high indeed. In general, a system of n elements has $2^{n^2} (2n-1)^2$ possible structures even disregarding the nature of the couplings. But full variety may not be possible because constraints exist on the possible states which the system can assume; indeed, *constraint is simply another way of defining organization.* If a system is free to take up *any* state, and all are equally probable, then its entropy is at a maximum and it is totally disorganized (KLÍR and VALACH, 1967, Chapters 3 and 4).

Ashby's law can, therefore, be put into slightly different words. When a system is affected by input disturbances which display a certain number of states, the output disturbances can be reduced by an interposed regulator in proportion to the number of states which it (the regulator) can display. In order to reduce the number of output states of the system to zero (i.e. to render its behaviour entirely invariant against full input variety), the regulator system must be capable of taking up *at least* the same number of states as the input disturbances. The regulator is then said to possess *requisite variety.*

Now the number of states a system can assume depends on the *resolution level* at which we choose to define it for our purposes (KLÍR and VALACH, 1967, section 2.3). Obviously if we decide to look at a situation in more detail, e.g. by collecting more information, by disaggregation and so on, there will be more elements and more connections to be accounted for and hence more variety even though the 'real-world object' remains the same. Variety is not something given and intrinsic, it is a result of our own choice in how we perceive a situation. Therefore, requisite variety too is only meaningful in relation to a system defined at a particular resolution level.

Another point to remember is that requisite variety is defined in relation to the output characteristics of the system being controlled. It is not a rigid condition in which output is absolutely invariant. Therefore, if a certain degree of variability within limits is acceptable, requisite variety is, by definition, that which will maintain output within those limits so that the viability of the system is not threatened. This is what ASHBY (1956) refers to as maintenance of the 'essential variables' within certain ranges.

In simple mechanistic systems, the essential variables are their critical ranges as determined from outside, usually by a human controller. When a navigator calculates a course, or a householder sets his central heating thermostat, they are selecting and calibrating the essential variables of steering a ship and keeping a house comfortable. But highly complex systems of the kinds which interest us – planning and urban systems – have typically internalized these processes; the controls are largely *intrinsic*. The governmental process of a planning system is thus fundamentally different as we learned in the last chapter. This has two aspects: the selection of the relevant policy variables and deciding the ranges within which they are acceptable.

> 'Thus all policy-making assumes that the policy maker possesses or can evolve standards by which to judge the desirable and the repugnant; assumes, in other words, that he is able to value. . . . Secondly, the recognition of policy-making as the regulation of *relations* stresses that the standards by which these relations are judged are not goals to be attained once and for all, but, like the mariner's course, must constantly be sought anew.' (VICKERS, 1968; p. 128 in 1970 edition)

Therefore, in simple equilibrial systems, the designer, working from outside the system, ensures that requisite variety is present in the control and this can be done in a once-and-for-all way. But planning systems, which are essentially dynamic configurations of human beings must constantly seek to define the conditions under which requisite variety is to be achieved and constantly to try to maintain it in the face of the 'turbulence' of the urban systems' behaviour (EMERY and TRIST, 1960).

It follows from the law of requisite variety that in the case of highly complex systems, their intrinsic controls must themselves strive for requisite variety and furthermore that since the systems they regulate are dynamic the control must itself be adaptive and dynamic. The key strategy is for the controlling system to 'map' within itself the variety of the controlled system and to do so, moreover, in an *anticipatory* fashion so that it has variety in appropriate forms to cope with the turbulence of the systems it is regulating.

But a regulator of this kind is not merely a *responsive* set of entities; it must also be *active* with respect to the controlled system, influencing it in ways determined by reference to the essential variables and their ranges.

The search for requisite variety in planning systems

Cybernetic theory suggests that there are a number of conditions necessary for the development of requisite variety in a regulator. We are going to discuss these in turn whilst gradually relating them to the context with which we are concerned, i.e. the planning function in local government.

First of all, one way in which complex regulators typically achieve requisite variety is by having a complex hierarchical structure similar to the structure of the systems they regulate. This similarity of structure is defined formally (see KLÍR and VALACH, 1967) as 'homomorphism', i.e. having similar shape or form. The conditions for homomorphism can be shown to be related to the law of requisite variety since in both cases it is *comparable degrees of complexity* which are involved. Now it has been observed (for example by ALEXANDER, 1965) that urban systems have structures which are referred to as 'semi-lattices' in the appropriate branch of mathematics i.e. topology. Semi-lattices can be visualized as hierarchical branching networks with greater cross-connectivity than simple branching structures of tree-like form. The principle of homomorphism, therefore, suggests that planning systems must themselves take on the adaptive lattice structure of the urban systems they regulate.

It does not seem possible to interpret regulatory behaviour in complex systems at one level of the hierarchy; such systems seem to depend on a succession of layers of control. Furthermore, BEER (1969) has shown that the control for any given level must be exercised by a 'metasystem' at the superior level. But, he goes on, the *language* of the metasystem is a metalanguage which, therefore, must

221

be translated both upwards and downwards. It is clear that in, say, a five-level hierarchy of control the language spoken in the topmost layer is completely meaningless to that in the lowest level.

An example may help to make this difficult but important point clearer. An industrial firm makes ball-bearings using machine tools. These tools have certain built-in controls which ensure certain conditions (diameter, surface texture, weight, etc.) of the product. But the suite of machines itself must be regulated, perhaps by a human supervisor, perhaps by a computer. The criteria for such control are quite different from those used by each machine to control the quality and quantity aspects of the ball-bearings. Furthermore, the functions of production, marketing, research and development, stocks, etc. must be controlled at a level above that of the control of the machines and this again operates in a different 'language', unintelligible to the lower levels. The firm's management is concerned with a yet higher level of analysis and action and the 'language' at this level is concerned with cash flows, rates of investment and dividends, etc. Above that are the concerns of the top management and the board – government policies, the consumer movement, industrial espionage, the shaping and reshaping of corporate goals in response to social, economic and political change as well as the demands of investors. The 'language' at this level of control is meaningless to supervisors or machines and thus *powerless to exercise direct control.*

The implications of this for local government and planning are obviously important. We could deduce from this general principle that the 'language' of the problems and needs of the individual, families and local groups in a community included statements about specific conditions of e.g. housing, traffic and child care and that a compatible language was used by those officials actually delivering those services e.g. numbers of dwellings, rooms, rents, rates, pedestrian crossing locations, foster homes and adoption cases. We would also deduce that the language of the much higher level of broad goals, objectives and policies, e.g. 'adequate accommodation for all citizens', 'accessibility and choice of transport mode', 'the highest possible standards of welfare services for the whole community' were *in themselves* meaningless to the individual and those who serve him directly. It would follow too that if the community were invited to participate in formulating and debating such statements that the response would be very poor. This is precisely what has happened to attempts to involve the community in such debates, the best documented British example being the meetings set up by the Greater London Council inviting debate on the Greater London Development Plan and its basic objectives which one commentator (HALL, 1970a) describes as 'so vague and general as to be anodyne'. Only when developed into the more detailed implications of broad policy (i.e. translated into a lower-level language) do we tend to find involvement and response.

This discussion has in fact led us to the second way in which a regulator system can achieve requisite variety. The demands made by the community and groups within it for specific types and levels of service, for more details about the implications of broadly-defined policies, the actions taken by local government which affect the community – all of these emphasize the importance of the *interface* between the planning and urban systems. For it is at this interface – between all sorts and conditions of public officials and all sorts and conditions of citizens – where all the understanding needed by a specific planning system originates. It is true that the general structure and behaviour of *all* local governments will be determined culturally within that society. The average Spanish local authority, for example, is like most others in Spain but quite unlike local authorities in, say, Sweden. They have developed from two quite different models of public authority – one basically French, the other basically Scandinavian. But the *specific* objectives and policies adopted by a *particular* local authority, the ways in which the dependent programmes of action and routine administration are carried out depend very heavily on what happens at the interface. It is here – often literally at a face-to-face meeting across a counter in the rents office, or in the development control section, or at the parents' evening at the local school, at the public enquiry – that the planning systems can learn most effectively about the problems in the urban systems, their type, the way they are changing, the effectiveness (or otherwise) of current actions, the way new problems are arising, the degree of misfit between urban-system problems and planning system structure.

Variety is obviously related to the *connectivity* which exists between the elements of a system. Therefore, the variety which a planning system possesses is directly related to the amount of interconnection

223

which exists between its various components. We have learned already that highly complex systems typically possess an intricate lattice-like structure and it is precisely this structural property that enables them to exhibit complex, high-variety, behaviour. Simpler branching, tree-like structures cannot possibly take up as many states as the richly interconnected lattice. This latter kind of structure, typical of living systems, allows interactions or exchanges to be effected along very many more channels than are minimally needed; this property is called *redundancy* in communication theory signifying that any given message can be transmitted along a very large number of channels. This is related to another very important property – the reliability of components and the reliability of the system as a whole. By reliability we mean the capability of transmitting patterns of information accurately between origins and destinations. Networks with very high connectivity (see HAGGETT, 1965, Chapter III) and associated redundancy are capable of being highly reliable as wholes even though their component elements may be unreliable (CHADWICK, 1971, p. 77).

We can now see the main requirements for achieving requisite variety in a system which is a regulator with respect to a system to which it is coupled, e.g. a planning system connected to urban systems. Firstly it should have a high degree of *external connectivity* with its environment, i.e. the system being controlled, so that there is the fullest possible transmission of information both outwards (i.e. actions on the urban system) and inwards (i.e. feedbacks about the outcomes of action). Secondly, there should be a high degree of *internal connectivity* to ensure high variety and redundancy so as to ensure reliability of the internal transmissions. Thirdly, such a lattice structure will usually take a hierarchical form in which the content of the transmissions along the channels connecting the parts or elements will be qualitatively different at the various levels or, as we put it earlier, in different 'languages'. This property will imply the need for 'translation' facilities within the planning system itself and between it and the urban systems.

Thus we have identified the central and crucial rôle of information transfer in a planning system.

Information and the cybernetic model of control

The transmission of information is essential to the maintenance of organization. This is true, of course, for all systems irrespective of their substantive make-up. The biochemical 'messages' which maintain organic functions serve precisely the same purposes as the price signals in a stock market and the code numbers called by an American football quarterback to his team-mates to transmit to them a specification of the patterns of play to be used. Later on in this chapter we shall have to introduce a rather specific meaning for the word 'information' but here we are using it in the most general sense as used in cybernetics (KLÍR and VALACH, 1967, 3.2). Change and growth are engendered by the transmission of information and the consequent increase in order or organization. Control or regulation occurs when selected aspects and amounts of information act upon a system and thus to affect its organization (KLÍR and VALACH, 1967, 3.3).

One of the distinctions which can be made between general systems models and cybernetic models is in the way in which each of them deals with the interactions between system elements. The general systems model will be interested in the structure of the system, i.e. in the pathways which are available for connections between elements but also in *what* is transmitted. Cybernetic models remain interested in these details but the emphasis is now shifted to the next level of abstraction which looks at the pattern of information transmitted along the various channels of connection; for it is the amounts and patterns of such transfers which determine whether control is effective or not rather than the precise nature of what is transferred. Ultimately, all information is reducible to binary form (yes/no, on/off, 1/0, black/white) since information is inseparable from matter; even the most complex 'messages' handled by the human brain are, nevertheless, made up of exceedingly large combinations of neuron states.

Information in this more abstract sense – the number of distinctions which can be made so that coded messages can pass – lies at the heart of cybernetic system analysis. In other words, it is the 'information or signal' emphasis in the relationships between system elements which characterize the cybernetic system (KLÍR and VALACH, 1967, p. 79). Control in simple equilibrium systems often

225

involves pushing levers and pressing buttons so that the outputs of a machine or set of machines remain within indicated limits. But higher level controls 'come to depend more and more on the transmission of *information* . . . [in which] the energy component is entirely subordinate to the particular form or structure of variations that the physical base or flow may manifest' (BUCKLEY, 1967, p. 47).

Open systems tend to lose pattern and organization by the operation of entropic processes. Steady-state systems are thus taking in information as fast as they lose it, morphogenic systems (BUCKLEY, 1967, pp. 58–62) – those characterized by 'biological evolution, learning and societal development' – take in information *faster* overall than they lose it. This, plus the development of an internal structure which best deploys the net gains of organization and pattern, enable high-order systems to elaborate and adapt their structure and behaviour.

Information then is of the greatest importance to the understanding of complex-system behaviour. In living systems, information intake is literally vital – not only in the form of very complex molecules of protein but also thoughts, images, facts and ideas in rich variety. Prisoners kept in solitary confinement may suffer impaired brain function and even death through 'information starvation'. Inappropriate coding can render information less useful and this phenomenon is associated with the presence of 'noise', i.e. extraneous information. Control mechanisms can be fooled or confused by these means. Finally, systems can suffer from the over-provision of information, i.e. of trying to take in more patterning or organization than currently they are able to 'digest', causing what MEIER (1962) and others have called 'information overload' in the individual person. In ASHBY's (1956) language the environment then has a 'variety' which is too high for the regulator, and until it adapts (by gaining variety) the system it is seeking to control is bound to go out of control. A football team defence which is thoroughly confused and outwitted by very intricate manoeuvres has gone 'out of control' if the attackers score a goal.

The place of information in urban-systems control

It is obvious that all aspects of the planning and governmental process require information though of quite different kinds. For example, goals cannot be discussed without reference to the political system within which the planning process is set, the distribution of power and the values held by various groups within the community, and the way these and other factors are evolving. These classes of somewhat elusive and ambiguous information must also figure in the design of various alternative courses of action together with a great deal of 'hard' data relating to social, economic and physical matters. Evaluation will require information which is as precise as possible with respect to the outcomes to be expected or required from each course of action as well as knowledge, of optimization techniques and the assumptions which lie behind models of rational choice.

We have already interpreted the correspondence in complexity between the objective (i.e. urban) system and the operative control (i.e. planning) system as an example of the workings of the law of requisite variety. If the planner's conceptions of the urban system is extended e.g. from simple land-use and traffic concepts to a much more ramified version in which a host of social, political and economic variables are included then the information system *must* expand correspondingly if anything like effective understanding and control is to be achieved.

Certainly a limited range and quality of information has definite effects on certain important aspects or stages of the planning process. Limited data will restrict the choice, say, of methods for modelling urban phenomena (MCLOUGHLIN, 1969, p. 235; CRIPPS and HALL, 1969).

This central importance of information results from the wholeness of the planning process. As CRIPPS (1969, ii/iii) puts it:

'The data bank and the model are, therefore, very much inter-connected within the information system. The existence of these two components do not necessarily build an information system, however, and to shape information technology appropriate to urban planning, we need to agree also on the shape of the planning process. In this way we can identify the points at which technology in the form of computer-organized and manufactured information is important. These problems need to be tackled before the question of information or data availability arises, since data as such merely indexes the variables we choose for system description. Nevertheless, data is a constraining influence on the kind of variables we can choose, and at this point in the process we shall no doubt have to modify earlier decisions made in designing the information system.'

Another very important problem which we shall have to tackle in our concluding chapter is referred to by Cripps. That is the relationship between information systems for planning and those which are intended to serve all the functions of local government. This question reflects also the questions of how planning relates to the other services performed by local government and to the several 'private-sector' (non-governmental) groups and institutions in the community and *their* inter-relations.

The place of information in the planning process seems at first sight to be a very gritty, practical business calling up visions of filing cabinets, computers, maps, charts and calculating machines. That is a perfectly reasonable view of the 'tip of the iceberg' of information; lying immediately below this tip is the bulky foundation which, in fact, is a conceptual model of the urban system being planned and of the planning process. This merely reflects the general truth that 'what is observed depends not only on the context in which a particular phenomenon is set, but in the manner in which one is prepared to view it' (CHORLEY and HAGGETT, 1967, p. 20).

In several ways it is difficult and limiting to insist on clear-cut differences between 'theoretical' and 'practical' matters. For example, modelling and simulation techniques, prodigious users of information, are both heavily dependent upon theories for their further development. BATTY (1970) has put this point very clearly both in words: 'In essence', he says, 'we see information as providing one of the bonds between relevant theory and relevant practice' and in the form of a diagram:

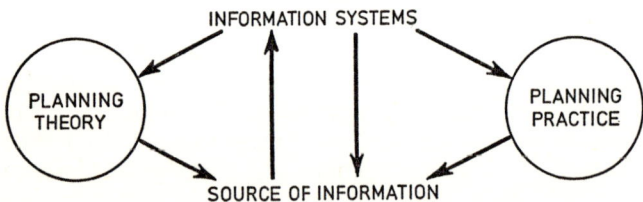

Figure 9.1: Theory, practice and information

These relationships explain why

'the development of planning through time is reflected by changes in the system and sources of information. Such changes may originate from planning theory or from practice, or may be affected by the rôle which planning assumes within the overall sphere of government.' (BATTY, 1970, p. 4)

Planning has also been described as 'the process of strategic choice' (FRIEND and JESSOP, 1969) which is made difficult because of various kinds of uncertainty. We have already referred to the general theoretical area of information, organization, entropy and uncertainty. Clearly the main theories developed there apply to urban planning also. This viewpoint has now been given official recognition for it is held that

'an information system is part of the mechanism for reducing uncertainty in the knowledge and understanding of the (physical, social and economic) environment. . . . But the information needed largely depends on the methods used in attempting to understand the environment: conversely, methodology is to some extent determined by the availability of data.' (DEPARTMENT OF THE ENVIRONMENT, 1972)

This recent governmental study considered the information needs of the whole cycle of planning activities but decided to concentrate on the background information needed to support the making of various plans. They also recognized that information would also be needed for continuous review, development control, public participation and 'general information for management . . . at the local authority level'.

However, there was a very important further emphasis in the study (p. 18) on the view that 'the end-product of planning activities was decision-making.' In other words, the reduction of uncertainty which information brings about serves the purpose of *choices or decisions* with respect to the urban system.

Data, information and intelligence

There has been considerable use of terms such as 'data bank', 'information needs' and 'intelligence systems' here and elsewhere and it will be helpful to try and clarify the distinct senses in which these terms will be used. Many writers use these terms without making a great deal of distinction between meanings, others seem to use them almost interchangeably. As far as the distinction between data and information is concerned, following the usage proposed by WHITE (1970)

'we define *data* as being raw (or unprocessed) and *information* as being cooked (processed or interpreted) . . . data form the base from which information is produced: that data are the facts, usually expressed in quantifiable form, which, when interpreted become the information on which decisions are based. . . .'

At this point we part company with Brenda White for we believe that the highly processed, evaluative, often tentative and speculative material, rich in value-judgements and opinions which is ultimately indistinguishable from the policy decision should be called *intelligence*. So we would identify three hierarchical levels:

data – raw material, the original empirical observation e.g. the census form completed by the householder, the interview record, the photograph, the return;

information – aggregated, transformed, tabulated and classified data presented in convenient form without evaluation, comment or discussion – e.g. volumes of statistics published by government agencies, urban reports appraising and commenting on a situation or a series of developments, a file of newspaper cuttings relevant to a particular set of issues;

intelligence – includes all that we regard as information but goes a crucial step beyond to include unstructured opinions, values, feelings and to include the implications of information for the making of policies, for the choice between alternative policies, for the foreseeable or actual outcomes and repercussions of putting policies into effect as programmes – and so on.

It should be clear that these three categories are by no means watertight and that it will often be difficult to distinguish with any certainty between data and information and between information and intelligence. For example, a discursive account of the analysis of ten years of house-building in a local authority area cannot fail to reflect and qualify the policies which governed those housing and redevelopment programmes; it would be very difficult to say whether such a document was information or intelligence. The distinctions between data, information and intelligence depend more on the context than on the nature of the material and what is information in one set of circumstances could be regarded as raw data in another, even within the same agency.

Even though facts are only relevant within some theoretical framework which suggest and guide an investigation, nevertheless, the disciplined and well-organized collection of data can threaten to overwhelm the investigator. This is surely an example of 'information overload'. One of the important characteristics of the computer is that it has promised 'to restore to the greatly strained geographical data-matrix some of the order that its rapid expansion threatened to destroy' (HAGGETT and CHORLEY, 1967).

Geography is the discipline most concerned with the development of data and information about spatial aspects of human behaviour and BERRY (1968a) has shown how its basic data matrix relates *characteristics* and *places*, whilst a series of such matrices can record the passage of *time*. More important, he has gone on to indicate (1968b) how the transformation of such matrices, using well established techniques of multivariate analysis, could provide the basis for relating spatial structure and spatial behaviour within a 'general field theory'.

But, in the opinion of many planners, such information systems stop short, usually, of what is really wanted. For the crude models currently employed by planners place an 'extraordinary premium on feedback' which can best be obtained and digested within an intelligence system (ALONSO, 1968). Institutional requirements may for a time force 'master plan' preparation on a planning profession increasingly in revolt against the very idea. Personal and professional mobility will usually result in a different set of individuals collecting feedback from planning programmes initiated and designed by others, now gone. But the feedback is vital to improving knowledge of urban systems and planning systems; hence the need for some form of intelligence system.

CHAPIN (1963) envisioned the general metropolitan plan, the policies instrument, the various programmes, development control codes and 'an informed community' as needed elements of a 'guidance system for urban development' activated very largely by feedbacks from outcomes to intentions. Such feedback from the urban system to the planning system will have the effect of modifying the planning system itself and, therefore, the more complex and flexible *intelligence* system is the most appropriate form to discuss. DUHL (1967) also believed that information seems to be the 'critical element' in planners' functions, rather than scientific techniques.

Increasingly, as the social-science impacts affect planning in practice (and in teaching and research) it is *socially relevant information* which is needed to sustain the planners' efforts (BROADY, 1965) and to enable him and others in the public service *and* the 'clients' to evaluate the services provided both quantitatively (ACKOFF, 1962) and qualitatively. Recent political developments in Britain over, say, the London motorway proposals and the work of the Roskill Commission on the siting of the Third London Airport show how important and how demanding qualitative evaluation is becoming. Arguments over how *far* we can quantify may lose sight of the fact that there will always be (in practice if not in theory) aspects of life which cannot be quantified and on which there will never be 'consensus' even of a partial and localized kind. It is this large area which brings about the need for *intelligence* as an aid to policy-and-decision-making, over and above the limited services provided by data and information. These are the vital issues we shall consider at the conclusion of this chapter. But before turning to the principles which ought to guide the development of data, information and intelligence systems in the future we shall examine the salient features of British and North American practice.

Current practice with respect to data, information and intelligence

The United States of America
A number of urban 'information systems' in the U.S.A. were examined by FRY (1968) who held that a good system would not be confined to physical aspects but would encompass a wide range of social and economic data also so as to provide 'a continuous quantitative background for the top-level decision-maker'. Fry did not find such a scheme among those he examined. Los Angeles City, however, has centralized all its data processing functions into a single Data Service Bureau and created a non-profit systems engineering corporation – the Los Angeles Technical Services Corporation (JOYCE and DESCHER, 1968). The city has launched a 'Community Analysis Program' designed to identify problems and to measure the social

and economic impacts of its improvement programmes. New York City is described as a 'rich laboratory' for the 'new breed of social-physical scientist' (SAVAS, 1968) and systems analysis is described as 'what's happening on the urban scene'. New York City was then setting up an observatory as a centre for basic urban research. This was to have four parts:

- a *Center for Urban and Program Analysis* comprising a 'think-tank' for problems and projects using systems analysis, simulation, control theory, information systems and management science; problem identification would be followed by the setting up of a P.P.B. system.
- an *Urban Data Center* one of whose main tasks would be 'to replace Greek letters with Arabic numerals' in mathematical models by developing 'cross-agency work on consistent data files'. It would support management and research in the Program Analysis Center. Using the best possible media (including graphics, press, tickertape) it would produce and disseminate regular 'State of the City' reports which would be open not only to the public sector but also *to the private sector* to aid in locational and other decisions. A major problem here is the issue of the confidentiality of individual data.
- an *Urban Research Consortium* to be set up mainly by universities in return for access to the Data Center. It would develop and test theories of urban growth and organization and participate in two-way flows of staff between local government and universities.
- an *Urban Documentation Center* (which (1968) already existed in embryo. It would produce 'a Thesaurus of urban bibliographic terms' and a 'Keyword-in-Context' abstracting and indexing service.

Great Britain

In reviewing current practice in Great Britain we can here draw on our own field investigation of several planning authorities as well as work carried out by other investigators.

CATER (1970), whose main theme was the information needs of planners, found very few authorities who examined the urban system in a logical way and that data collected was 'task-oriented' i.e. related to specific projects after which it was jettisoned. The *depart-mentalism* of local government fostered a compartmented approach to problems which led in turn to serious gaps in data related to problems when viewed holistically. Also there was considerable

233

duplication of data collection despite the finding that 'inter-departmental liaison was generally very good.' (CATER, p. 1)

She found also, as others have done, that co-operative 'data bank'
projects are all too often what WEBBER (1965) calls 'grab-bag
collections' of randomly assorted data each sub-set relevant to a
particular problem as viewed by one department at one particular
time. There was rarely, if at all, any shared conception of the urban,
social, economic and physical systems and thence an agreed minimal
data set which would enable shared, interdepartmental, community-
wide analyses of problems and policies to be made.

But many local government officers were acutely aware of current
shortcomings and there are several developments seeking to remedy
this state of affairs. The view of most authorities visited by Cater
was that there should be a new, separate 'Research and Intelligence'
department although a number of authorities had encouraged their
planning department to assume and develop this function.* The main
practical difficulties discovered by Cater were also familiar – no
consistency in definitions, areal units or dates of collection. The
computer, so great in its potential, was usually in the charge of the
treasurer's department and oriented towards payroll and other
'number-crunching' accounting procedures. Never was it conceived
of as a management tool to aid in the study of problems, policies and
decisions. Although 'several of the authorities visited had one or
more computer-readable topic files . . . yet no authority had a
completely computer-based information system.' (CATER, 1970, p. 8)

A broadly similar pattern was discovered by the author and his
colleagues. Of seventeen authorities visited only the Greater London
Council had an intelligence unit in the true sense. The investigation
focused on the needs of the planning department (rather than any
wider purposes of local government) and in particular, the information needs of the development control caseworkers. In practice, these
caseworkers made little use of *data* systems. On the rare occasions
when they judged that data was needed they sometimes asked
colleagues in 'development plan', 'design' or 'policy' sections of the
planning department or colleagues in other departments – usually

* This question of the (departmental) location of the research-and-intel-
ligence function is not simply a problem of bureaucracy but reflects strongly on
the nature of planning in public authorities and the rôle of intelligence systems.
We shall not develop this theme here but rather in the concluding sections of
this chapter.

the engineer's – to provide them. The data most often used by the caseworkers were land-use, census of population and traffic-study material (see Chapter 4).

Development control caseworkers and their colleagues are deeply involved in the information services proviced by local government. It is probably fair to say that with the exception of several authorities which clearly make a great effort to provide an efficient, helpful and friendly service 'over the counter' to the general public, such services in Britain are dreadfully inadequate. We say elsewhere that the planning function as a whole and the development control function in particular do not affect the average person or family so frequently as, say, the education, housing and refuse collection services. But when planning does affect a family, a group of houses or part of a community the problems raised tend to be more troublesome. This is not only because people find problems of physical development – whether by the public authority itself or by private initiatives – unfamiliar because they are less frequent. It may also be the case that the forces which lie behind the physical development proposals – government, the banks, and insurance companies, public corporations, as well as building and engineering contractors, retailing organizations and so on – are little understood by the average person. But there are also a host of quite small physical developments occurring all the time. Some of them require planning permission; others may not but will come within the ambit of the building bye-laws, public health inspector, the highway authority and a host of other central and local government officials. Although each development or change may be quite small in itself – new street lighting, 'yellow line' regulations, the widening of a short length of road, the change-of-use of a wine merchant's premises into a supermarket – in combination they can affect the lives of people in the neighbourhood considerably. Perhaps most disturbing of all is the rumour that 'they' are going to build a block of flats, or chop down some trees, or extend the clearance order, or route traffic along this road in a one-way system, or allow a noisy industry to occupy the spare land at the end of the street, or fence it off so the kids can't play (*see* Rosalind Brooke in ROBSON and CRICK, 1970 on the 'civic rights' aspects of informing people).

All of these different but overlapping aspects of the relationship between government, local government and the public require information of many different kinds organized in as many different ways. Planners dealing with the physical environment are *part of the whole interface between local government and its 'clients'*.

Development control information for policy analysis

MCLOUGHLIN and WEBSTER (1971) found an almost complete absence of feedback from the outcomes of decisions on applications for planning permission to the caseworkers who were responsible for framing the recommendations. It was, therefore, hardly surprising that development plan staff were not systematically informed as to what was happening in the way of physical developments and change of use, etc.

The majority of caseworkers, of course, 'kept an eye on things' as they went about their daily rounds outside the office but otherwise reliance was usually placed on the Completion Notices, copies of which may be sent on by the building inspectors, the updated O.S. maps and the planning department's own 'enforcement officers' (see Chapter 4). In London, the boroughs were able to refer to the G.L.C.'s annual review of new physical developments and changes-of-use but unfortunately this was always in arrears. Although Aberdeen had an established system of using inspectors, none of the information they collected seemed to filter through to the policy workers.

We are distinguishing here between *two kinds of feedback*: first the simple and direct feedback to the caseworker, indicating very crudely how effective his activity is; especially whether refusals are *not* in fact contravened and whether or not the conditions attached to per-missions are observed. Information about the extent to which permissions are in fact implemented by subsequent development is really a feature of the second kind of feedback, i.e. to the policy workers (both strategic and detailed design) from development control activity.

DONNISON and BRANCH (1971) suggest that development control information can be used to aid the control process proper, to provide certain administrative statistics and that

> 'there should be a "feedback" to the plan-making process itself . . . [which] . . . could, for example, be used to identify areas in which there is a pressure for growth. The degree of success in catering for

236

it, or opposing it as the case may be, could be measured against the policy that has been applied. In this way the relationship between planning decisions and subsequent development could be fruitfully explored. Finally, the changes taking place as development occurs can be monitored.'

These authors refer to the inward-looking nature of most information systems for development control; they are designed to improve the operation of the control side of the office in an 'O and M' sense with little, if any, awareness of the needs or potentials of other sections, departments or the public in a context of public policies, control and initiative.

But a number of local planning authorities are becoming aware not only of the significance of data, information and intelligence systems within the planning process but also of the potential which information gathered for the development control process and issuing from it, can be an invaluable part of the whole information or intelligence system and 'have adjusted their methods of working so as to be able to review development plans on a continuous rather than on a periodical basis' (BLAKE, 1970). In the London borough of Brent, the planning department has been assigned the information/intelligence rôle on behalf of the authority as a whole. Development control records form an integral part of the data bank. The building inspectors' records of completed, approved development are supplemented by regular field checks.

The information of planning decisions and completions is used: 'to show trends in the amount, type and location of new development as well as the amount of development "in the pipeline" by way of outstanding consents. Secondly, it is used to update the land-use survey information.' It is also used to assist the actual process of development control – 'e.g. keeping track of when temporary consents are due to terminate and by feeding back information on completions so that checks can then be carried out as to whether the conditions attached to a planning consent have been complied with'. Those who designed and initiated the Brent data bank envisage it used for model-building on a continuous basis. They emphasize the sheer volume of dedicated work necessary to set it up but are confident of a high rate of return. They point out the amount of routine work involved in maintaining the system and how a great deal of interdepartmental co-operation is required. They are sure that comprehensive automatic data processing systems will be 'essential if local development plans are to be kept under continuous review'.

The West Sussex County Planning Department (see WILLIS, 1972) has had a 'Planning Applications System' operational since early 1967 with the two principal aims:

> first, 'to indicate when required, how much development of what kind has been approved or refused and when and where . . . in order to improve the information base for the planning function'. More specifically it will help 'to ensure that the planning authority is fully aware of the overall demands on land and how much demands change over time . . . to assist in the provision of an up-to-date picture of the land use in the Administration County . . . to evaluate the continued relevance of current plans and policies [and] to provide the statistical returns required by Central Government.'
>
> secondly, 'to provide, when required, information for the better management of the work of Development Control'. More specifically to establish a 'reminder system' indicating the impending expiry of temporary planning consents and to help in the preparation of statistics for reporting (quarterly) to the County Planning Committee.

The Sussex system clearly derives from a sophisticated view of the planning process and the relevance of control as a means of *monitoring* of the actual course of change and as an *error-activated* device wherein outcomes in terms of physical developments are compared with the intentions embodied in plans and policies.

The evolution of a comprehensive information system, nevertheless, seemed to be confined, in the minds of the West Sussex planners, to planning functions as embodied in the Planning Acts and discharged in the planning departments.

Another system of comparable sophistication is that set up by the Greater London Council in response to the recommendations of the 1963 Royal Commission on London Government which led to the 1965 London Government Act. The Act created the two-tier system comprising the G.L.C. and the boroughs and the G.L.C. was given responsibility for setting up an *Intelligence Unit* which would provide a continuous service of data, information and intelligence not only for the G.L.C. but also for the boroughs. This is one of the best staffed and best equipped intelligence units in the country and produces work of the highest quality and relevance. But at the time of the study (1970) by McLoughlin and Webster the data collected from the boroughs and the G.L.C. about the applications for planning permission and the subsequent decisions were not analysed in ways which were explicitly or directly concerned with the design, monitoring or review of policies.

WHITE (1970) investigated the information needs of planners in practice and in academic life using very wide interpretations of these terms. She approached her investigation from the point of view of the forms of sources rather than content. She found that maps and plans, data from their own surveys and their office records were the most frequent sources of operational information used by practising planners. This seems further evidence of the inward-looking nature of work in the planning office. Planners were found to make little use of abstracts and bibliographies but more use of references in books and journals. Discussions with colleagues within the same office or department was the most common personal source of information. Planners seem not to read very widely or deeply in the journal literature in spite of their expressed desire to 'keep up to date'; but seminars, conferences and symposia are rated highly for this purpose.

Brenda White recommended: improving the *physical availability* of sources in planning organization and general libraries; making planners *aware of the wide range of sources which now exist*; providing planners with 'packaged, concentrated information' supplied direct and of immediate applicability to practical situations.

In general, the data, information and intelligence systems for statutory planning in Britain are very poorly developed. We have described some of the most sophisticated in order to highlight the very unsatisfactory nature of the majority. Some of the best developed data systems are associated, whether in practice or in research agencies, with rapid growth of mathematical models of urban systems and this aspect of information in planning deserves separate consideration.

Models, computers, data and information

The rapid increase in the use of models in British planning (e.g. see CATER, 1970) is paralleled by the use of the computer in local government and academic research (e.g. see WILSON, 1968; HARRIS, 1968). The relationship is more than mere association. Planners need models because of the perceived complexity of the urban systems which they deal with and if these are to be explored in a quantified fashion the computer is indispensable. Certain quantified analyses of urban phenomena simply *could not be done* before high-speed computers became available during the 1960s; the most obvious case is the study of traffic flows on a network of roads. The use of models depends upon theories and in turn leads to the development of fresh or revised hypotheses for testing. Finally, the data collected depends upon the theory being employed – that which is believed best to 'explain' the phenomena in which the planner is interested (BATTY, 1970, p. 3).

'Models are made necessary by the complexity of reality . . . [they] . . . convey not the whole truth but a useful and comprehensible part of it.' (HAGGETT, 1965, p. 19.) One of the best accounts which put models into the widest context of the planning process as a whole, is that given by WILSON (1968). He shows how models are relevant to the rich interactions between planners (who depend on research) and researchers (who must understand planning). He goes on to show how models can be useful in varying degrees in all the major kinds of work which planners do.

All of this reinforces the view that the decisions about data and information systems cannot be divorced from the planner's conception of the urban system in which he is interested. This does *not* mean that planners articulate these systems in setting up filing systems and data banks or designing computer routines. But what they should realize is that in defining a data bank they are thereby *implicitly* defining the range of systems which they can investigate, the range of policy areas which they can analyse and the content of the programmes which can be monitored and evaluated. This lack of *explicit* recognition of the inter-relatedness of theory, models, data, policy and action

'leads to the development of data systems with an emphasis on the collection and storage of data for its own sake. The retrieval of

240

data from such systems is rarely designed to make specific contributions to the formulation of policy and monitoring of change which is carried on in other parts of the information system.' (CRIPPS, 1970)

Once computers and models are operational within a planning agency they can process, store and retrieve information, carry out all kinds of analyses of that information and make predictions or forecasts (HARRIS, 1968). But although there are serious threats involved, the most serious perhaps being that to the privacy of the individual (see e.g. SHUBIK, 1967) it is our belief, shared with WILSON (1968) that 'the computer's rôle in the planning process will be determined by the higher goals of planners rather than by its own revolutionary impact.'

The continuous interactions we have spoken of – and especially that between data and theory *via* computerized models – demand a great deal of flexibility. Clearly the most difficult side of the relationship here is the data which by its very nature tends to be inflexible with respect to definitions, geographical areas and so on. The strategies which could be employed to keep data as flexible as possible in realistic ways we shall discuss below in conclusion.

Intelligence systems and urban management

We are now in a position to identify the principles which should guide the design and operation of the data, information and intelligence systems for urban planning. To do so we shall have to say things about the internal structure and function of local government and the relations between planning and the other services.

One of the biggest problems faced by those involved in these developments is the large time-lags which exist between theory-development and the usual style of practice in planning. Thus WEBBER (1965) says that although the 'new scientific urbanists' admit none of the old disciplinary loyalties and that a 'unity of diversity' is emerging, we haven't yet got a new methodology; current practice (in the U.S. but equally true of Britain) reflects older outlooks. Those involved in the design of information systems may, therefore, face problems which transcend the mere technology of the programme. Data can be very costly and, therefore, the initial content of the data files comes under scrutiny from senior people. They are likely to query and possibly reject as of little relevance data which do not relate to their own ideas about cities and planning.

One of the crucial problems in the initial stages is delimiting the content of the intelligence system (which as we have seen is almost synonymous with defining an 'urban system of interest').

It should by now be clear that we are discussing not just an 'urban' or 'local government' or least of all an 'urban planning' intelligence system to aid in control of towns or local authorities. Instead we are discussing *the general principle of intelligence in the regulation of complex open systems*. For, although BEER (1969) begins writing about corporate management and planning he claims for the scheme which he puts forward that 'the model, if it is valid at all, is invariant' and can be applied as well to governments and nations as to firms.

Beer puts forward a model of organization which tries to overcome the dilemma of management, i.e. that it seems better to procrastinate rather than to plan because a manager will always have better information tomorrow; that

> 'when tomorrow comes and provides more information, in principle he must *change his decision* . . . a corporate plan refers to an indefinitely long series of tomorrows and to a complex set of decisions, and the quanta of information which accrue daily may in the long run significantly change any given contributory decision. Thus it turns out that corporate planning is a continuous process, directed towards the adaptation of contemporary decisions about the future to the continuously present state of knowledge.' (BEER, 1969, p. 398)

Adaptation then is the crux of planning though not its ostensible object which is *decisions and events* – the objective of planning is

> 'the continuous adaptation of the enterprise towards continuing survival . . . there is no plan, to be determined now and adhered to, which will guarantee that survival. There is, however, a planning process which is continuous, aimed at adapting the enterprise to a changing environment – and fitting it, therefore, to exploit its opportunities.' (loc. cit.)

Beer then goes on to state his central thesis i.e. that we are concerned with *adaptive organization* on a general principle of maintaining viability i.e. of surviving. Examples of such adaptive behaviour all have a *hierarchical* structure and this must be accepted as

242

one of the 'givens' of cybernetics. He puts forward a five-level hierarchy in which level 1 (the lowest) is 'where the action is' and operations are actually carried out; level 2 damps down any tendency toward oscillation in level 1 while level 3 maintains internal homeostasis and level 4 external homeostasis by reporting on and analysing the organization's environment. Level 5, which completes the hierarchy, is a 'look-out' facility for mapping out viable strategies.

This model of management and planning is one in which 'the entire organization must needs fulfil the function of a controller' and works by free interchange of rich supplies of information. *The source for all of the information ingested by an open system is the environment and the point of contact is the interface between planning and action.*

The source of information for the urban management and planning system is the environment of that system, the urban systems-of-interest themselves. In local government the major 'sensors' will be at two levels in the hierarchy – at what Beer calls level 1, that is the operational level and at level 4, the staff function which collects and distils direct from the outside world. This is the 'research and intelligence unit' of recent local government history and as can be seen it 'sits squarely on the central command axis' (BEER, op. cit. p. 411) i.e. it is totally integrated into the gubernatorial process and *not* somewhere off to one side 'advising'.

Nor are level 1 elements merely doing 'what they are told' but as they carry out their tasks day-in day-out they are receiving and passing upwards information about the external world *without which urban management would simply not be possible.*

It is now being argued that the function of local government should *be* governing or managing the urban systems of interest in a unified and concerted way. It is also argued by many that the purpose of such government is to enable those systems to survive and adapt in the face of the 'buffetings' of change. *This requires an intelligence system which is central to and pervasive of the governing institutions.*

Thus there is a central and pervasive 'rôle of intelligence systems in urban-systems planning' (WEBBER, 1965) which transcends the detached, value-free rôle of the data bank kept for the 'private' use of a department in local government. The urban intelligence systems must recognize that

'facts about societal things and events are seldom value-neutral. They inevitably intervene into the workings of the systems they

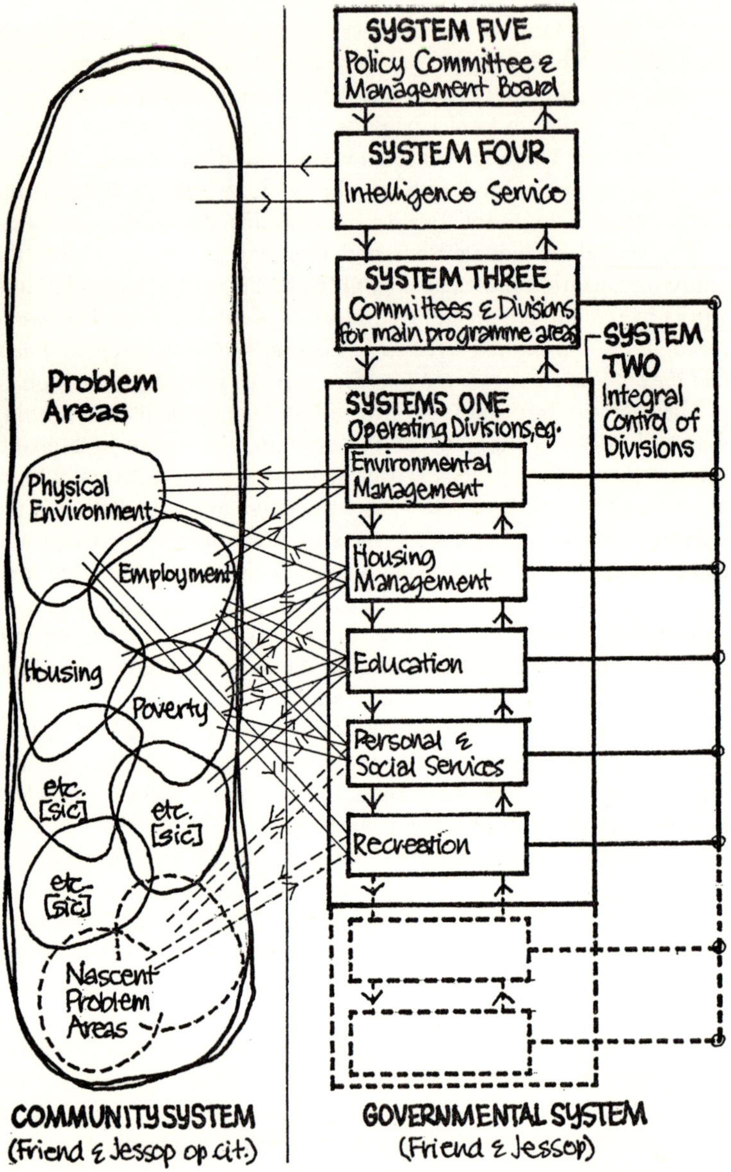

Figure 9.2: Information-flow relationships within government and between government and community

describe. The information supplier, whatever his motives and methods, is therefore inevitably immersed in politics. . . . To play the rôle of scientist in the urban field is also to play the rôle of intervener, however indirect and modest the intervention may be.' (WEBBER, p. 295)

Webber concludes his arguments by reminding us that there are few decision rules relevant for the multitude of overlapping publics and that the urban analyst is inevitably a 'policy-shaper if not a policy maker' because those who publish urban information, especially about possible futures, have gone a long way towards helping those futures to come about. The most effective and helpful action for planners may simply be to *provide better information about the urban systems of interest* – of interest that is to all the groups, and individuals on the urban scene. Thus those who operate the urban intelligence centres are helping with

'the injection of the *scientific morality* into urban policy-making. . . . Partisanship, parochialism and partial knowledge are inherent to the urban system as they are to science. The intelligence centres can never eliminate them. The new planners must accept them as facts, no less real and valid than rents, transport costs, interest rates and topographic conditions. By more systematically accounting for these variables, however, and by then exposing alternative action and value hypotheses to critical and systematic examination, those in the information-and-planning sciences may help to eliminate the most negative consequences of partisanship and ignorance.' (p. 296)

We have said already that information about urban systems and especially about how they affect the individual enquirer is an aspect of civic rights (BROOKE, 1970) and the need to communicate to the great diversity of people and groups highlights the diversity which the intelligence system must possess. For example, it must be capable of giving central government a highly sophisticated analysis of the changes which affect the area as a whole and which may be significant at a national level; but at the same time it has to be able to explain in a suitably simple and direct way – probably verbal and face-to-face – what the effect of a clearance order is to a housewife who rents furnished accommodation in a redevelopment area.

Obviously such an intelligence system cannot be contained with a department nor a finite number of staff members, nor occupy a finite suite of rooms. We repeat, what we are discussing here is *pervasive*

*networks of data and information exchange which are so inter-
connected as to constitute an intelligence system.* Now obviously there
will be a core of personnel which is devoted wholly to intelligence-
system duties and looking after its central hardware, writing most of
the major reports, seeing that the links in the networks are all
functioning properly, developing new links, enlarging old ones and
so on. This will be a 'staff' function attached to the office of the chief
executive. But the intelligence system does not comprise a finite set
of people; it includes at different times and in different ways a very
large proportion of a local government's staff who must receive
information at the interfaces with the client groups, central government, universities and other institutions and also those in intermediary rôles – project managers and other 'line' executives part
of whose responsibilities is the collation, editing, interpretation and
transmission of information both 'upwards', 'downwards' and 'side-
ways', towards or away from top management centres.

It is a serious mistake to regard intelligence systems as finite 'units'
which are somehow *in* but not *of* institutions of government. It is
this concept, together with the erroneous assumptions about value-
free data and detached 'positivist' analysis which allows such units
to become embarrassments to those who set them up and often
ensures their expedient demise. A pervasive intelligence system is not
something tacked on to the institution but *built in to it*. It follows that
as the institution adapts, so will its intelligence systems; in fact, the
relationship is reciprocal for the intelligence systems embodying a
'look-out' facility (BEER, 1969) should be largely instrumental in
bringing about periodic adjustments and innovations in the structure
of the *adaptive* organization.

It is some time now since PERLOFF (1965) indicated some 'new
directions in social planning' and showed how both institutions and
programmes would have to be adaptive and responsive to the
evolution of problems and solutions. He showed too that coping with
some of the biggest problems of urban societies required much closer
integration of physical and social planning into the form of area-
based services focused on the household as its key unit of concern
and caught up in a 'continuous process of neighbourhood improvement' (p. 302).

Action would be focused on neighbourhood improvement
programmes working towards gradual upgrading of physical and

social services (quicker where redevelopment or specially-supported projects were to be invoked). The broadly-based social planning process would include:

(a) monitoring problems/outcomes;
(b) research action/promotion;
(c) pilot projects;
(d) programme costing and evaluation;
(e) budgeting control;
(f) recruiting people from wide 'pools of competence';
(g) securing public involvement;
(h) strengthening planning/programming in constituent agencies;
(i) reporting/evaluating programmes;
(j) keeping public informed at all times through wide range of media. (p. 303)

Perloff concludes with the note that the rôle of social planning

'is to focus the community's attention on theoretical social problems and issues . . . and on ways of achieving (objectives) in the face of the inevitable diversity and conflict. To be effective it has to help key decision-making units ranging from the individual family and business firm to the social agency, the local Health and Welfare Council and the municipal governments, so that these various units can see where the common interest lies and how they might advance the broad community goals while advancing their own ends.' (PERLOFF, p. 303)

Thus, as Perloff says in his abstract the new information tools allied to the new planning methods:

'would feed the social planning process with a constant stream of information bearing as closely as possible upon the substance of objectives of the programme, enabling continual refinement of method, providing new guides toward solution.'

247

Government, community and governance

We have advocated a view of government which sees its principal function and fortification as a set of institutions performing certain essentially brain-like functions within society. This view derives from cybernetics because this new science is concerned with the communication of meaningful patterns of information around the networks of highly complex adaptive systems. It is certainly not the only possible model for studying governmental and planning processes (see ROSE, 1971) and, indeed, like any other model it raises certain difficulties and ambiguities. Nevertheless, a number of important issues in governance such as purposive behaviour, rationality, control, stability, change and communication are the subject matter of cybernetics which does shed new light on these abiding problems of public and political life. Increasingly there are demands that government should be more *responsive* to currents of change, that its actions should be more *relevant* to problems and their evolution, that it should be more *accountable* to the community and that it should operate better as an important part of a 'social learning system' (SCHON, 1971) and play a major rôle in anticipating, exploring and willing the future. These processes place heavy reliance on communication networks both within the formal organs of government and its planning systems and between them and the community and its urban systems.

The sheer complexity of the conjoint system resulting from rich interlinkage between the governmental planning systems and the urban community systems suggests a number of things. Firstly that government should not be regarded as a responsive entity bending to winds of change blown from elsewhere outside it. Government can and does contain individuals and groups who may be highly innovative and 'afire with faith in what people ought to want' (VICKERS,

248

1968). Their desire and ability to engender parametric social changes contrasts sharply with the model of disjointed incrementalism in public life. But equally, for government to act effectively as regulator system it needs requisite variety and this needs the input of information from the enveloping community system. The relevance, responsiveness and adaptability of government depends critically on its connections with the community so that facts, ideas, demands and suggestions can be transferred within the formal institutions of government.

Government is the set of formal, legally defined institutions with legitimate power but the process of *governance* must involve the conjoint system which embraces both government and community. The whole policy realm of national parks and access to the countryside originated in the communities of northern industrial towns who demanded the right to share the hills of Derbyshire and Yorkshire with aristocratic grouse-shooters. Latter-day students of social administration may conclude that new policies and agencies for dealing with the problems of the inner parts of our largest cities have their roots in ideas first raised and debated by the communities of Notting Hill, Sparkbrook, Moss Side and Gorbals. But other initiatives – structure plans, country parks, comprehensive schools, traffic management – can be traced to officials in central and local government and academics interested in these problems. No clearly identifiable group, no 'us' or 'them' can be clearly defined or ascribed the prerogative for initiating change. Mechanistic analysis of simple and obvious cause-and-effect relationships is only possible when dealing with much smaller systems than human society.

Equally, the recognition of high complexity rules out simplistic debate as to whether the functions of government and the processes of governance are concerned with stability *or* change. Cybernetic analysis of highly complex systems reveals that stability depends upon change, so that both must co-exist. Much depends on the time-scale because for example a community reasonably expects commitment by government which will stabilize the conditions of 'delivery' of particular services (housing, transport, education) over certain periods of time but also expects the possibility of change in those arrangements from time to time. Government and community are both concerned with stability and change. It is especially important for both to have the capability to change subsystems and elements in relatively short time-spans so as to ensure responsiveness and relevance; but that may be conditional on the stability of the capacity to initiate and accomplish such changes. In Chapter 9 we have argued that this capacity may depend almost completely on the existence and the character of intelligence systems within government and linking government to the community. Such intelligence systems would be pervasive and have a network structure.

> 'Where social, organizational or interpersonal networks are in question, there is the concept of channels of relationship among elements, which make it easier or more likely for transactions of a certain kind to occur among elements than if those channels were not present.' (SCHON, 1971, pp. 190–1)

Responsiveness, relevance and foresight in governance, the ability to deal effectively with current problems, to anticipate those which could emerge, will depend not only on formally defined organizational networks but on those informal networks which 'have long seemed to enable people to get things done when the formal networks failed'. These latter networks are increasing in importance and requiring more people who can build, operate and move around in them. These people are represented by the Russian 'tolkatch', the American 'fixer', and the 'reticulist' as recently christened by POWER (1971).

Intelligence systems in government, linking planning and urban systems, government and community, strategic policy and programmed or routine action, together with the multitude of network operators are all implied by a cybernetic model of governance. Such a model is essentially about management, planning, decision and control but in an overarching and generic sense. This book, however, has a particular focus on physical or environmental planning at all levels from broad 'structure' planning to detailed design, action and regulation. Such as emphasis marked the earlier chapters on the objects of British statutory planning and details of its practice. It is now time to try and locate such activities and strategic planning and development control within the sort of framework we have been sketching. We shall now emphasize these statutory physical planning functions but the interconnected, holistic nature of our frame of reference will require us to say things about local government structures and functions in general.

Detailed physical planning and development control

The research project on which we have drawn extensively throughout this book considered the future of statutory planning in local government as well as studying current practice. A wide variety of views was revealed among caseworkers and other officials about the future of development control and related aspects of physical planning. Some people believed that the 1968 Act would not make much difference to control and design because the reforms it initiates concentrate on the strategic policy levels. This was a widely held view and confirmed our impressions of a certain degree of alienation between strategic work and casework. Officers in Durham told us that 'we don't take much notice of the existing County map' partly because 'land-use allocations are not much used in making decisions; they are made with respect to county policy as a whole and the merits of the application.' The control chief in the Peak Park office remarked that 'things will remain much the same' because the old-style (1947 Act) development plan for rural areas had never been a land-use plan as it was in towns. One officer felt that 'control has been left to get on with the job without any backing of information or detailed plans.' By contrast, some people thought that great changes would ensue from the 1968 Act. There was a welcome for its greater flexibility so that policies could be interpreted by the officers in broader terms than land use, road alignments and the like. Several people said that it would remove the present distinction between control and plan work but usually this view referred to detailed rather than strategic plans. One interesting view was put forward by officers in Camden who suggested that the plan/control distinction could disappear to be replaced by one between short-term and long-term working groups; the short-term group would contain both 'design' and 'control' functions. However, very few people realized that if structure plans were to be expressed partly in terms of numerical values of population, employment, traffic, land development ratios and so forth, then control would have to work in the same 'language' – just as land-use plans can be related to land-use controls so the socio-economic factors in plans will require appropriate measures for their implementation.

All in all there was some evidence of considerable confusion and uncertainty about control in the future. This is hardly surprising considering the scant attention it has received from government compared with the very considerable effort which has gone into 'the future of development plans'. A feature of the investigation as a whole was the very different degree and type of response from caseworkers and 'plan' officers. For example, most caseworkers talked in terms of the 1968 Act, its provisions and procedures, whilst development plan, design and research officers tended to talk about planning in general. This certainly lends some weight to the widespread view that case-workers are too busy, have not time to think, to reflect, to read, to form and re-form their views of a professional activity in the public service whereas their colleagues may be more fortunate.

However, there was a general welcome held out by both 'plan/policy' officers and control staffs for the 1968 Act's new local plans – the 'action area' and especially the 'district' plans. One officer held that 'development control will find the structure plan useless and will have to wait for local plans to be prepared.' A Camden officer hoped that the district plans would contain 'wholesale intentions for an area' and yet be 'flexible at the same time'.

Many planners to whom we spoke looked forward to a three-level hierarchy of operations with strategy at the top and action/control at the bottom linked by the district plan which thus assumed great importance as a pivot or link element. The relationships between action areas, district plans and development control were stressed both in Luton (where 'control' and 'design' are integrated) and in Durham (where they are not). Officers in these and several other authorities believed that *detailed plans could 'almost arise from the work of development control'*. In other words, the caseworker comes to have a very rich and detailed understanding of the area for which he is responsible – of the physical environment and its potential, of its work and its people. To discount or discard this valuable source of information (as is mostly the case at present) would be foolish in the future; the hope is that local plans will provide the formal framework for such methods of working.

Often this point was put in a rather different way – namely, that *development plan people should have a better understanding of the implications of their policies* – both before and after they were adopted and implemented. A plan officer would help to make a better plan and would do a better job in reviewing it if he could experience, as directly as do his caseworker colleagues, the effects on school children, bus drivers, shoppers, industrialists and old people of the policies he is recommending or helping to monitor. 'A plan is only as good as its implementation' said a Leicester caseworker, pointing out that plans were implemented to a considerable degree by development control. The process of formulating and reviewing policies, but especially the more detailed physical plans, could gain immeasurably if development control were more closely associated with it.

Perhaps this desire for deeper and more realistic understanding of policies by executives and vice versa underlies the widespread feeling that in future, development control decisions would have to be much more explicitly founded in rational arguments than in the past. 'Officers will have to be more convincing . . . and more knowledge-able' we were told in Durham, and in the G.L.C. officers felt that casework in the future, as now, would consist mainly of 'making wise decisions which would be justified by exposure to public scrutiny'. An officer in Herefordshire gave examples of what he called 'develop-ment control mythology', i.e. beliefs which underlay certain import-ant classes of planning decisions which were subsequently shown to be without foundation. For example, the number of applications for houses outside towns and villages roughly equals those inside. When allowance is made for the 'damping' effect of known planning policies the unconstrained demand must be considerably higher. And yet it is Herefordshire's policy (and that of many other counties) to 'contain' existing settlements severely. As this officer said, this poses crucial questions as to 'What is planning for? – what people want, or what they ought to want?'

Suggestions varied as to how this greater rationality would come about. For many it was via scientific method and this usually meant more numerical measures of relevant variables caught up in an intelligence unit by urban-regional models which were in part 'fed' with data emanating from development control work. Understand-ably, this view was mostly found among the younger officers. As one said, 'I feel that if we are going to use rationality and numeracy in plan-making we must also use it in control which will thereby be integrated.' Development control, one officer thought 'is clearly a sort of information service for development plan', though in highly informal ways. In Luton, they hoped for the reverse process whereby models would help the development control officer to answer the question 'what happens if we approve?'

Some comments and speculations about the future included references to *data and intelligence systems*. These would include the mathematical models which would help with the 'what would happen if' type of questions, but going beyond this to embrace *qualitative* analyses of problems, public comments, entrepreneurial pressures, the incidence and effects of public controls and initiatives. Development control was seen as being an integral part of such systems – as 'one of the sensors in a multi-channel monitoring system'. Properly organized systems would digest the proliferating detail of development control work and interpret it for policy workers in appropriate terms.

Many caseworkers looked forward to a further development of the educative, counselling, persuasive, helpful styles of contact with the community via applicants and others. 'People will still want to know about individual properties and how they are affected' said an officer in Leicester, echoing a widely held view.

One of the most interesting views of all was the suggestion that *development control should be integrated not only with detailed physical planning but with many other kinds of public activities of a detailed, executive kind.* A senior 'plan' officer in Herefordshire suggested that 'anything concerned with development should come under a Central Intelligence Unit serving all departments. All relevant information – for example, about population and employment, should be circulated in the form of 'state-of-the-county' reports at intervals, elucidating important trends. Development control activity should be included in this.' He felt, as did a number of people, that detailed physical controls at present administered by planning, engineering and health officials under several Acts should be integrated in the interests of good administration.

Some officers in Leicester went further, one calling for '*a multi-functional District Officer* system related to fairly small areas with a small "H.Q." staff providing overall guidance and intelligence'. Another went so far as to suggest that if all the 'human scale' activities and services were properly integrated 'they could leave the planning department altogether'. Certainly, the 'Ombudsman', counselling, educative and informative rôles performed by many development control people extended far beyond the narrow confines of zoning and aesthetic controls. The undoubted success and public appreciation of, for example, Leicester's counter service, Luton and Herefordshire's ex-policemen who subtly and gently enforce planning law are present-day examples of what could be important parts of the inter-face between planners, other public servants and their various 'clients' (SCHON, 1971).

The White Paper (Feb. 1971) on Local Government said that 'planning control raises issues of close local interest' and, therefore, that 'by far the greater number of planning control decisions' should be dealt with by second-tier local authorities, leaving a much smaller proportion of 'strategic and reserved decisions' to be taken by the first-tier authorities. There have been difficulties in operating a two-tier system in Greater London since 1965 but this is not because of faults inherent in a two-tier administration. We believe that an hierarchical system has considerable theoretical justification and many parallels in complex-system control. But once again we must stress the need for 'language' consistency between intention and regulation within each level. The problem in London has been the transfer of *all aspects* of certain cases to the G.L.C. for determination because *some aspects* raised issues of metropolitan significance. This has made for confusion and cumbersome procedures because it has required the G.L.C. to examine and determine the *details* of cases as well as their broader implications. So long as such examination is made in relation to the 'Initial Development Plan' – a detailed, land-use type of document – then the consistency principle is upheld. But in future when all cases must be judged in relation to the strategic G.L.D.P. this will no longer be so and the details must in logic be reserved for the London boroughs to decide. Since a two-tier system will be general throughout Britain, all development control cases must be considered both from a detailed and from a strategic view-point. The majority of cases will not of themselves raise strategic issues whereas their cumulative direct or side-effects will in time produce considerable changes. The requirement is, therefore, that *all cases should be considered by both tiers.* This may well mean that the upper-tier 'examination' in the majority of cases will be simply a recording of details (e.g. floor area, activity types, employees, rooms, etc.) in data files. The need for inter-authority intelligence systems is obvious and we shall deal with that below.

The 'legislating for taste' aspects of development control should be removed as unnecessary and undesirable. Cybernetic theory suggests that diversity is a precondition of learning and the imposition of taste norms is, therefore, likely to depress rather than elevate public taste. In any case development control touches on such a minute aspect of total visual experience that its effects in its present form are negligible. Detailed control of the appearance of all buildings and other structures represents a piece of irritating and needless bureaucracy and for that reason alone should be ended.

But the *selective and intensive* use of such control has much to commend it. Visual control in 'Areas of Special Control', safeguarding fine individual buildings, groups of trees, views and so forth is both necessary (since 'the market' would not do so) and widely accepted and supported. Such provisions should be continued, strengthened where necessary and extended to cover all developing agencies *including government departments and nationalized industries.*

In the interests of good administration and responsiveness to the needs of the public, development control should be related very closely not only to detailed physical planning but to the whole range of activities in local government which are concerned with the local environment. In addition to the present range of jobs done by development control workers and their colleagues in detailed design sections, *a new kind of 'line' department perhaps called 'environmental management'* would also deal with all the normal building and civil engineering work of the authority, traffic management, landscape design and management, building inspection and similar matters.

This new kind of department would deal not only with day-to-day routine administration but also with *projects* involving physical developments of all kinds. In doing so, the department would normally provide the *development project management* function and thus call upon and co-ordinate the skills and resources needed for all other departments. Because of the rich interactions between the physical environment and other aspects of life, such work should relate closely to the work of other departments and agencies performing a service directly to individuals and households. The conversion of houses into flats, the creation of parking areas, the creation of 'play-streets' are problems of income distribution, information and education as much as of physical form and design. As DONNISON has said, 'if planning is to take increasingly comprehensive account of the impact of and the interrelationships between, all local services' their planners should be kept 'in closer touch with those administrating the schools, housing services, personal social services and other branches of local government' (the *Guardian* 15 March 1971).

This line of argument leads us towards conclusions relevant to local government organization and management as a whole and we shall mention this topic as such later on. Our main conclusion so far is worth restating however; that development control is logically and usefully linked with detailed physical planning; this link should be strengthened and extended to encompass a comprehensive service of *local environmental management*; development control can have very little, if any, direct relationship with structure planning and similar expression of broad and general policy; this leads us to consider the conclusions to be drawn from our work as far as structure planning is concerned.

Structure planning and other forms of public policy making

General-systems views of some key aspects of urban-regional structure and dynamics poses a number of important questions for strategic and structure planning. One of the most significant reviews of this field has been made by BERRY (1964). He looked at the work of Zipf on the rank-order of urban settlements by size, that of Clark on the pattern of densities within cities, developments of central place theory (especially the work of Christaller and Lösch) and the empirical tests which have latterly been carried out by means of multivariate 'social area analysis' on the early work of Hoyt, Harris, Ullman and others.

Berry was able to show a formal link between Zipf's work on rank-ordering and that of Clark on density distributions. The former is related to the Yule or log-normal distribution and as a society and its economy grows more complex and diversified so the rank-ordering approximates more closely to such distributions. Clark's negative-exponential density distribution can be defined for any particular settlement by two parameters only – the central density and the exponent value of 'gradient'. Since the central density is a function of the size of the 'primate' city and the latter is a function of its age, i.e. the point at which it entered the system of cities, the two phenomena of rank-order and density gradient are linked. Both are, according to Berry, 'the steady-state distributions of a stochastic

257

process' in which *entropy* is tending to increase. But the entropic drift is constrained by the increase in the number of types of activity found in the set of cities and within each individual settlement; this concept is the concern of central place theory. The process by which types of businesses, institutions, activities and so on grow and diversify can be regarded as increasing *information*, i.e. the converse of entropy, and thus tends to prevent settlement-systems from reaching their most probable state. This notion is related to the ideas of MEIER (1962) who put forward the view that cities were systems for maximizing the range of 'contact choices' and tended to operate on the principle of 'conservation of information'.

Berry concluded that:

'cities and sets of cities are *systems* susceptible of the same kinds of analysis as other systems and characterized by the same generalizations, constructs and models. *General Systems Theory* provides a framework for such inquiry into the nature of systems; indeed Boulding calls it "the skeleton of science".'

Berry thus anticipated the work of the 'new geographers' which was shortly to follow, notably that of STODDART (1967) and HARVEY (1969).

Now the variables in the models which Berry reviews – e.g. city size, density configurations, number and types of activities – are among those which are the direct concern of structure plans as defined by statute and in Ministerial advice (see Chapter 6). The views of Berry (although challenged by WILSON, 1970b) suggest that such variables, constituting urban subsystems of interest for structure planners and 'comprehensive' planners generally, *possess high degrees of intrinsic control*. If that is so, what is the point of formal, deliberate attempts to control extrinsically by the use of structure plans, land-use and floorspace controls, specification of central places and their activities and so on? Does it mean that such planning is superfluous and, therefore, a waste of skilled manpower and other resources which could be diverted to other social purposes? Does it imply some intellectual and operational modifications to the idea and practice of structure planning as presently conceived? Cybernetics and general-systems theory, having raised these issues in the first place, can reasonably be expected to offer at least the beginnings of some answers.

Cyberneticians themselves are in dispute about the meaning of self-organization or intrinsic control and, therefore, about strategies for the management of complex systems (BEER, 1966, Chapter 14). One viewpoint is that many complicated conditions must be fulfilled, the other that any complex system left alone will tend to organize itself. Beer is in favour of the latter viewpoint for he argues that 'organization is an attribute of the observer of the system rather than of the system itself.' Thus one may either design a system to achieve goals (and this is held to be very difficult indeed) or one may seek to constrain an existing system in such ways that its self-organizing properties move it towards the goals specified. The strategy involved is to understand the system's dynamics so as to exploit its own entropic drift and by *selective* (i.e. low-variety) intervention to encourage it to move towards identified goals. The governance of very complex systems must (see Chapter 7) operate very largely in a realm where the pattern and connectivity of information flows is of the essence of organization. A principal task of government and its planner-managers is, therefore, the continuing one of organizational design. In particular the key subsystems which are largely homeo-static should be identified and provided with rich interconnections by the establishment and constant husbandry of information inter-changes. This high-level control and monitoring system (represented by levels 3, 4 and 5 in Figure 9.2) would recognize a number of 'quasi-independent domains' each of which was largely self-organizing but would interconnect them in such ways as to exploit this property at the high level of ultra-stability. As Beer puts it, 'government depends on informational processes rather than upon mandatory powers' and its central tasks are identifying and debating goals, building institutional structures and processes to serve these goals and especially creating information stocks and flows which serve these purposes.

Structure plans and planning as currently understood may be far too 'mandatory' in orientation. Both the general-systems analysis of its subject fields (Berry) and the cybernetic analysis of self-organiza-tion (Beer) suggest that structure planning should be integrated within the highest levels of (local) government, contributing to and drawing upon its central purposes of goal-formulation and debate, policy analysis and the development of intelligence systems. Structure planning would thereby become an analytical and normative exercise of a continuing kind. It surely can and must be alert to crisis situations and be prepared to take swift interventionist action (since 'quasi-independent' self-regulating domains *can* produce localized pathological results).

There can be no direct and simple connections between development control (or environmental management) and structure planning (or any of the strategic policy issues dealt with by upper-tier authorities). Instead this relationship will be indirect and complex but *it must, nevertheless, be established consciously and with determination.* The way in which a constantly changing and proliferating set of local tangible problems is related to a more durable (but necessarily evolving) set of strategic policies is by means of an intelligence system.

Those local government officers who told us that broad policies would be all the more relevant if better connected with implementation (e.g. detailed design projects, control) are supported in their view by cybernetic theories of learning. These latter require rich and complex feedback connections between the level of action and all superior hierarchical levels. Such patterns of connection ensure manifold directions of the flow of information. Thus both instructions for action and also reports on the outcomes not only depend upon the networks of the intelligence system, but also help to sustain it. One of the system's major requirements is the ability to translate between the languages of each level.

The Greater London Development Plan Inquiry exemplifies several of these points. For example, many of the questions and objections levelled at the plan arise from the level of action – What will happen to my house? to that school? to this group of trees? Such questions of detail are the province of control and detailed planning and in the language in which the physical environment is perceived. The G.L.C. staff and the inquiry itself has had to become a translation system in order to relate most of the objections and questions to the plan itself.

This does not mean that the strategic level can never consider cases. Indeed it can do so and must do so but only those aspects relevant for the language of structure or strategy. As we said earlier, the physical design details of cases will be considered in relation to detailed plans and local programmes whereas the strategic aspects of the case will be considered at the upper-tier level. *Only rarely will these be obvious in individual cases.* Usually such strategic implications will appear after the event and by aggregation of individual cases. Better response to such matters – e.g. the likely effects on traffic flows, the telephone system, the demand for labour, the expenditure pattern of a locality – will be achieved through the planning system *learning to be a better forecaster.* This, in turn, is likely to come about via better conceptual and analytical models of the urban systems of interest for policy and action arising from the work of the intelligence system.

Broad strategies must consider the means of their implementation. The introduction of structure planning threatens to produce statements of ends without considering the means (as in the G.L.D.P. for example). The making of policy (including its examination and analysis, its public questioning and challenge, its reformulation, its implementation via public and private investments and public administrative action and control) should be a continuous process. Much lip-service has been paid to this principle by professional town planners but it has never been clear what it means. It seems that the need to provide information for the intelligence systems of government, to carry out day-to-day action and to relate this to higher and higher levels of analysis until a policy realm is reached, logically demands *continuous policy work.* If we provide rich interconnection between policy and action, then *policy making, etc. must be a continuous process.*

Strategic or structure planning must, therefore, become closely involved with the higher levels of the government systems. There is the need to express, to communicate and to analyse various important facets of such policy work, e.g. the manpower and cash-flow implications, the demand for physical resources, the consumption of energy implied, etc. Equally it is necessary to indicate the location and intended use, the rate of consumption, etc. of the resources of land implied by current policies. But this is not a 'comprehensive plan' any more than a statement about manpower or capital budgets is a comprehensive plan.

Truly comprehensive policy statements by government should have at least as much variety as the urban community systems being governed; it is then obvious that no single functional department of government can do so and likely that all aspects of government must be involved in 'comprehensive' policy work. Structure plans cannot fulfil a useful function in their present form. First, the idea of comprehensiveness is highly suspect; second, however subtle the review provisions may be, a plan is still a *thing* whereas a *process* is required; thirdly, the basis of structure plans is land use and location and so-called social and economic aspects appear as subservient inputs to spatial considerations; finally, they may obscure the need for *regular statements about land development, land resources and land management aspects* of the current policies taken as a whole (MCLOUGHLIN and THORNLEY, 1972).

Since planning must be a truly continuous process of the higher levels of government and a learning process concerning 'strategic choice' (FRIEND and JESSOP, 1969), it seems that the present interpretation and orientation of structure planning should be modified quite drastically. At least, structure planning should be more concerned with an ongoing process of strategic choice and become much more closely integrated with all the other aspects of corporate planning and urban management. There are clearly implied links between the subject concerns of structure plans and the housing, transport, educational, recreational and social services. But none of these services is required to produce something as finite (and positively rigid) as a statutory plan. A truly comprehensive process of service planning and corporate (inter-services) planning implies not only continuity, flexibility and responsiveness but also firm strategic decisions, explicit commitments of resources in terms of capital, manpower and land. Policies and plans of various kinds should, therefore, be seen as the outputs of a continuous planning process within the context of overall urban management. The weakness of statutory physical planning is its inherited emphasis on the *plan* itself rather than the process of strategic choice which produces it. Its overriding strength is that it forces the planning system to 'come clean' i.e. to be publicly committed about its intentions. In a period of some devolution of power and responsibility from central to local government it may be necessary to consider legislation which would introduce a requirement to publish regularly and with certain minimum levels of specific information, policy statements and plans for all the services administered by each local authority. STOCKPORT COUNTY BOROUGH COUNCIL (1972) has done so voluntarily; this might be adopted as a statutory requirement in local public life.

Major statements of policy must be relatively brief and to-the-point so as to command attention and communicate their message. But since the objects of policy are complex there is necessarily a very considerable loss of variety. The real world of education, housing, transport, etc. is far, far more complex than the sort of broad treatment which must of necessity be given to policy statements. *This variety reduction limits the regulating power of the policy statement as such according to the law of requisite variety.*

If administrative actions and day-to-day decisions are to have a rational basis in policy then the policy statements need translating into the language of action. This can be done in a variety of ways – for example by producing successively more detailed statements. But in order that the increased variety should be most appropriate and useful for the realm of administrative action the increasing variety must also be sought in the action level. Furthermore, if the various publics who represent the client groups for local government services are to participate in any useful (i.e. influential) way, then this participation must be in an appropriate language. *The public does not respond to high-level general statements of policy because it is logically impossible to do so.*

To make participation possible we need policy expressions which are sufficiently explicit and are also in terms which are relevant to the client groups rather than the bureaucracy. These conditions are likely to arise in circumstances when general policy statements (e.g. about the Greater London's celebrated 'motorway box') are challenged by the public. All of this argues strongly against the notion of policies being expressed in terms which, because of their formality, inhibit their evolution and adaptation. The conceptual model for the 1968 Act structure plan is the architectural, engineering or civic design project which is specific (and rightly so) since it is close to the level of action. Such a model is logically and operationally useless as a strategic policy vehicle and as the G.L.D.P. Inquiry shows is likely to gain the higher variety needed in many ways. In doing so, of course, the original low-variety 'structure plan' is transformed into something quite different.

The needed variety is to be gained mostly from connections with the action level and with 'challenge' procedures like administrative inquiries. But the former are continuous and it seems logical to suggest that the latter should be also. We conclude that *means must be sought to institute some continuing forum for challenging and*

263

debating the policies of local government. Many problems have to be faced, e.g. the independence of the forum from the authority itself, its power to call evidence and examine witnesses and also the problem of ensuring that the poor and the inarticulate can have their points made and their questions asked with at least the equivalent force and skill as anyone else more fortunate.

All of this discussion, centred on the physical planning service at both the detailed and the strategic level seems to confirm the 'organic' models of organizational *structure* advocated generally by BURNS and STALKER (1968) and BEER (1969). It also seems to confirm the management *processes* associated with such structures by the Maud and Mallaby reports and by STEWART (1971).

Such models indicate a variety of specific agencies within the authority which are expressly charged with the delivery of particular services. They are above all implementation or effector agencies. They do not possess policy-making functions and responsibilities; these are developed by other levels in the hierarchy such as the management board of senior officers, the chief executive and the policy committee (of elected members). There may be intermediary levels between the implementing agencies and the policy groups; these 'programme divisions' will usually group together a number of closely related implementation agencies.

The structure and behaviour of such organizations is characterized, on the one hand, by a considerable flexibility in the grouping and regrouping of service agencies at the level of implementation and, on the other hand, by a relative stability of the structure at the level of policy formulation and debate. Thus an authority may regularly reorganize in detail the agency structures for local traffic management, psychiatric casework, refuse collection and the school meals service in response to feedback from officers and clients about the delivery of the service. But the arenas for developing and reviewing policies for the physical environment, the social services, education and housing will be subject to much slower evolution since they are concerned with strategic choices involving large time spans. Although electing and budgets may be annual affairs, the issues with which they deal are more enduring.

There is much more 'horizontality' in such management structures and the networks which link people and their departments in a lateral sense are more explicitly recognized either on an *ad hoc* basis (e.g.

interagency working parties) or in a more enduring way (e.g. through the intelligence service and its ubiquitous officers). There is far less 'verticality' in such management systems. Departments are essentially service-delivering agencies with shorter ladders of command to their chiefs than in the present conventional local government structures. And whilst service chiefs will undoubtedly make contributions to the development of policy (as we argue they should) the policy rôle proper will lie elsewhere; it too will be characterized by the horizontality of the management board and the pervasive intelligence system. In essence these structures and processes involve the disappearance of one of the major characteristics of British local government practice and that is the strong vertical *department*, dominated by one or two *professions* and with a continuous chain of command and communication between policy and implementation *with respect to one service at a time.*

The new model of local government as a planning system or regulator is much more homomorphic with the complex urban community system to which it relates. It is a logical outcome of admitting that 'everything in the city affects everything else.' Sometimes clearly and directly, more often in diffuse and indirect ways, major urban problems in housing, personal welfare, transport and employment are linked to the specific circumstances of a family, a student, a locality and a factory. The governmental systems in recognizing this are having to adapt their own structure and behaviour accordingly so that the complex interdependencies between *all* policies and *all* actions are accounted for.

The empirical studies of development control and the associated studies of other kinds of planning-department work in Britain suggests that a closer integration of control and detailed planning is occurring and at the same time that both of these sorts of activity are gradually but perceptibly becoming separated from 'strategic' and structure planning. Cybernetic and general systems analysis suggests that from a theoretical standpoint we would expect this to occur and that broadly speaking it is logical to encourage this restructuring. Furthermore, similar analyses suggest that this breaking down of the 'vertical' link should be accompanied by much more 'horizontal' connectivity between the various parts of the levels at which design and control on the one hand and structure planning on the other occur.

Such developments clearly imply the disappearance of the vertically defined 'town planning department' with its associated command hierarchy, career structure and the professionalism which sustains it. This change in the 'triangular' interaction between departmentalism, professional bodies and educational policy is likely to have important repercussions for the Royal Town Planning Institute and on educational innovation itself. (For much fuller discussions see McLoughlin's chapter in COWAN, 1973 and COCKBURN, 1973 respectively.)

People for planning*

These structures and processes are not abstract generalizations. They exist and can be made to exist only by giving them, quite literally, the flesh and blood of all the various kinds of people who work in them. We have suggested that at the level of service delivery and policy implementation a grouping of all services related to *local environmental management* is needed. What sort of people will be needed for the variety of tasks in such a service? To begin with there will be a continuing need for the present development control and building regulation functions. We noted earlier the importance of an 'across-the-counter' service of guidance, help and information to the public about many aspects of the local environment and their rights and responsibilities. All of these people who will have daily contact with the public will have further responsibilities for contributing to the intelligence service. As an integral part of their duties, they will be required to report on trends and patterns not only in quantitative statistical terms but also in qualitative written and verbal forms expressing their vague 'hunches' and considered opinions. Much of this information may be of a fairly routine nature such as the categorization of development applications and decisions, floor areas, dwelling units and so on. But this will receive also a preliminary, qualitative analysis in which the officer points out what seems an unusually large number of applications for launderettes and informal inquiries about conversion of houses for multiple occupation. These facts and valuations will be transmitted 'upwards' and 'across' the authorities' intelligence system to contribute (when

* Much of the material which follows was initially drafted by and developed in discussion with Judith Webster.

merged with many other similar inputs) to early warnings of the need for policy review or completely fresh interventions.

In addition to these routine functions a local environmental management agency will have to call regularly on the services of various 'pools of competence' (SCHON, 1971). The authority will need to employ, for example, architects, engineers, landscape designers, housing managers, traffic managers, estate managers, lawyers and social services workers of all kinds. Particular projects will require different mixes of these and other skills and effective direction by project managers possessed of the necessary qualities of understanding and leadership. The need for this level of management is not confined to specific projects such as redevelopment, renewal or estate development; the routine administration of the day-in-day-out services requires equally skilled service managers.

Promotion and career development with such a new set-up will depend on many old-established and sensible criteria such as experience and proven ability. But entry to the local government service will obviously require at a minimum, some specific skill or set of skills. The service will need people who know a lot about some particular subject or problem: road design, teaching five-year-olds to read, planting trees and bushes, buying and assembling land for development, placing children in foster homes. But such specific skills which ensure an immediate useful contribution to the whole business of urban management will realize less than their full potential unless those who possess them also understand how to link their own efforts with those of many others and understand too something of the workings of urban and planning systems.

In particular, those who will do the development control job will probably need to have a number of skills and aptitudes which are quite different from present-day caseworkers. Future development control personnel will still need to understand the physical environment and the legal, engineering and other physical processes involved in changing it. But they will also need ability in dealing with many different kinds of people in face-to-face situations, how to help the inarticulate, soothe the angry and bombastic, explain to the puzzled. They will have to understand and be skilled in both exploiting and contributing to urban intelligence systems for all sorts of hard and soft data and information. This will involve writing reports on current and prospective trends, sharing in group discussions and

267

seminars on the problems of an area and in case conferences. Most of these skills can be formally taught in appropriate courses but some will have to be learned on the job and supplemented and extended by in-service and post-experience training. These latter kind of courses will help younger officers with some experience to move on and take more responsible posts in the environmental management service, in other service departments or in the intelligence service.

All of these requirements imply a rather higher level of formal education than many caseworkers now enjoy (leaving aside the graduates) and a much more relevant preparation for the demands of casework itself: the present state of affairs with its obvious 'mismatches' is very largely the result of *departmentalism and its associated professionalism*. 'Town planning' departments have long ladders of promotion to chief planning officer in which entry to and advancement within the service depends largely on possession of the Royal Town Planning Institute qualification. So long as this is the case, development control staffs will be frustrated: either by being under pressure to pursue a largely irrelevant course of studies; or if they are already qualified (in R.T.P.I. terms) they will feel that they are doing a less demanding job than, say, a university degree has fitted them for.

It is for these reasons, and for the juxtaposition they have with the 'plan and research whizz-kids' that development control officers feel themselves to be the Cinderellas of the planning department. But their job is, at its best, no mere bureaucratic routine grind; rather it is a vital element in ensuring the implementation of policies, in the interface between government and community, a 'window on the world' for the urban intelligence systems. Those who do these jobs must not be frustrated and disheartened by the irrelevances of professionalism and departmentalism. Fresh educational initiatives and new professional attitudes are needed so that development control can play its fullest part in urban management.

For a number of years now there has been discussion about the need for a so-called 'urban design' skill. To some people this has been conceived of as 'architecture writ large' i.e. of the design of *ensembles* of buildings and spaces. This would go beyond the 'city beautiful' traditions of beaux-arts civic design and encompass a wider knowledge of modern urban functions, land development processes and economics, traffic circulation and so on. Other people would go still further and attempt to embrace in the educational and training

268

programmes an adequate understanding of social problems and processes, community and governmental organization and so forth. The Royal Institute of British Architects' 'Urban Design Diploma' and Manchester University's graduate programme in urban design provide examples of these initiatives.

People trained in these ways could undoubtedly make valuable contributions to urban problem-solving. But the organizing framework for thought and action is still physical in these cases. Alongside such people we need many others whose 'core' of knowledge and capability is in *other* fields – urban economics, political science, social administration, human communication, community development, programme budgeting, etc. They too must be able to reach out and *connect* with the work of others. Requisite variety in local environmental planning and management will not be achieved by new kinds of 'generalist' but rather by a diversity of inter-related skills all possessing mutual understanding.

The problem of staffing the structure or strategic planning operation raises comparable issues in education, training and professionalism. We discussed the scope and content of such activities and their relationships with the whole realm of policy making in local government in Chapters 6 and 7. Such work will require a rich mixture of knowledge, skills and abilities: structure planning itself clearly implies the need for people skilled in demographic and economic analysis, forecasting techniques generally, modelling of social and economic systems emphasizing the spatial dimension. The newer disciplines of urban sociology, urban economics and urban geography are obviously relevant. But the application of such knowledge cannot take place in a vacuum. It must be refreshed and guided by insights from the general public, elected representatives and community organizations of many kinds directly. And as we have noted several times before, the several indirect results of 'interrogating' the whole of the intelligence system itself will continually help in identifying problems and in testing the feasibility of possible policies and programmes.

But structure planning must be closely related to all the other kinds of planning going on in the local authority – in education, social services and transport, for example – and this implies the need for structure planners to have three additional kinds of understanding. First of all, they must understand how the other major services work,

269

how the administrators of those services tackle their problems, what assumptions they tend to make and how their judgements are formed. They must understand how, for instance, the policy alternatives in education relate to those of structure planning (spatial disposition, land development, transport, etc.) and how each policy field affects the others. Secondly, working in this policy realm involves studies and proposals which are essentially political, though elected representatives must take the final decisions. All of those officers who work on policy development must, therefore, by education and training no less than by experience and individual character, be aware of the urban political process in general and the specific issues which it faces from time to time. To work, for example, on housing studies and policy alternatives is to contribute to the formulation of the issues themselves and to help define the terms of the political debate. Finally, the interactions between structure planners and other officers and public authorities and between officers, elected members and the public requires considerable skill in various kinds of communication: the building, maintenance and operation of communication networks with fellow-officials and others; the use of written, graphical and verbal modes of communication, the arts of persuasion, exploration and discussion.

This *diversity* of skills needed for structure planning is the predominant impression to be gained. Such a wide mixture could not possibly be found in any single individual to be labelled a 'structure planner'. It overlaps to some extent the examination syllabus of the Royal Town Planning Institute but extends significantly beyond it in several directions. Several 'clusters' of needed skills can be discerned:

Mathematics, statistics, the 'new geography' and model-building;
Socio-economic analysis and forecasting; urban sociology and economics;
Intelligence, information and data-systems operation, cybernetics;
Land resources management and ecology;
Transport and communications;
Public and social administration; 'reticulist' skills;
Political science and local government; decision-making theory and practice.

This list is not intended to be definitive and even less is it neatly parcelled. The most useful and creative individuals will probably have studied in two or three of these areas; no one could be expert in all of them. But what does seem to be a common essential in addition to this knowledge is what COCKBURN (1973) calls 'planning capability'. The essence of such capability is *an understanding of how governmental planning systems actually operate*, their internal relationships and their liaisons with other public authorities and the community. One of the key rôles for the new planner-managers will be the seeking of ways and means for continuous adaptation of the structure and functions of the authority to keep it relevant for and responsive to the ever shifting problems of the community in whose service it operates.

The changes implied by this discussion are another reflection of the law of requisite variety. But no hidden hand will identify them clearly and put them into operation. These changes, like changes in the urban systems themselves, are the subjects of deliberate choice and the exercise of will. They are part and parcel of the whole business of control and urban planning.

References

ACKOFF, R. L., (1962) Towards qualitative evaluation of urban services, *Report of the Conference on Public Expenditure*, Baltimore.

ALEXANDER, Christopher (1964) *Notes on the synthesis of form*, Cambridge, Mass., Harvard University Press.

ALEXANDER, Christopher (1965) A city is not a tree, *Architectural Forum 124*, 58–62 (April issue) and 58–61 (May issue). (*See also Design 206*, 46–55.)

ALONSO, William (1968) Predicting best with imperfect data, *Journal of the American Institute of Planners 34*, 248–55.

ALTSHULER, Alan (1965) The goals of comprehensive planning, *Journal of the American Institute of Planners 31*, 186–95.

ANSON, D. J. and A. J. SHELTON (1971) Social aspects of improvement, *Journal of the Royal Town Planning Institute 57*, 229–30.

ASH, Maurice A. (1966) The linear-city fad, *Town and Country Planning, 34*, 150–2.

ASHBY, W. Ross (1956) *An introduction to cybernetics*, London, Chapman and Hall.

ASHWORTH, William (1954) *The genesis of modern British town planning*, London, Routledge and Kegan Paul.

BABCOCK, Richard F. (1966) *The zoning game*, Madison, Wisconsin, University of Wisconsin Press.

BAIR, Frederick H. (1970) *Planning cities*, Chicago, American Society of Planning Officials.

BARR, John (ed.) (1971) *The environmental handbook*, London, Ballantyne/ Friends of the Earth.

BATTY, Michael (1970) *Spatial theory and information systems*, (U.S.R.U.-WP-3/0), University of Reading, Dept. of Geography (mimeo).

BEER, Stafford (1960) Below the twilight arch: a mythology of systems, *General Systems 5*, 9–20.

BEER, Stafford (1966) *Decision and control: the meaning of management cybernetics*, London, John Wiley.

BEER, Stafford (1969) The aborting corporate plan *in* Erich JANTSCH (ed.) *Perspectives of planning*, Paris, O.E.C.D.

BERRY, Brian J. L. (1968a) A synthesis of formal and functional regions using a field theory of spatial behaviour, pp. 419–28 *in* BERRY and MARBLE (eds.) *Spatial Analysis: a reader in statistical geography*, Englewood Cliffs, N.J., Prentice-Hall.

BERRY, Brian J. L. (1968b) Approaches to regional analysis: a synthesis, pp. 24–34 *in* BERRY and MARBLE (eds.) *Spatial Analysis: a reader in statistical geography*, Englewood Cliffs, N.J., Prentice-Hall.

BLAKE, John (1970) (pseud. 'A correspondent') Computer-continuous review of development plans, *The Surveyor*, 8 May 1970, 30–1.

BRAVERMAN, M. H. and B. G. SCHRANDT (1967) Colony development of a polymorphic hydroid as a problem in pattern formation, *General Systems 12*, 39–51.

BROADY, Maurice (1965) Hampshire census project, *Journal of the Town Planning Institute 51*, 300–2.

BROADY, Maurice (1967) Social theory and planning, *New Society 9*, 232–5.

BROADY, Maurice (1968) *Planning for People*, London, Bedford Square Press (The National Council of Social Service).

BROOKE, Rosalind (1970) Civic rights and social services, 36–51 *in* ROBSON and CRICK (ed.) *The future of the social services*, Harmondsworth, Penguin.

BUCHANAN, Colin *and others* (1963) *Traffic in Towns* (The 'Buchanan' Report) London, H.M.S.O. A shortened version was published by Penguin Books in 1964.

BUCHANAN, Colin *and others* (1966) South Hampshire Study (3 volumes), London, H.M.S.O.

BUCKLEY, Walter (1967) *Sociology and modern systems theory*, Englewood Cliffs, N.J., Prentice-Hall.

BURNETT, F. T. (1969) Open space in new towns, *Journal of the Town Planning Institute 55*, 256–62.

BURNS, Tom and G. M. STALKER (1968) *The management of innovation* (2nd ed.) London, Tavistock.

CADWALLADER, M. L. (1959) The cybernetic analysis of change in complex social organisations, *American Journal of Sociology 65*, 154.

CATER, Erlet (1970) Information needs of planners – a survey, (U.S.R.U.-WP-4/0), University of Reading, Department of Geography (mimeo).

CENTRE FOR ENVIRONMENTAL STUDIES (1971) *Proceedings of the C.E.S.-R.T.P.I. conference on structure plan preparation*, (CES-CP-4), London, Centre for Environmental Studies.

CHADWICK, George F. (1971) *A systems view of planning*, Oxford, Pergamon.

CHAPIN, F. Stuart (1963) Taking stock of techniques for shaping urban growth, *Journal of the American Institute of Planners 29*, 76–87.

COCKBURN, Cynthia (1970) *Opinion and planning education*, (CES-IP-21), London, Centre for Environmental Studies.

COCKBURN, Cynthia (1973) (ed). *Educational objectives for urban and regional planning*, Oxford, Pergamon (in press).

COMMITTEE ON THE MANAGEMENT OF LOCAL GOVERNMENT (1967) (The 'Maud' Committee) *Report*, London, H.M.S.O.

COMMITTEE ON THE STAFFING OF LOCAL GOVERNMENT (1967) (The 'Mallaby' Committee) *Report*, London, H.M.S.O.

COMMITTEE ON THE PROBLEM OF NOISE (1963) (The 'Wilson' Committee) *Noise: Final Report*, Cmnd. 2056, London, H.M.S.O.

COMMITTEE ON THE QUALIFICATIONS OF PLANNERS (1950) (The 'Schuster' Committee) *Report of the* —. Cmnd. 8059, London, H.M.S.O.

COWAN, Peter (ed.) (1973) *The future of planning*, Report of a C.E.S. working group. London, Heinemann.

CRIPPS, Eric L. (1969) *An introduction to the study of information for urban and regional planning*, U.S.R.U.-WP-1/0, University of Reading, Department of Geography (mimeo).

CRIPPS, Eric L. and Peter HALL (1969) An introduction to the study of information for urban and regional planning, pp. 23–81 *in Information and Urban Planning, Volume I*, (CES-IP-8), London, Centre for Environmental Studies.

CULLEN, Gordon (1971) *The concise townscape*, London, Architectural Press. (First published 1961 as 'Townscape'.)

CULLINGWORTH, J. B. (1965) Milner Holland; London's housing: towards an agreed policy, *New Society 5*, 16–19.

CULLINGWORTH, J. B. (1972) *Town and Country Planning in Britain* (4th edition), London, Allen and Unwin.

DAKIN, John (1963) An evaluation of the 'choice' theory of planning, *Journal of the American Institute of Planners 29*, 19–27.

DAVIDOFF, Paul (1965) Advocacy and pluralism in planning, *Journal of the American Institute of Planners 31*, 331–8.

DAVIDOFF, Paul and Thomas A. REINER (1962) A choice theory of planning, *Journal of the American Institute of Planners 28*, 103–15.

DAVIES, Jon Gower (1972) *The evangelistic bureaucrat: a study of a planning excercise in Newcastle-upon-Tyne*, London, Tavistock.

DELAFONS, John (1969) *Land-use controls in the United States* (2nd edition), Cambridge, Mass., M.I.T. Press.

DEPARTMENT OF THE ENVIRONMENT (1971) *Town and Country Planning (structure and local plans) regulations 1971*, Statutory Instrument 1971 No. 1109. London H.M.S.O.

DEPARTMENT OF THE ENVIRONMENT (1972) *General information system for planning*, A report proposed by a joint local authority, D. of E. and Scottish Development Department Study team.

DEPARTMENT OF THE ENVIRONMENT AND THE WELSH OFFICE (1971) *Town and Country Planning (structure and local plans) regulations, 1971: and Memorandum*, Circular 44/71 (D. of E.) and Circular 114/71 (W.O.), London and Cardiff, H.M.S.O.

DEUTSCH, K. W. (1961) On social communication and the metropolis, *General Systems 6*, 95–100.

DONNISON, David (1970) Liberty, equality and fraternity, *Three Banks Review*, December 1970.

DONNISON, David (1972a) Ideologies and policies, *Journal of Social Policy 1*, 97–117.

DONNISON, David (1972b) Micro-politics of the inner city (paper for the Inner City conference, Oxford, July), London, Centre for Environmental Studies.

DONNISON, R. D. and S. M. BRANCH (1971) An information system for development control, *Journal of the Town Planning Institute 57*, 21–4.

DUHL, Leonard and John POWELL (1963). *The urban condition*. New York, Basic Books.

DUNN, Edgar S. (1970) A flow network image of urban structures, *Urban Studies 7*, 239–58.

EAGLAND, R. M. (1971) General improvement area – implementing a scheme in Gloucester, *Journal of the Royal Town Planning Institute 57*, 35–6.

EASTON, David (1966) Categories for the systems analysis of politics *in* EASTON (ed.) *Varieties of political theory*, Englewood Cliffs, N.J., Prentice-Hall.

EMERY, F. E. and E. L. TRIST (1960) Socio-technical systems *in* F. E. EMERY (ed.) (1969) *Systems thinking*, Harmondsworth, Penguin Books.

EWALD, William R. (ed.) (1968) *Environment and Policy: the next fifty years*, Bloomington, Ind., the University of Indiana Press.

FOLEY, Donald L. (1960) British Town Planning: one ideology or three? *British Journal of Sociology 11*, 211–31.

FRIEDMANN, John (1967) A conceptual model for the analysis of planning behaviour, *Administrative Science Quarterly 12*, 225–52.

FRIEDMANN, John and William ALONSO (eds.) (1964) *Regional development and planning*, Cambridge, Mass., M.I.T. Press.

FRIEND, John and Neil F. JESSOP (1969) *Local government and strategic choice*, London, Tavistock.

FRY, R. E. (1968) Urban information systems in the U.S.A.: a review and commentary, *Quarterly Bulletin of the G.L.C. research and intelligence unit 3*, 3–7, London, Greater London Council.

GANS, Herbert J. (1968) *People and plans*, New York, Basic Books.

GITTEL, M. (1966) A typology of power for measuring social change, *American behavioral scientist 9*, 23–8.

GOSS, Anthony (1963) *The architect in town planning*, London, Royal Institute of British Architects.

GREATER LONDON DEVELOPMENT PLAN INQUIRY (1971) *Transcript of the proceedings of the 126th day.*

GREGORY, S. A. (ed.) (1966) *The design method*, London, Butterworths.

GRIFFITH, J. A. G. (1966) *Central departments and local authorities*, London, George Allen and Unwin.

GROSS, Bertram M. (1965) What are your organisation's objectives: a general system approach to planning, *Human Relations 18*, 195–216.

GROSS, Bertram M. (1966) *The state of the nation: social systems accounting*, London, Tavistock.

GROSS, Bertram M. (1967) The coming general systems model of social systems, *Human Relations 20*, 357–74.

HAGGETT, Peter (1965) *Locational analysis in human geography*, London, Arnold.

HAGGETT, Peter and Richard J. CHORLEY (1967) Models, paradigms and the new geography *in* CHORLEY and HAGGETT (eds.) *Models in geography*, London, Methuen.

HALL, Peter (1970) *Theory and practice of regional planning*, London, Pemberton Books.

HALL, Peter (1970a); in *London under stress*, London, Town and Country Planning Association.

HAMILTON, H. R. *and others* (1969) *Systems simulation for regional analysis: an application to river-basin planning*, Cambridge, Mass., M.I.T. Press.

HARRIS, Britton (1968) Computers and urban planning, *Socio-economic planning sciences 1*, 223–30.

HARVEY, David (1969) *Explanation in geography*, London.

HEAP, Desmond (1968) *The new town planning procedures – how they affect you*, London, Sweet and Maxwell.

HEAP, Desmond (1969) *An outline of planning law* (5th edition), London, Sweet and Maxwell.

HIRSCHMAN, A. O. and C. E. LINDBLOM (1962) Economic development, research and development, policy making: some converging views. *Behavioural Science 7*, 211–22.

HOWARD, Ebenezer (1898) *Tomorrow: a peaceful path to reform*, republished 1965, edited by F. J. Osborn as: *Garden cities of tomorrow*, London, Faber and Faber.

JACKSON, John N. (1972) *The urban future*, London, Allen and Unwin.

JACOBS, Jane (1961) *The life and death of great American cities*, New York, Random House.

275

JONES, J. Christopher and Dennis C. THORNLEY (eds.) (1962) *Conference on, design methods*, London, Butterworths.

JOYCE, R. and C. DESCHER (1968) Putting the city in the computer, *Journal of Housing 25*, 294–7.

KEEBLE, Lewis (1961) *Town planning at the crossroads*, London, Estates Gazette.

KLÍR, Jiri and Miroslav VALACH (1967) *Cybernetic modelling*, Prague, SNTL, 1965. English translation 1967, London, Iliffe Books.

LEGGATT, R. W. (1968) Older houses and their environment, *Journal of the Town Planning Institute 54*, 379–85.

LICHFIELD, Nathaniel (1956) *The economics of planned development*, London, Estates Gazette.

LICHFIELD, Nathaniel (1966) Cost-benefit analysis in urban redevelopment: a case study – Swanley, *Urban Studies 3*, 215–49.

MANDELKER, D. R. (1962) *Green belts and urban growth*, Madison, Wisconsin.

MARUYAMA, Mogoroh (1963) The second cybernetics: deviation-amplifying mutual causal processes, *General Systems 8*, 233–41.

MEIER, Richard L. (1962) *A communications theory of urban growth*, Cambridge, Mass., M.I.T. Press.

MEYERSON, Martin (1960) Utopian traditions and the planning of cities, pp. 233–50 *in* Lloyd Rodwin (ed.) *The future metropolis*, London, Constable.

MCKENZIE, W. J. M. (1967) *Politics and social science*, Harmondsworth, Penguin.

MCLOUGHLIN, J. Brian (1969) *Urban and regional planning: a systems approach*, London, Faber and Faber.

MCLOUGHLIN, J. Brian and Judith N. WEBSTER (1970) Cybernetic and general-system approaches to urban and regional research: a review of the literature, *Environment and planning 2*, 369–408.

MCLOUGHLIN, J. Brian and Judith N. WEBSTER (1971) *Development control in Britain*, Manchester, The University, Centre for Urban and Regional Research, (mimeo).

MCLOUGHLIN, J. Brian and Jennifer THORNLEY (1972) *Some problems in structure planning: a literature review*, (CES-IP-27), London, Centre for Environmental Studies.

MINISTRY OF HOUSING AND LOCAL GOVERNMENT (1954) *Town and country planning (development plans) (amendment) regulations, 1954.* Statutory Instrument 1954 No. 933, London, H.M.S.O.

MINISTRY OF HOUSING AND LOCAL GOVERNMENT (1955) *Report of the Ministry . . . for the period 1950/51 to 1954*, Cmnd. 9559, London, H.M.S.O.

MINISTRY OF HOUSING AND LOCAL GOVERNMENT (1956) *Report of the Ministry . . . for the year 1955*, Cmnd. 9876, London, H.M.S.O.

MINISTRY OF HOUSING AND LOCAL GOVERNMENT (1958) *Trees in town and city*, H.M.S.O.

MINISTRY OF HOUSING AND LOCAL GOVERNMENT (1960), *Control of advertisements regulations, 1960.* Statutory Instrument 1960 No. 695. London, H.M.S.O.

MINISTRY OF HOUSING AND LOCAL GOVERNMENT (1963a) *Use Classes Order*, Statutory Instrument 1963 No. 708, London, H.M.S.O.

MINISTRY OF HOUSING AND LOCAL GOVERNMENT (1963b) *General development Order*, Statutory Instrument 1963 No. 709, London, H.M.S.O.

MINISTRY OF HOUSING AND LOCAL GOVERNMENT (1965a) *London Government: The Town and Country Planning (Local Planning Authorities in Greater*

London) Regulations 1965, Statutory Instrument 1965 No. 679, London, H.M.S.O.

MINISTRY OF HOUSING AND LOCAL GOVERNMENT (1965b) *The Town and Country Planning (Development Plan) Direction, 1965*, Circular 70/65, London, H.M.S.O.

MINISTRY OF HOUSING AND LOCAL GOVERNMENT (1967a) *Management study on development control*, London, H.M.S.O.

MINISTRY OF HOUSING AND LOCAL GOVERNMENT (1967a) *The management of local government*; 2 volumes (The 'Maud' Committee report), London, H.M.S.O.

MINISTRY OF HOUSING AND LOCAL GOVERNMENT (1967c) *London Government: The Town and Country Planning (Local Planning Authorities in Greater London) (Amendment) Regulations, 1967*, Statutory Instrument 1967, No. 430, London, H.M.S.O.

MINISTRY OF HOUSING AND LOCAL GOVERNMENT (1969a) *General Development Order*, Statutory Instrument, 1969, No. 276, London, H.M.S.O.

MINISTRY OF HOUSING AND LOCAL GOVERNMENT (1969) *Development Control Policy notes*, see series introduced with Circular 23/69.

MINISTRY OF HOUSING AND LOCAL GOVERNMENT (1970) *Development plans: a manual on form and content*, London, H.M.S.O.

MINISTRY OF HOUSING AND LOCAL GOVERNMENT AND MINISTRY OF TRANSPORT (1962) *Town centres: approach to renewal* (Planning Bulletin No.1), London, H.M.S.O.

MINISTRY OF LOCAL GOVERNMENT AND PLANNING (1951) *Town and country planning 1943–1951*, Cmnd. 8204, London, H.M.S.O.

MINISTRY OF TOWN AND COUNTRY PLANNING (1950) *Development by government departments* (Circular 100/50), London, H.M.S.O.

MUMFORD, Lewis (1961) *The city in history*, London, Secker and Warburg.

NATIONAL SOCIETY FOR CLEAN AIR *Clean air year book* (annual), London, N.S.C.A.

NEEDLEMAN, Lionel (1965) *The economics of housing*, London, Staples Press.

NEEDLEMAN, Lionel (1968) Rebuilding or renovation? A reply, *Urban Studies 5*, 86–90.

ODUM, Howard T. (1971) *Environment, power and society*, New York, Wiley-Interscience.

OGDEN, R. H. (1970) Pedestrian precinct in Bolton, *Journal of the Town Planning Institute 56*, 142–6.

OZBEKHAN, Hasan (1969) Toward a general theory of planning *in* Erich JANTSCH (ed.) *Perspectives of planning*, Paris, Organisation for Economic Co-operation and Development.

PAHL, R. E. (1968) *Spatial structure and social structure* (CES-WP-10), London, Centre for Environmental Studies.

PANTLING, D. J. and A. J. SHELTON (1970) An approach to district planning, *Journal of the Town Planning Institute 56*, 147–9.

PARKINSON, Ewart (1970) Renewing the urban environment, *Journal of the Town Planning Institute 56*, 264–7.

PERLOFF, Harvey S. (1965) New directions in social planning, *Journal of the American Institute of Planners 31*, 297–304.

PLANNING ADVISORY GROUP (1965) *The future of development plans*, London, H.M.S.O.

POWER, John (1971) *Planning: myth and magic* (Conference paper), London and Coventry, Institute of Operational Research.

PRINGLE, J. W. S. (1956) On the parallel between learning and evolution, *General Systems 1*, 90–110.

RAPOPORT, A. (1966) Some system approaches to political theory *in* David EASTON (ed.) *Varieties of political theory*, Englewood Cliffs, N.J., Prentice-Hall.

REX, John A. (1968) The sociology of a zone of transition *in* R. E. PAHL (ed.) *Readings in urban sociology*, Oxford, Pergamon.

RIDGEWAY, T. A. (1965) Cambuslang : redevelopment in a growth area, *Journal of the Town Planning Institute 51*, 407–10.

ROBSON, William A. and Bernard CRICK (eds.) (1970) *The future of the social services*, Harmondsworth, Penguin.

ROSE, Richard (1971) *Models of governing*, Paper presented at the I.S.S.C. conference on the comparative analyses of highly industrialized societies, held at Bellagio, Italy, August 1971. Glasgow, University of Strathclyde, (mimeo).

ROYAL COMMISSION ON ENVIRONMENTAL POLLUTION (1970) *First Report*. Cmnd. 4585, London, H.M.S.O.

ROYAL COMMISSION ON LOCAL GOVERNMENT IN ENGLAND (1969) *Report* (The 'Redcliffe-Maud' report), London, H.M.S.O.

SAVAS, E. S. (1968) Information systems in a New York urban observatory, *Socio-economic planning sciences 1*, 203–8.

SCHON, Donald (1971) *Beyond the stable state*, London, Temple Smith.

SCHÜTZENBERGER, M. P. (1954) A tentative classification of goal-seeking behaviour. *Journal of Mental Science 100*, 97–102.

SELF, Peter (1971) *Metropolitan planning: the planning system of Greater London*. Greater London Papers No. 14 London, London School of Economics and Weidenfeld and Nicolson.

SENNETT, Richard (1970) *The uses of disorder: personal identity and city life*, New York, Knopf; London, Allen Lane, The Penguin Press (1971).

SHARP, Evelyn (1969) *The Ministry of Housing and Local Government*, London, Allen and Unwin.

SHARP, Evelyn (1970) *Transport planning: the men for the job*, London, H.M.S.O.

SHUBIK, M. (1967) Information, rationality and free choice in a future democratic society, *Daedalus 96*, 771–8.

SIBERT, Eric (1969) Aircraft noise and development control – the policy for Gatwick airport, *Journal of the Town Planning Institute 55*, 149–52.

SIGSWORTH, E. M. and R. K. WILKINSON (1967) Rebuilding or renovation? *Urban Studies 4*, 109–21.

SIMMIE, James L. (1971) Physical planning and social policy, *Journal of the Royal Town Planning Institute 57*, 450–3.

SIMON, Herbert A. (1956) Rational choice and the structure of the environment, *Psychological Review 63*, 129–38, republished *in* EMERY, F. E. (ed.) (1969) *Systems thinking*, Harmondsworth, Penguin Books.

SOUTH HAMPSHIRE TECHNICAL UNIT (1970) Research techniques in structure planning – experience from the South Hamphsire Plan, *Journal of the Town Planning Institute 56*, 211–33.

STEWART, John D. (1971) *Management in local government: a viewpoint*, London, Charles Knight.

STEWART, John D. and Tony EDDISON (1971) Structure planning and corporate planning, *Journal of the Royal Town Planning Institute 57*, 367–9.

STOCKPORT C.B.C. (1972) *Position statement* (10 volumes), Stockport, the Council.

STODDART, David R. (1967) Organism and ecosystem as geographical models *in* CHORLEY and HAGGETT (eds.) *Models in geography*, London, Methuen.

TELLING, A. E. (1970) *Planning law and procedure* (3rd edition), London, Butterworths.

THOMAS, David (1970) *London's green belt*, London, Faber and Faber.

THORBURN, Andrew (1971) Preparing a regional plan: how we set about the task in Nottinghamshire/Derbyshire, *Journal of the Town Planning Institute 57*, 216–18.

THORNLEY, Jennifer (1973) *Aspects of urban management*, Paris, O.E.C.D. (in press).

TOMLINSON, Graham (1970) Housing improvement, *Journal of the Town Planning Institute 56*, 342–7.

TOWN PLANNING INSTITUTE (1963) Planning administration: the establishment of separate planning departments – a statement of policy by the Town Planning Institute, *Journal of the Town Planning Institute 49*, 76.

TOWN PLANNING INSTITUTE (1964) *Survey of membership and of planning staffs*, London, Royal Town Planning Institute.

TOWN PLANNING INSTITUTE (1970) Report of joint R.I.B.A./T.P.I. working party on techniques for local planning, *Journal of the Town Planning Institute 56*, 279–84.

VICKERS, Geoffrey (1968) *Value systems and social process*, London, Tavistock. Also available from Penguin Books (1970)

WADE, B. F. (1971) Some factors affecting the use of new techniques in planning agencies, *Environment and Planning 3*, 109–14.

WANNOP, Urlan A. (1972) An objective strategy: the Coventry-Solihull-Warwickshire sub-regional study, *Journal of the Royal Town Planning Institute 58*, 159–66.

WATER RESOURCES BOARD *Annual Report*, London, H.M.S.O.

WEBBER, Melvin M. (1965) The rôle of intelligence systems in urban systems planning, *Journal of the American Institute of Planners 31*, 289–96.

WHITE, Brenda (1970) *Planners and information*, London, Library Association.

WHITE, Morton and Lucia WHITE (1960) pp. 214–32 *in* Lloyd Rodwin (ed.) *The future metropolis*, London, Constable.

WILLIS, Jeffrey (1972) *Design issues for urban and regional information systems* (CES-WP-71), London, Centre for Environmental Studies.

WILSON, Alan G. (1968) Models in urban planning: a synoptic review of recent literature, *Urban Studies 5*, 249–76.

WILSON, Alan G. (1970a) Forecasting 'planning', *in* Peter COWAN (ed.) *Developing patterns of urbanisation*, Edinburgh, Oliver and Boyd.

WINGO, Lowdon (ed.) (1964) *Cities and Space: the future use of urban land*, Baltimore, Md., Johns Hopkins Press.

Abbreviations

C.D.A.   Comprehensive Development Area
C.E.S.   Centre for Environmental Studies
F.S.I.   Floor Space Index
G.L.D.P. Greater London Development Plan
G.D.O.   General Development Order
P.A.G.   Planning Advisory Group
P.P.B.S. Planning, Programming and Budgeting Systems
S.T.M.   Supplementary Town Map

Subject Index

Author Index

Greater London Development Plan
Enquiry, 158, 223
Gregory, S. A., 135
Griffith, J. A. G., 57, 62, 179
Gross, Bertram M., 190, 215

Haggett, Peter, 208, 224, 228, 231, 240
Hall, Peter, 111, 227
Hamilton, H. R., 216
Harris, Britton, 240, 241
Harvey, David, 258
Heap, Desmond, 47, 49
Hirschman, A. O., 214
Howard, Ebenezer, 15

Jackson, John N., 149
Jessop, Neil, F., 146, 163, 168, 183, 229, 262
Jones, J. Christopher, 135
Joyce, R., 232

Keeble, Lewis, 20
Klír, Jiri, 183, 194, 195, 199, 211, 212, 219, 221, 225

Leggatt, R. W., 120
Lichfield, Nathaniel, 31, 136
Lindblom, C. E., 214

Mandelker, D. R., 20
Maruyama, Mogoroh, 196
Meier, Richard, L., 188, 189, 226, 258
Meyerson, Martin, 23
McKenzie, W. J. M., 214
McLoughlin, J. Brian, 143, 184, 218, 227, 236, 239, 262
Ministry of Housing and Local Government, 40, 60, 62, 75, 76, 77, 81, 91, 103, 110, 119, 121, 125, 143, 171, 172
Ministry of Local Government and Planning, 19, 118
Ministry of Town and Country Planning, 80
Ministry of Transport, 125
Mumford, Lewis, 23

Needleman, Lionel, 131

Odum, Howard, T., 207
Ogden, R. H., 120
Ozbekhan, Hasan, 183, 205, 206

Pahl, R. E., 187
Parkinson, Ewart, 120
Perloff, Harvey S., 246, 247
Planning Advisory Group, 21, 22, 126, 141
Power, John, 150, 250
Pringle, J. W. S., 199

Rapoport, A., 195, 196
Reiner, Thomas, 188
Rex, John A., 198
Robson, W. A., 235
Rose, Richard, 161, 177, 182, 248
Royal Commission on Local Government in England (the 'Redcliffe-Maud' report), 62

Savas, E. S., 233
Schon, Donald, 248, 250, 255, 267
Schrandt, B. G., 200
Schützenberger, M. P., 214
Self, Peter, 76
Sennett, Richard, 33
Sharp, Evelyn, 45, 67, 171, 173
Shelton, A. J., 131
Shubik, M., 241
Sigsworth, E. M., 131
Simmie, James L., 32
Simon, Herbert, A., 215
South Hampshire Technical Unit, 166
Stalker, G. M., 201, 264
Stewart, John D., 64, 179, 180, 264
Stockport C.B.C., 178, 262
Stoddart, David R., 208, 209, 210, 211, 212, 258

Telling, A. E.,
Thomas, David, 20, 166
Thorburn, Andrew, 134
Thornley, D., 135
Thornley, Jennifer, 25, 143, 262
Tomlinson, Graham, 120
Town Planning Institute, 66, 135, 154
Trist, E. L., 220

Valach, Miroslav, 183, 194, 195, 199, 211, 212, 219, 221, 225
Vickers, Geoffrey, 167, 202, 204, 220, 248

Wade, B. F., 201
Wannop, Urlan, 134
Webber, Melvin, M. 234, 241, 243, 245
Webster, Judith N., 184, 218, 236, 239

White, Brenda, 230, 239
White, Lucia, 23
White, Morton, 23
Wilkinson, R. K., 131
Willis, Jeffrey, 238
Wilson, Alan G., 212, 240, 241, 258
Wingo, Lowdon, 24
Welsh Office, 130, 148